Nineteenth-Century Major Lives and Letters

Series Editor: Marilyn Gaull

This series presents original biographical, critical, and scholarly studies of literary works and public figures in Great Britain, North America, and continental Europe during the nineteenth century. The volumes in *Nineteenth-Century Major Lives and Letters* evoke the energies, achievements, contributions, cultural traditions, and individuals who reflected and generated them during the Romantic and Victorian period. The topics: critical, textual, and historical scholarship, literary and book history, biography, cultural and comparative studies, critical theory, art, architecture, science, politics, religion, music, language, philosophy, aesthetics, law, publication, translation, domestic and public life, popular culture, and anything that influenced, impinges upon, expresses or contributes to an understanding of the authors, works, and events of the nineteenth century. The authors consist of political figures, artists, scientists, and cultural icons including William Blake, Thomas Hardy, Charles Darwin, William Wordsworth, William Butler Yeats, Samuel Taylor, and their contemporaries.

The series editor is Marilyn Gaull, PhD (Indiana University), FEA. She has taught at William and Mary, Temple University, New York University, and is Research Professor at the Editorial Institute at Boston University. She is the founder and editor of *The Wordsworth Circle* and the author of *English Romanticism: The Human Context,* and editions, essays, and reviews in journals. She lectures internationally on British Romanticism, folklore, and narrative theory, intellectual history, publishing procedures, and history of science.

PUBLISHED BY PALGRAVE MACMILLAN:

Shelley's German Afterlives, by Susanne Schmid
Coleridge, the Bible, and Religion, by Jeffrey W. Barbeau
Romantic Literature, Race, and Colonial Encounter, by Peter J. Kitson
Byron, edited by Cheryl A. Wilson
Romantic Migrations, by Michael Wiley
The Long and Winding Road from Blake to the Beatles, by Matthew Schneider
British Periodicals and Romantic Identity, by Mark Schoenfield
Women Writers and Nineteenth-Century Medievalism, by Clare Broome Saunders
British Victorian Women's Periodicals, by Kathryn Ledbetter
Romantic Diasporas, by Toby R. Benis
Romantic Literary Families, by Scott Krawczyk
Victorian Christmas in Print, by Tara Moore
Culinary Aesthetics and Practices in Nineteenth-Century American Literature, edited by Monika Elbert and Marie Drews
Reading Popular Culture in Victorian Print, by Alberto Gabriele
Romanticism and the Object, edited by Larry H. Peer
Poetics en passant, by Anne Jamison
From Song to Print, by Terence Hoagwood
Gothic Romanticism, by Tom Duggett
Victorian Medicine and Social Reform, by Louise Penner
Populism, Gender, and Sympathy in the Romantic Novel, by James P. Carson
Byron and the Rhetoric of Italian Nationalism, by Arnold A. Schmidt
Poetry and Public Discourse in Nineteenth-Century America, by Shira Wolosky
The Discourses of Food in Nineteenth-Century British Fiction, by Annette Cozzi
Romanticism and Pleasure, edited by Thomas H. Schmid and Michelle Faubert

Royal Romances, by Kristin Flieger Samuelian
Trauma, Transcendence, and Trust, by Thomas J. Brennan, S.J.
The Business of Literary Circles in Nineteenth-Century America, by David Dowling
Popular Medievalism in Romantic-Era Britain, by Clare A. Simmons
Beyond Romantic Ecocriticism, by Ashton Nichols
The Poetry of Mary Robinson, by Daniel Robinson
Romanticism and the City, by Larry H. Peer
Coleridge and the Daemonic Imagination, by Gregory Leadbetter
Dante and Italy in British Romanticism, edited by Frederick Burwick and
    Paul Douglass
Romantic Dharma, by Mark Lussier
Jewish Representation in British Literature 1780–1840, by Michael Scrivener

FORTHCOMING TITLES:

Robert Southey, by Stuart Andrews
Playing to the Crowd, by Frederick Burwick
The Regions of Sara Coleridge's Thought, by Peter Swaab

Jewish Representation in British Literature 1780–1840

After Shylock

Michael Scrivener

JEWISH REPRESENTATION IN BRITISH LITERATURE 1780–1840

First published in 2011 by
PALGRAVE MACMILLAN®
in the United States—a division of St. Martin's Press LLC,
175 Fifth Avenue, New York, NY 10010.

Where this book is distributed in the UK, Europe and the rest of the world,
this is by Palgrave Macmillan, a division of Macmillan Publishers Limited,
registered in England, company number 785998, of Houndmills,
Basingstoke, Hampshire RG21 6XS.

Palgrave Macmillan is the global academic imprint of the above companies
and has companies and representatives throughout the world.

Palgrave® and Macmillan® are registered trademarks in the United States,
the United Kingdom, Europe and other countries.

ISBN: 978–0–230–10289–7

Library of Congress Cataloging-in-Publication Data

Scrivener, Michael Henry, 1948–
    Jewish representation in British literature 1780–1840 : after Shylock /
Michael Scrivener.
        p. cm.—(Nineteenth-century major lives and letters)
    Includes bibliographical references.
    ISBN 978–0–230–10289–7 (hardback)
    1. English literature—19th century—History and criticism. 2. Jews in
literature. 3. English literature—18th century—History and criticism.
4. Jews—Great Britain—Intellectual life. 5. Judaism and literature—Great
Britain. I. Title.

PR151.J5S44 2011
820.9′3529924—dc22   2011005269

A catalogue record of the book is available from the British Library.

Design by Newgen Imaging Systems (P) Ltd., Chennai, India.

First edition: September 2011

10 9 8 7 6 5 4 3 2 1

Printed and bound in Great Britain by
CPI Antony Rowe, Chippenham and Eastbourne

Contents

ACKNOWLEDGMENTS

For this book, which had a long gestation period, I thank several institutions and many people. Wayne State University has generously given me several research grants and sabbatical leaves permitting me to study archival material in London, principally at the British Library and the University College of London University Library. As a recipient of a fellowship from the John Simon Guggenheim Memorial Foundation in 2007–08, I was able to research and write for a year, working in the British Library and the Jewish Theological Seminary Library in New York.

From the citations within the book one will see the numerous scholars to whom I owe much. The following people have been generous with their ideas and I express my gratitude, although the book's flaws are entirely my own and cannot be attributed to any of the following: Charles Baxter, Simone Chess, Bryan Cheyette, Arthur Efron, Todd M. Endelman, Frank Felsenstein, Michael Galchinsky, William Galperin, Jaime Goodrich, Renuka Gusain, Terence Alan Hoagwood, Heidi Kaufman, Lisa Maruca, Ann Nichols, Judith W. Page, Ross Pudaloff, Michael Ragussis, Sheila A. Spector, Arthur F. Marotti, Irving Massey, Victoria Myers, Nadia Valman, Renata M. Wasserman, Karen Weisman. I offer my warmest thanks to Marilyn Gaull, the editor of the Nineteenth-Century Major Lives and Letters Series. I dedicate the book to my grandson Xavier Zeller and his wonderful parents, Corey and Kay Zeller.

I have used all or part of the following two essays and am using them with permission:

"The Philosopher and the Moneylender: The Relationship between William Godwin and John King," in Robert M. Maniquis and Victoria Myers, ed., *Godwinian Moments: From Enlightenment to Romanticism* (University of Toronto Press, 2010), 333–62.

"Rethinking Margin and Center in Anglo-Jewish Literature," in Sheila A. Spector, ed., *Romanticism/Judaica: A Convergence of Cultures* (Ashgate Publishing, 2011), 157–68.

INTRODUCTION

My study of Jewish representations concentrates on Romantic-era British writing, roughly between 1780 and 1840. By the logic of my argument I am forced to go back to George Granville's *The Jew of Venice* (1701) and ahead to Grace Aguilar's *Essays and Miscellanies* (1853), but otherwise the focus stays mostly within Romanticism.

Was Romanticism good for the Jews? Yes and no.

Representations of Jews and Judaism do not necessarily correspond with actual Jews and religious practices. Indeed, these representations, even when authored by Jews, reinforce fictions that strengthen prejudice and stereotypes, harming Jewish bodies. The medieval fictions of ritual murder and satanic possession led to torture and murder. The argument of Daniel Jonah Goldhagen's *Hitler's Willing Executioners* (1996) that several centuries of German "eliminationist antisemitism" led to the Shoah assumes that Jewish representations have powerful consequences.[1] From image, narrative, symbolism, and affective engagement to actual political and military deeds there are complex mediations and translations—what Homi Bhabha calls "negotiations"—but intangible representations eventually have physical outcomes.[2]

Bryan Cheyette, several years before Goldhagen's book, offered three compelling ideas that apply to literary criticism of Jewish representations: that antisemitic texts do not necessarily lead to mass murder; that the negative stereotypes are not eternal myths but rather historical constructions; and that the categories of philo- and anti-semitism, which enable false moral judgments, should be replaced by the single category of "semitism," signifying Jewish representations of any kind, either positive or otherwise.[3] Because literary meaning depends on historical contingencies, even stereotypes that endure over many centuries—the ritual murderer, the Shylock—do not function in exactly the same way in every historical moment. Medieval Christian antisemitism, according to historians like Robert Chazan, did not express unchanging hatred of Jews but reflected instead fundamental changes in Christianity itself, particularly a new focus on a humanized Christ and his suffering at the hands of Jews.[4] From the eighteenth to the nineteenth centuries antisemitism became more racial than religious, reflecting the prestige of science. Cheyette's rejection of the moralistic philo-and antisemitic categories for the more neutral "semitic" calls attention to some of the ironies of labeling. Philosemitism invariably has an agenda, explicit or concealed, for converting or marginalizing actual Jews and Jewish practices. Michael Galchinsky cites the Anglo-Jewish joke: What is a philosemite? An antisemite who loves Jews.[5] Even that most philosemitic of nineteenth-century British novels, George Eliot's *Daniel Deronda* (1876), perpetuated stereotypes in representing the Cohen family as congenitally commercial and suggested furthermore that Jews do not belong in Britain but only in their own country in the Middle East. A narrative whose central logic is a *judenrein* (clean of Jews) Britain and money-obsessed Jewish shopkeepers is not completely sympathetic to Jews, but of course this complex novel has other meanings, far from anti-Jewish.

For conceptual rigor and linguistic precision it would be beneficial to dispense entirely with "semitic" and its prefixes, for the terms have problematic origins and create confusion. When Wilhelm Marr (1819–1904) coined *"Antisemitismus"* in 1879, he was trying to make hatred of Jews—*"Judenhass"*—sound scientific and modern.[6] The Hebrew language's affiliation with other "Semitic" languages notwithstanding, hatred of or acceptance of Jews has nothing to do with "Semites," nor do Jews constitute a "race," for racial thinking has been wholly discredited. Nevertheless, the words anti- and philosemitism still have currency, for good or ill. When I sparingly use philosemitism, I understand that it carries its own agenda not wholly unlike outright antisemitism. Even if one agrees with Cheyette that anti- and philosemitism as conceptual categories have enabled superficial moral judgments, one still has to make moral statements and discriminations. If those discriminations are simplistic, then the fault rests with the overall interpretation and not just with those two terms.[7]

Romantic Jewish representations as a whole are ambivalent. Freud's collaborator Eugen Bleuler (1857–1939) initially developed the concept of ambivalence, of which there are three kinds: of the will, the intellect, and the affects. Psychoanalysis defines affective ambivalence as an emotional condition within which "affirmation and negation are simultaneous and inseparable."[8] A classical Freudian instance is the son's Oedipal love/hate for the father. The theory of Melanie Klein (1882–1960) posits ambivalent instinctual affects from the start, so that only a splitting of good and bad manifestations of the object makes the emotions manageable.[9] Kleinian splitting and Oedipal displacement describe some versions of antisemitic stereotypes, notably the Shylock figure as the bad, castrating father, but Bleuler's other two kinds of ambivalence, of the will and intellect, illuminate identity construction and conversion to and away from Judaism.[10]

Ambivalence, a central concept of postcolonial theory, has long played a role in Jewish studies, notably in Sander Gilman's groundbreaking study, *Jewish Self-Hatred* (1986). According to Gilman, "Self-hatred results from outsiders' acceptance of the mirage of themselves generated by their reference group—that group in society which they see as defining them—as a reality."[11] Jews, like other vulnerable minorities (blacks, homosexuals), deflect the negative stereotypes with an ambivalent construction of good and bad versions of the social group, heaping scorn on the bad (clannish Yiddish-speaking *Ostjuden* [Jews from Eastern Europe]; greedy Shylocks) to vindicate the good (benevolent Nathans and Shevas; biblical patriarchs; Christian converts; assimilated anti-Zionists). Tracing this process from the early modern period to the present, Gilman shows Jews repeatedly accepting the stereotypical and hegemonic "mirage" as real but not definitive and final. The self-hatred strategy is often futile, for the mirage is a dialectical force that makes the most positive counterconstructions sinister and worthless: assimilation is seen as soulless mimicry, and conversion as insincere and impossible, for Jews are assumed to have an unchangeable essence.

Homi Bhabha's ideas on ambivalence with the most relevance to Jewish studies are his discussion of stereotypes, which he conceives as not simply "wrong" but as "an ambivalent mode of knowledge and power."[12] The stereotype, according to Bhabha, is a "complex, ambivalent, contradictory mode of representation, as anxious as it is assertive."[13] Disputing Edward Said's more monolithic notion of Orientalist "discourse/power," Bhabha writes that stereotyping "is not the setting up of a false image which becomes the scapegoat of discriminatory practices. It is a much more ambivalent text of projection and introjection, metaphoric and metonymic strategies, displacement, over-determination, guilt, aggressivity; the masking and splitting of 'official' and phantasmatic knowledges to construct the positionalities and oppositionalities of racist discourse."[14] If stereotypes are textual, systematic, and complexly meaningful, then the interpretive task is to describe and understand them.

Ambivalence characterizes Jewish stereotypes like Shylock. Europe's conflicted views on commerce, banking, trade, usury, and capitalism form the background for Shylock's emergence. One of the likely sources for Shakespeare's *The Merchant of Venice* depicts a virtuous Jewish moneylender and an unscrupulous Christian merchant, and another possible source for the story of the pound of flesh portrays the Jew as the victim not the executor of the bond.[15] Shakespeare's character is more rounded than the coarse stereotype that will be named after it, and the theatrical figure itself has been realized on stage and interpreted by readers in numerous ways. The Romantic Shylock of Edmund Kean (1789–1833) is more sympathetic than the demonic creature performed earlier for a half-century (1741–89) by Charles Macklin (1690–1797), or the comic villain invented by George Granville (1666–1735) in his *Jew of Venice* (1701). Literature of the Romantic era is not uniformly less hostile to Jews, however; William Cobbett (1763–1835), the populist author and reformist politician, one of the most popular writers of his day, exploits the crude medieval and Shylock stereotypes to provoke hatred against Jews.

Just as the movement for Jewish emancipation was stirring to life in the 1830s, Dickens's Fagin, unforgettably drawn as despicably satanic in George Cruikshank's illustrations, kept alive the medieval libel of Jewish ritual abuse and murder of Christian boys in the popular novel *Oliver Twist* (1837–39). With Shylock, Fagin is English literature's most memorable Jew, who might have delayed Jewish emancipation for a generation.[16] How Dickens, one of the greatest English novelists, represented Jews is instructive because as a humanitarian liberal he inserted a benevolent Jew, Riah, in *Our Mutual Friend* (1864–65) largely in response to Jewish protests against Fagin. According to Anthony Julius, Dickens reworked "pre-existing themes" and "stock subjects"—imagining a dangerous interaction between a male Jew and Christian children—to transform the raw cultural material into something vividly inventive and strikingly well defined.[17] Fagin, like Shylock, is discovered as much as he is created because the overdetermined stereotypical elements have long existed in multiple forms. Dickens defended the Jewishness of Fagin as realistically reflecting London criminality when Ikey Solomons (1785–1850) was most active (1810s–20s) as a receiver of stolen goods,[18] but even if true, Fagin is represented like no other character in the novel. In the versions of the novel before the 1867 revisions, the narrator and the characters almost always call him "the Jew," who has no familial context, and all of whose characteristics evoke Jewishness in its worst light. Physically ugly with a huge hook nose, red-haired like the stage Jew or Satan or Judas, corrupter of the innocent Christian children whom he exploits until he sends to the gallows, Fagin is an inhuman miser who cares only for money.[19]

For Edgar Rosenberg, it is a mistake to look for realism in stereotypes, which will always be extreme exaggerations: "A fiction may be all the more convincing and durable for being a basic distortion."[20] Fagin like Shylock has convinced and endured, to be sure, but I want to press the issue of how stereotypes work in literature. Introduced into the fiction, the stereotype aligns characters and themes decisively, spreading his or her semiotic power in every direction. Jewish villain Fagin makes Nancy into the Jew's daughter, a literary descendant of Jessica, for Fagin has raised her from childhood. She undergoes a conversion to middle-class Christian values but she cannot leave her world completely behind, as she is a hybrid character like Jessica. Her inability to transfer completely to middle-class respectability is homologous with the impossibility of a racialized Jew ever becoming anything else. Indeed, she refers to "God's wrath for the wrong I have done," making her permanent membership in the underclass a consequence of divine judgment, something like the situation of the Wandering Jew.[21] In *Our Mutual Friend* (1864–65), where Dickens makes amends for Fagin with the saintly Riah, the avaricious moneylender role is played by a Gentile, Fledgeby, but the stereotype of the Shylock survives. Fledgeby rather than Riah is acting like Shylock, which is a minimal way to subvert the stereotype because the text encourages a reading that Fledgeby behaves like a Jew and Riah like a Christian. Something similar occurs in *The Christmas Carol* (1843), where Scrooge never is identified explicitly as Jewish, but he, as Jonathan H. Grossman has pointed out, appears to be Jewish in everything but name: he hates Christmas, which he has never celebrated; he and his partner Jacob have "Old Testament" names; he seems critical of his nephew for marrying a Christian; biblical allusions authorize the view that Scrooge should convert to Christianity; even after his manic conversion to Christmas appreciation, he expresses a dark humor and remains isolated, not a real part of anyone's community.[22] Even without the explicit identification, many casual readers of the story and viewers of the film versions have always taken Scrooge as being Jewish. On the charge of conscious racism, Dickens is innocent, but in creating *The Christmas Carol* his imagination cannot resist reshaping the stereotypical raw materials.

Ambivalence marks Romantic Jewish representations in a pervasive way. The most read novelist before Dickens, Walter Scott, created the sympathetic Jewess, Rebecca, but in *Ivanhoe* (1819), the novel of English origins in the union of Anglo-Saxons and Normans,

there is no place for Jews, who are dispatched instead to Spain. The
Romantic poets romanticized the Wandering Jew figure as a fellow
rebel and exile/prophet oppressed by unjust authority and alienated
by social restrictions, but with few exceptions had little interest in
knowing much about the Jews among whom they lived. Although
the Benevolent Jew of Romantic writing is generous to Christians,
he also is invariably old and sexually inactive, in effect neutered. The
attractive Jewesses in Romantic texts are in love not with Jewish but
always Christian men. Biblical Israelites and Hebrews figure hero-
ically in Protestant theology and religious constructions of the End
Times, but there is little patience with and much disdain for actual
Jews living in Petticoat Lane. Millenarianism, greatly stimulated by
the French Revolution and Napoleon's presence in the Holy Land,
assigned a key role to living Jews, but the script—return to Zion and
conversion to the true faith of Jesus—was written wholly in English
according to the King James Bible. If the Christian God is going
to reappear, the Jews will have to do their part; the prevailing wisdom is that toleration of Jews and contempt for Judaism promises
the best results. Cobbett's style of savage antisemitism, which had
its enthusiasts to be sure, competed with the so-called philosemitic
approach of humanely treating Jews in order to liquidate Judaism.
The hostility to Judaism is not uniform, however, because another
current of cultural discourse upholds Judaism as a defense against
secularism. As the established religious certainties are under attack
by science, rationalism, and Enlightenment, Christians strategically
use Judaism—the Old Testament—to provide a secure foundation
for the religion of the New Testament. Against the Higher Criticism
of the Bible there are the ever refined, constantly revised prophetic
readings of the older Testament to confirm the truths of the newer.
Yet another angle on Judaism is Hebrew republicanism, using the
Mosaic commonwealth as a model for democratic and even socialis-
tic politics. Coleridge (1772–1834) in his radical twenties fashioned
a communistic Christianity relying on Hebrew republicanism, and
Thomas Spence (1750–1814) founded a left-wing movement, active
from the French Revolution through the Chartist agitation, on the
Jubilee of Leviticus 25.

Although the number of English Jews in the early nineteenth century was small, the impact of figurative Jewishness on British culture
was large: religion; the Empire; minorities; commercial morality; secularism anxieties; populist mobilization against concentrated wealth;
the appeal of radical individualism and an idealized alienation; and
protosocialist republicanism. Taken together, these make up much

of the British culture at the time. Jewish representations, which may seem to be a parochial concern, in fact function like Freud's return of the repressed: expelled and excluded, they keep coming back, raising uncomfortable questions.

Of course actual Jews, not just anxious Christians, also produced literary representations. The Anglo-Jewish writing in English—there was also a Hebrew language literature—revised already-existing genres and conventions. How to define Anglo-Jewish writing raises a few difficulties. In chapter 2, my claim for Menasseh ben Israel as the first Anglo-Jewish writer can be challenged because he lived in London for only two years, but my argument rests on the following: the writer was Jewish, and he wrote and published a few texts in English. In chapter 5, I focus on John King's daughters, Sophia and Charlotte, as Anglo-Jewish writers, even though they married Christians and apparently converted to the faith of their husbands. Neither wrote on Jewish subjects, but their writing—lyric poetry and gothic fiction—yields rich meaning viewed in the Anglo-Jewish context, not just the roman à clef angle disclosing details about growing up in an Anglo-Jewish household but also the uniquely Anglo-Jewish aspects of performing gender and assimilation.

Two other kinds of texts require some discussion. In chapter 3, "The Pedlar," I draw upon the Old Bailey court *Proceedings* to retrieve the testimony and language of Jews who are defendants, victims, and witnesses in criminal trials. One never gets the unmediated voice of actual Jews, but the court record provides something close. Awash in stereotypes and bad faith idealizations, this study needs the language of ordinary Jews as a contrast and counter. The second kind of text can be called subliterary, the so-called "Jew Songs" from the *Universal Songster* and the popular theatre. Many anonymously composed, others written by Grub Street doggerel scribes, a few by recognizable authors, the highly conventional and stereotypical songs were probably authored by non-Jews but one can never know for sure. As examples of Romantic urban popular culture, the songs meaningfully express how the dominant culture figured its Jewish minority.[23]

An important structure shaping how the dominant culture figured Jewishness is the pattern established by Shakespeare's comedy, *The Merchant of Venice.* Shylock and Jessica shadow Jewish Romantic representations sometimes strongly and sometimes faintly. The Benevolent Jew negates the Shylock figure without transcending it, while Jessica undergoes mitosis, one part becoming *la belle juive*, the exotic and alluring beauty, while the other part becomes the embodiment of spirituality and piety. Nadia Valman has written persuasively on the ambivalent nature of the nineteenth-century Jewess.[24] Permutations of the Jessica character, whether conversionist or loyal to Judaism, reflect the ambivalence evident in Shakespeare's depiction. The flood of conversionist texts in the early nineteenth century—in fiction, sermons, religious tracts—discussed by Michael Ragussis, Nadia Valman, and Cynthia Scheinberg depict a patriarchically oppressive Judaism from which sensitive women only want to flee, as Jessica fled her father, the moneylender.[25]

Chapter 4, "The Moneylender," concentrates on John King (1753–1824), an actual Jewish moneylender who wrote and published over a dozen books and pamphlets. In some respects he corresponds with the negative stereotype of the Shylock figure. A scoundrel involved in numerous illegal schemes from blackmail to fraud and prostitution, he left his Jewish wife and children for an Irish aristocrat who also had a taste for the pleasurable life. King was intelligent, politically radical, charmingly sociable, philosophically curious, and religiously involved with Christian millenarianism and Jewish messianism. The relationship with his two literary daughters was ambiguous, to some extent following the Shylock and Jessica pattern. His friendship with William Godwin is surprising on both sides, as one would not expect the bon vivant King to enjoy the company of the former Dissenting minister, nor the compulsively serious philosopher to associate himself with the unrespectable King.

Chapter 1, "Anglo-Jewish Writing, Literary Criticism and History," situates the book in relation to the critical literature on Jewish representations from the late nineteenth century to the present. Chapter 2, "1656 and the Origins of Anglo-Jewish Writing," explores the readmission debate initiated by Cromwell, who wanted Jews to resettle in England after four centuries of exclusion. The chapter examines the debate's role in establishing the major literary genres relating to Jews: the antisemitic diatribe opposing Jewish settlement authored by William Prynne; the proposal that Jews colonize Ireland in James Harrington's ambiguously philosemitic political treatise, *Oceana*; and Menasseh ben Israel's several essays arguing for readmission and rebutting the major slanders against Jews and Judaism. Chapter 3, "The Pedlar," draws upon several kinds of texts—songs, trial records, fiction, poetry—and develops the representations of the most common occupation of Romantic-era Jews living in London. While chapter 4, "The Moneylender," is on a real moneylender, John King, chapter 5, "The Jew's Daughter," explores the varieties of the Jessica figure, from King's own literary daughters who rejected Judaism to Walter Scott's Rebecca in *Ivanhoe*. Chapter 6, "Exiles and Prophets," has several points of departure: the experience of the *conversos* in the Iberian peninsula, as Jews were forced to assume a Christian public appearance, as well as the experience of Christians who experienced positive identification with Jews and Judaism, from converts like George Gordon to radicals like Thomas Spence, who took his political ideals from Leviticus. Deploying the concept of Richard Popkin—Christian Jews and Jewish Christians—the chapter illustrates the hybridization that marked much of Romantic writing.[26] The conclusion revisits the issue of stereotyping and reiterates the themes of ambivalence, anxious boundary crossings, unstable identities, and gendered resistance to stereotypes to repel the notion that an inquiry into Jewish representations is exhausted by the anti- and philosemitic categories.

CHAPTER 1

JEWISH REPRESENTATIONS,
LITERARY CRITICISM AND HISTORY

If Anglo-Jewish history has been marginalized, as Todd Endelman, David Feldman, David Katz, and other historians have protested, Jewish representations and Anglo-Jewish literature have been marginal as well, for many of the same reasons.[1] Even the relatively small number of Jews in Britain distracts one from perceiving that around 1800, "London was a major center of urban Jewish life" and that "more Jews lived in London than in any other city" except Amsterdam.[2] After the wave of East European immigration in the last three decades of the nineteenth century, London's Jewish community numbered almost two hundred thousand, where it still remains. The historical experience of Jews in Britain, however, has been instructively meaningful in numerous ways: how the Protestant majority treated one of its minorities from the Jew Bill of 1753 to the Aliens Act of 1905 with a mixture of tolerance and intolerance, in one of the West's earliest attempts to deal with a multicultural reality; how Protestant millenarianism led to philosemitism's various constructions of what Jews were and how they should behave; how Jews became part of the British Empire's involvement in the Middle East; how the Hebrew Bible and the Hebrew language became central in the Protestant attempt to achieve theological coherence in relation to modernity; how Jewish bankers provided essential support to the British state; and how someone like Benjamin Disraeli became one of Britain's most important prime ministers; and, finally, how from the eighteenth century the mass of ordinary Jews—pedlars, artisans, shopkeepers, factory workers—experienced modernity with its pleasures and perplexities. The historical literature on the British Jews is now too substantial both in terms of its quantity and quality to ignore.

Ignoring the Jewish presence, however, has been routine in literary studies. According to James Shapiro, the "reluctance" of cultural materialists studying early modern culture "to deal with Jewish questions undoubtedly has much to do with problems that the cultural Left has had in reconciling itself to Zionism and Israeli policy, with the prevailing legacy of Marx's account of the 'Jewish Question,' and with the fact that in their view Jews no longer constitute a disadvantaged or threatened social group." Although the New Historicists have written extensively on a wide range of victimized Others, they have ignored Jews, "the Other of Others in the Renaissance."[3] Sander Gilman observes that "one of the most recent forms of Jewish self-hatred is the virulent Jewish opposition to the existence of the State of Israel."[4] Delegitimizing Israel has been a signature aspect of the Left at least since the 1967 Six Day War. In Anthony Julius's study of antisemitism in England, he comments that "Israel is the only state in the world whose legitimacy is widely denied and whose destruction is publicly advocated and threatened."[5] Israel's military and economic success and American Jewry's relative prosperity after World War Two, along with the relative decline since then of overt antisemitism, have diminished the perception of Jewish victimization. Moreover, older antisemitic narratives of Jewish domination are gaining new life, from the charges of the undue influence of the "Israel Lobby" to accusations by long-time journalist, Helen Thomas, that "Congress, the White House and Hollywood, [as well as] Wall Street are owned by the Zionists."[6]

Some literary scholars and historians, however, have studied the literature about Jews and Judaism by both Gentile and Jewish writers. An area of concern, completely undeveloped in the literary criticism before the 1980s, is how figurative Jewishness functions in terms of articulating national identity in the eighteenth and nineteenth centuries. For James Shapiro texts like Shakespeare's *Merchant of Venice* turn to Jewish questions to answer English questions about "social, religious, and political turbulence."[7] The public protests against the Jew Bill of 1753—which provided for naturalization procedures for some Jewish immigrants—were animated, according to Shapiro, by anxiety over English identity: "if even a Jew could be English what could one point to that defined essential Englishness?"[8] As Shakespeare became the national poet in the eighteenth century, Charles Macklin's version of *The Merchant of Venice* stabilized English identity as not-

Jewish, not-Shylock; the play in effect supported repeal of the Jew Bill.[9] Michael Ragussis continues this vein of critical analysis on the Georgian theatre. Working with the "four nations" model of British cultural conflicts, he demonstrates how the eighteenth-century plays used theatre as a site of "contestation" over different national and ethnic commitments. Framed by the Scottish Act of Union (1707) and the Irish Act of Union (1800), as well as the Jew Bill (1753) and the Chelsea Murder Case (1771) when a Jewish gang killed a servant during a robbery,[10] the mainstream London theatre—a "multiethnic spectacle"—represented symptomatically the ethnic rivalries and conflicting approaches to national identity.[11] Although Jews were routinely stereotyped as Shylocks and sexually predatory nouveaux riches, as well as stigmatized linguistically with a grotesque foreign dialect (Shakespeare's Shylock spoke the same English as Antonio, it will be recalled), Jews pushed back with their own audience protests against Thomas Dibdin's *Family Quarrels* (1802) and their effective boycott of Marlowe's *Jew of Malta* (1818).[12] Not only are there hundreds of plays with Jews, Scots, and Irish, but the most popular plays in the later eighteenth century feature Jewish characters: Richard Sheridan's *Duenna* (1775) and *School for Scandal* (1777), Hannah Cowley's *Belle's Stratagem* (1780), and Charles Macklin's *Merchant of Venice* (1741–89).[13]

Ragussis's earlier book, *Figures of Conversion* (1995), demonstrates how national identity themes are worked out in the nineteenth century through the figure of conversion, as Protestant Britain is invested in a millenarian narrative that requires Jews, liberally and tolerantly treated, to convert to Christianity. In the first half of the century religious societies carried out conversionist efforts by distributing tracts and pamphlets, while women fiction writers produced Evangelical novels and stories. The Jewess is central in these narratives, for she is the victim of patriarchal and repressive Judaism, eager to embrace the more spiritually satisfying faith of Christianity.[14] Michael Galchinsky sees Walter Scott's *Ivanhoe* and its Rebecca linking the spiritually inclined Jewess with the proselytizing Christian woman, who really writes about herself when she writes about converting Jews.[15] Similarly, according to Nadia Valman, paralleling anti-Catholic tropes of religious ritual, legalism, materialism, and masculine domination, the conversionist stories aimed at Jewish women promoted a moderately feminist emphasis on women's intellectual rights while at the same time denigrating the intellect itself for the feminine "heart." Protestant women used converting Jewesses to advance their own religious, political, and social interests.[16] For the second half of the century the emphasis in Jewish representations turned racial in both Ragussis's and Valman's accounts, as scientific racism replaced religion as the dominant shaper of meaning.

English identity is the theme of Heidi Kaufman's study as well, as she dates the racializing discourse back to the early eighteenth century and assumes that the religious discourse was always linked with the racial. English Protestant writers used figurative Jewishness to claim English supremacy among the nations, pushing aside the original notion of Jewish chosenness.[17] Likewise, Cynthia Scheinberg identifies three things that make Jews, despite being a small minority, central to British Victorian culture: the role of Judaism and Jews in the Protestant defense of its theology against the scientific theories and practices of Darwin and the Higher Criticism of the Bible; the role of Jews for defining a superior Anglo-Saxon race; and the role of Jews as a religious minority in relation to the national Protestant identity.[18] Eitan Bar-Yosef's *The Holy Land in English Culture 1799–1917* illustrates how Jerusalem and The Holy Land figured in the English Protestant imaginary, turning England into the New Jerusalem and the English into the new Jews—the "real" Jews chosen by God. With a running commentary correcting errors in Edward Said's *Orientalism*, Bar-Yosef's study carefully reads the English discourse about the Holy Land distinguishing between actual restorationist-Zionist currents and more phantasmatic appropriations.[19] In both Kaufman and Bar-Yosef, the figure of Jewishness is used primarily for constructing English identity. In such a context, the question of xenophobic or tolerant attitudes toward Jews is practically irrelevant. Actual flesh and blood Jews were about the last thing on the minds of the English.

While English Christian writers busied themselves with Jewish matters, Jewish writers in the eighteenth century, according to David Ruderman, struggled to be taken seriously on philological and literary controversies about the Hebrew Bible, interpreting so-called Old Testament prophecies, evaluating the Newtonian science and reconciling it with theological assumptions, testing the ideas of Deism in relation to Judaism, developing models of political radicalism with Jewish resources, and finally "Englishing" Jewish culture. Ruderman discloses a host of eighteenth- and early–nineteenth-century Anglo-Jewish writers, both Anglophone and Hebrew-language, who eagerly followed the twists and turns in the most recent debates of the Enlightenment.[20] For the Romantic period to the end of the nineteenth century and beyond, recent scholars have opened up a new canon of Jewish writers such as Emma Lyon, Marion and

Celia Moss, Grace Aguilar, Maria Polack, and others. The two anthologies of essays edited by Sheila Spector on Jews and Romanticism provide new readings that make visible an Anglo-Jewish literary and intellectual tradition that had escaped scholarly attention.[21] The terms on which the Anglo-Jewish texts are brought into the canon are not self-evident, but the prevailing model of interpretation is to integrate the Anglo-Jewish presence by treating it as a minority discourse connected to both the dominant discourse and other minority discourses, emphasizing the dialogue among the ethnic minorities, the debate about English and British identity, and the struggle to articulate an Anglo-Jewish voice "nested" (Kaufman)[22] but not wholly determined by the dominant culture. Another kind of approach, such as Ruth Wisse's, highlights Jewish authenticity as a counter to powerful non-Jewish representations, has much merit, but I will devote more attention in this book to the former model, delineated clearly in a recent article by Bryan Cheyette.[23]

INTERPRETING JEWISH
REPRESENTATIONS, 1880–1971

One way to get a better critical understanding of Anglo-Jewish writing and its implications for Jewish and literary studies in general is to return to the earlier scholarship. By reviewing the work of David Philipson, Edward Calisch, Hijman Michelson, Meyer Landa, Frank Modder, Edward Coleman, Jacob Cordoza, H. R. S. Van Der Veen, Edgar Rosenberg, and Harold Fisch, I hope to put this body of work in conversation with contemporary scholarship to open up new questions and gain a fresh perspective.

When David Philipson (1862–1949), an American-born Reform rabbi, began lecturing in the 1880s on the *Jew in English Fiction*, American antisemitism was at a new level as the banker Joseph Seligman (1819–80) was turned away from the Grand Union Hotel in Saratoga, New York, in 1877, while the pogroms in Russia a few years later in 1881–84 would lead to massive Jewish immigration; "the number of Jews in the country grew," according to Philipson, "from the small number of 250,000 in 1881 to the present [late 1930s] 4,250,000, the largest concentration of Jews in the modern world."[24] According to Nadia Valman, Philipson's literary criticism was part of an effort to oppose the anti-Jewish hostility occasioned by the new immigration.[25] Running counter to the Enlightenment narrative of emancipatory progress in which Philipson is invested is the eruption of antisemitism—discursive, symbolic, violent, and political.

Because literary representations are powerful and because the novel is the most popular genre, fictional Jewishness has immediate relevance for Philipson and his audience. According to Philipson, "misrepresentation…has inflicted on innocent victims the greatest harm. Passion and prejudice readily communicate themselves from the page to the reader. Then ignorance, too, has impressed its seal on many a work whose influence all argument and all proof have in vain attempted to counteract. And that the Jew has suffered in this respect can not be denied."[26] After quoting some lines from Marlowe's *The Jew of Malta*, in which Barabas expresses his violent desires, Philipson comments: "No wonder that a populace, ignorant, unthinking, superstitious, should be goaded on to all excesses imaginable, when they heard such words as these."[27] Literary criticism as diagnostic and prescriptive of Jewish representations operates as a defender of Jewish interests, almost as if it were functioning like the Anti-Defamation League. Praising Richard Cumberland's Sheva, Walter Scott's Rebecca, and George Eliot's Mordecai, damning Charles Dickens's Fagin and Anthony Trollope's Melmotte, Philipson downplayed aesthetic criteria for the politics of representation. He criticized even Jewish writers like Abraham Cahan (1860–1951) when they concentrated on what he called the negative aspects of the Jewish ghetto. He did not quarrel with the realism of Cahan's fictions, such as *Yekl: A Tale of the New York Ghetto* (1896), only the political wisdom of displaying such an unseemly picture of Jewish life to the Gentiles.[28] Philipson acknowledged that Cumberland's play *The Jew* (1794) was clumsily simplistic, but it was seen at the time as good for the Jews. The excessive praise that Philipson and other early critics bestowed on Scott for his heroine Rebecca is that she was both an aesthetic and a national triumph, "intensely Jewish" and not simply beautiful, according to Philipson.[29] Edward Calisch was no less effusive in extolling Rebecca: "an ideal figure of true Jewish womanhood, faithful in the defense of her people, her religion, and her honor." Moreover, she acts as a counter to the "frivolous and false" Jessica of Shakespeare's *Merchant of Venice*.[30] Calisch's connecting Rebecca with Jessica anticipates the current practices of a critic like Michael Ragussis, who reads Rebecca in terms of a revisionary intertextuality;[31] but neither he nor Philipson is disturbed by the eroticizing of the Jewess and making her an exotic "*belle juive*." Philipson and the early critics saw Rebecca as undermining antisemitism rather than being also inscribed in some ways by antisemitic discourse, as is the more current view.

Few critics now will subscribe to the mechanistic view of literary representations that Philipson and Calisch assumed, but it is a truism that literary representation entails politics and the exercise of power. According to Edgar Rosenberg (1960), there is profound difference between political actions and artistic representations, but the distinction has little currency with the "superstitious mass of men" who are apt to mistake distorting fictions for reality.[32] Rosenberg's dispute with the earlier generation of critics—Meyer Landa, Hijman Michelson, Calisch, Philipson—was that they were "parochial," "provincial," and "ill-humored" for calling antisemitic stereotypes unrealistic when, in fact, stereotypes have their own separate logic not directly tied to social realities. To criticize stereotypes, which by their very nature are unrealistic, for a *lack* of realism is to confuse art and life, literature and experience; the earlier critics ignore the possibility that "a fiction may be all the more convincing and durable for being a basic distortion, with deep-seated attractions for the superstitious mass of men." For Rosenberg the enlightened Jewish representations lack the aesthetic allure of stereotypes.[33] Rosenberg also rejects the progressive view of antisemitism expressed by Frank Modder, another early critic, for whom Enlightenment was slowly but surely eroding superstition.[34] A refugee from Hitler's Germany, Rosenberg pointed to the persistent popularity of the antisemitic villain in literature and suggested that antisemitism functions in terms of scapegoating.[35] That the energies and power of popular art might be more firmly attached to social irrationality and injustice than to Arnold's sweetness and light has occurred to other critics as well, including other German Jewish refugees like Theodor Adorno and Max Horkheimer.[36] The traditional Jewish suspicion of art for ethical reasons reflects the encounters with Greek, Roman and Christian, as well as other civilizations and cultures. Rosenberg's pessimistic understanding of antisemitic representations is similar to how Harold Fisch in 1971 discusses what he calls the "dual image" of the Jew in literature, as devil or saint. Fisch dismissed Cumberland's sentimental play *The Jew* not so much aesthetically as ideologically, for it is representative of an Enlightenment liberalism that is no longer credible; Lessing's *Nathan the Wise*, a much better play, is still unpersuasive: "The age of liberalism has unfortunately passed away" and "we can see that human nature is not changed by merely preaching a sermon on tolerance." Moreover, "The assumption common at the time that differences of race and tradition are only skin deep does not hold in the light of modern history and the modern science of anthropology."[37] Rosenberg dispelled the gloom of his argument by proposing a countermyth to that of Shylock, namely, the myth of the Jew as artist, as a "man" of irony, on the margin of the social world.

Drawing upon the ideas of Leslie Fiedler on Joyce, Kafka, Proust, and Freud, Rosenberg saw in Fiedler's Jewish modernism a way for art's power to align itself *with* rather than *against* the Jew.[38] Fisch's own hope in the future rested with Jewish nationalism and a Jewish literary renaissance in North America and Israel. Antisemitic stereotypes interested Fisch primarily in terms of Jewish writers working out identity themes in the Diaspora and in Israel. For Fisch, the important writing was in Israel, not the Diaspora, where the whole problem of antisemitic representations, as it was framed by Philipson and the earlier critics, dissolves.[39] Now Jewish writers are the central concern, representations by non-Jewish writers only a marginal issue.

Neither Rosenberg nor Fisch, as post-Shoah critics, shared the Enlightenment assumptions of those who believed that historical understanding would eliminate the antisemitic stereotypes. As Modder in 1939 phrased it, when "ignorance" diminishes, so too does antisemitic "hostility."[40] Typical of earlier critics is the view that antisemitism was a residual medieval attitude that perversely survived into modernity.[41] Calisch, after depicting a hopeful arc of progress from the expulsion of 1290 to the late–nineteenth century emancipation, brooded nevertheless over the Aliens Act that indicated widespread hostility to Jewish immigrants.[42] Indeed, in the view of Nadia Valman, Calisch had a tragic sense of literature in relation to society.[43] Landa's 1927 study of the Jew in drama concluded optimistically but registered unease at the persistence of racial theory, which was not only like medieval prejudice in its hatred but also unlike it in its scientific pretensions.[44] Michelson's study confidently and rationally analyzed antisemitic stereotypes, which were traced largely to the effects of the New Testament and the Christian Church, but its depiction of the antisemitic atmosphere of 1926 was ominous and conflicted, for he could not reconcile what ought to be—the full integration of the Jew into modern society—and what is—pervasive and intractable hatred.[45]

Although the Shoah discredited the myth of inevitable progress, the establishment of Israel in 1948 and other hopeful developments, especially in the English-speaking countries, inspired an historian like William Rubinstein to describe the story of Anglophone Jews as a spectacular success story;[46] he did not fail to note the British and European antisemitism that demonizes Israel, although even this prejudice he described as predominantly leftist and not necessarily mainstream.[47] Israel dominates the contemporary hermeneutic moment, just as Zionism and immigration did with the earlier criticism of Philipson, and as the Shoah did with Rosenberg and Fisch.

The position from which the pre-Shoah critics condemned antisemitic representations was Enlightenment universalism. Philipson and
Calisch were vehemently anti-Zionist but retained a messianic insis-
tence on the Jew's role in moving society to a radically new transformation. Michelson's version of the messianic moment began with
a deconstruction of the concept of a Jewish race, pointing out that
most Jews could "pass" as southern Europeans and some could pass
anywhere in Europe, so that their "obstacle" to social integration was
not external:

> In their case it is only their ancient culture and its consequences that
> has made them and still makes them stand apart and that will continue
> to do so, unless the great miracle shall happen one day, the dream of so
> many idealists, the miracle by which all cultures will be thrown aside
> as so many worthless worn out garments and man will stand naked
> and innocent as Adam stood in Paradise, with this difference that the
> new Adam will know that he is naked and glory in it.[48]

This lyrical and Blakean passage stands out in these earlier studies, but
one finds messianic desire in another idea in the criticism: as prejudice
against Jews was symptomatic of social and economic inequality, so
the elimination of such prejudice would signify the achievement of
justice. For Michelson, Christian-majority societies needed to overcome antisemitism in order to achieve righteousness, thus rendering Jewish representations a central, rather than marginal concern.
By this logic, a writer as aesthetically unremarkable as Cumberland
had a role to play in the anti-antisemitic canon. A parallel might be
the aesthetically unremarkable and historically problematic television
miniseries *The Holocaust* (1978), by Gerald Green; although weak as
art and history, it initiated important and valuable public discussion.

Whether productions like Gerald Green's *The Holocaust* do more
harm than good is a debatable question, and contemporary critics
are more likely than earlier to discuss the harm.[49] It is a mistake,
however, to think that the earlier critics ignored aesthetic matters.
They all routinely made aesthetic judgments about texts, and several
of their commentaries resonate with us now. First, Philipson, Calisch,
and Modder dealt with Anglo-Jewish writers and not just the Jewish
characters in Scott, Dickens, and Eliot; and they read Disraeli, despite
his Anglican affiliation, in terms of literary Jewishness. However,
they declined the opportunity to theorize on the scandal of Disraeli's
boundary-crossing. Although Philipson vehemently insisted that Jews
were exclusively a religious group and not a national or racial group,

he treated not just Disraeli, but also Heine, another Christian convert, in terms of literary Jewishness. In this case, his critical practice did not match his anti-Zionist theory.

Second, Philipson's frame of reference was broadly European, not exclusively Anglo-American, for he contextualized Zangwill's fiction by relating it to similar texts by German Jews: Leopold Kompert (1822–86); Karl Emil Franzos (1848–1904); Joseph Seligmann Kohn (1803–50); and Heine (1797–1856).[50] Critics routinely now aim for broad contexts to understand Anglo-Jewish writing, whether the interpretive category is gender, modernity, race, transatlantic interactions, or colonialism.

Third, sometimes the interpretive frame gets beyond a simple polarity of philo- and antisemitic, as when Philipson and Calisch bring in Heine's and Arnold's Hebraic and Hellenic contrast.[51] Bryan Cheyette and Michael Ragussis have followed them in illustrating how this binary category functions for Victorian and Edwardian conceptions of Britishness and Jewishness. Rather than separating the sheep and goats into philo- and antisemitic writers, which the earlier critics saw as their primary interpretive task, current critical practice emphasizes the nuances of ambivalence at the levels of national and individual identity. An example is Cheyette's most recent reading of Matthew Arnold in his essay "On Being a Jewish Critic." Moreover, ever since Sander Gilman's groundbreaking study, *Jewish Self-Hatred* (1986),[52] critics such as Endelman[53] have written about the internalization of dominant norms in writers like Amy Levy (1861–89) and Julia Frankau (1863–1916). Nadia Valman, however, depicts Levy and Frankau as lucid, courageous, and exemplary naysayers to the apologetic platitudes and complacent materialism of the Anglo-Jewish establishment,[54] against whom Gilman's concept of Jewish self-hatred is deployed.[55] By using the concept of self-hatred, however, one already is practicing the newer criticism.

Fourth, Michelson deconstructed the notion that Britishness and Englishness were purely of Anglo-Saxon construction. Citing Joseph Addison's *Spectator*, Michelson pointed to the biblical influence on English authors, even the influence of the Hebrew language as an "Oriental" contrast to the "coldness and indifference" of European languages. Associating Hebrew with force, energy, warmth, and animation, Addison in *Spectator* 405 celebrated the positive effects of the hybridized language and literature.[56] According to Calisch, the King James Version of the Bible is in some ways authentically Jewish, including the influence on the translators of David Kimchi's commentary.[57] An important current in modern criticism emphasizes the cultural mixing of Jewish and English. Sheila Spector's work on Christian Kabbalah in Blake and the Yiddish and Hebrew translations of Byron is congruent with Bryan Cheyette's writing on Joyce's *Ulysses* as a complex revision of the Hebraic and Hellenic categories that decenter Anglo-Saxon Protestant Englishness,[58] as well as Judith Page's description of Hazlitt's and Kean's undermining of Macklin's antisemitic version of Shylock.[59] A similar emphasis in recent Anglo-Jewish historiography mainstreams the Jewish presence.[60] According to Ragussis, as England becomes Great Britain, it needs Jewishness in order to define itself.[61] The version of modernism we read in Leslie Fiedler and Bryan Cheyette situates the imaginary Jew at the center of that enterprise.

The half-century of Anglo-Jewish criticism from the time of the East European and Russian immigration of the 1880s to the Shoah struggled on the symbolic terrain of the negative stereotype, not surprisingly in the Hitler era. Although the criticism was not wholly instrumental in trying to protect a threatened Jewish community, all of the commentary was tied to the anti-antisemitic project of the time. From historical distance, one sees what Philipson and his fellow writers could not at the time: the wrongheadedness of the anti-Zionism, the futile poignance of the universalism, the unfortunate spurning of the great Yiddish literature being produced precisely when Philipson and Calisch were commenting on Jewish representations, and of course, the unimaginable catastrophe of the Shoah. As history tramples indifferently on every generation's illusions, one notices that the universalist rhetoric of the Reform rabbis and their vehement anti-Zionism, both of which were mainstream Jewish tendencies, are now more characteristic of the harshest Jewish critics of Israel on the Left.

There are three areas of striking difference between the older and current literary critics: the dialectic of minority and dominant discourse; the inclusion of diverse genres, not just the novel and drama; and the broad contextualization of literary texts in terms of cultural, postcolonial, gender, and feminist studies.

The earlier critics did not treat Anglo-Jewish writing as minority discourse (in relation to the "four nations," women's, and Afro-British writing), but only in relation to the dominant culture. Modder, for example, treated the writing of Aguilar and the Moss sisters as wholly instrumental in relation to Jewish emancipation; their writing lacked literary significance as such. Disraeli, however, possessed more than propagandistic value, so his writing was treated as literature.[62] Philipson wholly ignored Aguilar and the Mosses, while Calisch praised Aguilar but complained of her sentimentality and "diffuse" style.[63] Philipson, like Modder, devoted a whole chapter to Disraeli, treating him largely as a philosemitic author with whom he quarrels on a few issues.[64] One large difference between current and earlier critics is the model of Jewish integration. From the eighteenth century to the Shoah, that model was shaped by an exchange: Jews give up public Jewishness in exchange for Gentile toleration of private Jewishness; this was the model first articulated in eighteenth-century Germany and revolutionary France.[65] One can be a Jew in the synagogue and at home, but in the public spaces one is British and English. The multicultural model of Jewish integration rejects the hegemony of a majority culture, and situates Jewish difference with other cultural differences—sexual, ethnic, and religious. Difference is to be affirmed and not concealed in public spaces. The historian Bill Williams rejects the older model of Jewish integration with his phrase, "the anti-Semitism of tolerance," by which he signifies the tacit social contract under which British Jews are to be tolerated: discreetly Jewish at home or at synagogue, they are just like the British in every other way—not excessively socialist or religiously fervent, no Yiddish culture or Zionist fervor, no peculiar, un-Protestant religious practices that obtrude themselves into the public awareness.[66]

While Williams writes about actual Jews, Ragussis and Cheyette write about the figure of the Jew in texts that construct English and British identity, usually against Jewishness but sometimes with Jewishness. As soon as fiction and drama become part of minority discourse, they operate semiotically and not just aesthetically. For the older criticism, the semiotic meaning was almost always along a philo- and antisemitic axis, so that Philipson and the others only occasionally saw the various ways discursive Jewishness articulated the central preoccupations of the dominant culture. As minority discourse, Jewish textuality is also positioned with and against other minority discourses. Racial science, which from the eighteenth century identified Jews in relation to Anglo-Saxons, black Africans, and Semites, powerfully shaped literary meanings from Scott's *Ivanhoe* (1819) to Disraeli's *Tancred* (1847) to George Du Maurier's *Trilby* (1894). Ragussis shows how British national identity in the eighteenth and nineteenth centuries was constructed in popular culture through theatrical versions of ethnic identities, including Jewish identity. A neglected area of investigation is the Jewish/Irish nexus. English Jews had an easier time than their fellow Jews on the continent perhaps because the Protestant English hated and felt threatened by the Irish Catholics rather than the Jews. One can see an ethnic payback by Charles Macklin in his *Love à la Mode* (1759), where the Irish hero triumphs over the contemptible Jew, and especially in Macklin's version of Shylock, because the scapegoating formula works the other way as well: the more Jews are hated as un-English outsiders, the more acceptable Irish Catholics appear as fellow Christians. The default position in the work of the liberal Anglo-Irish writer Maria Edgeworth was uniformly antisemitic, until she was provoked by the American Jew, Rachel Mordecai, into writing her remarkable novel of reversals, *Harrington* (1817). One sees instances in the nineteenth century where Jews and Irish join forces against the Anglo-Saxon establishment: the political radical, John "Jew" King, collaborates with the Irish ultraradicals Patrick Duffin and Davenport Sedley, blackmailing aristocrats and royals.[67] In London's poor districts, the Irish and Jews both clash and cooperate, if the transcripts of criminal trials are used as evidence; but in literary representations, Anglo-Jewish writers, like Grace Aguilar, accent the similarities between Jews and Protestants while equating Catholicism with the Inquisition. One must not forget, however, that Daniel O'Connell (1775–1847), the Great Emancipator and political leader of the Irish Catholics, strongly supported Jewish emancipation. According to Galchinsky, Jews were not the primary or only Other against which the English culture defined itself; also important in the discursive efforts to patrol the borders of imperial British identity were the Irish, Catholics, Indians, Arab Muslims, and Africans.[68]

The earlier criticism of Jewish representations was generically narrow, limited largely to the culturally prestigious novel and drama. The recent recovery of Anglo-Jewish writing, however, includes a broad generic diversity—Judith Montefiore's diary, religious writing, literary history, translations, prints and caricatures, theological polemics, not just poetry, drama, and fiction. Critics now read Jewish texts semiotically and rhetorically, not just according to the anti- and philosemitic focus.

Finally, the earlier critics, without exception, for both good and ill, practiced a strong or weak version of identity politics, an inevitable entanglement in their own present situation. I was moved by their identity commitments, from Philipson's earnest and messianic anti-Zionism to Landa's comments in the 1920s on the excellence but obsolescence of the Yiddish theater. Identity politics in relation to literary criticism is nothing new. From the 1980s we have had the diasporic affirmations of the Boyarin brothers, on one side, and the Zionist affirmations of Ruth Wisse, on the other side, and other positions somewhere in between.[69] These identity commitments shape canon and theoretical understanding. The two contentious issues now are the state of Israel and the evaluation of antisemitism. Especially in the wake of the Second Intifada that began in the fall of 2000, criticism even of older texts allegorizes the present situation. For example, is Amy Levy a self-hating Jew or a lucid critic of a decadent Jewish establishment that mimics the Gentile authorities? Evaluating antisemitism now and historically is both inevitable and intellectually challenging in any kind of writing on Jewish representations. Is antisemitism what Ragussis calls the "dirty secret" of British liberalism, or is it as insignificant as Rubinstein claims?[70] Even if one does not share Rubinstein's neo-Conservative ideology, his argument on antisemitism for British and American exceptionalism is largely persuasive. However, Philip Roth's comic account of antisemitism in *The Counterlife* (1987) as being far worse in London than in New York is brilliant as literature and seems true. Neither statistics, which Rubinstein orchestrates effectively, nor aesthetic impressions and anecdotal experiences are sufficient to settle the controversy over antisemitism in British culture and literature. Rubinstein and others who slight the importance of British antisemitism fail to acknowledge fully that racist hatred is also destructive in its less physical manifestations in terms of intimidation, humiliation, and symbolic aggression, all things impossible to quantify.

Frank Felsenstein illustrates well the ambiguous nature of British antisemitism: the Lancaster school of the nineteenth century used to punish student misbehavior by making "the culprit parade from class to class decorated in the garb of a pedlar while the other boys followed behind imitating in a taunting fashion the dismal tones of Jewish street hawkers." Joseph Lancaster (1778–1838) could not understand objections to this or did not think it would encourage anti-Jewish feelings, for he believed that hostility to Jews was not because they were Jews but because of the way they cried "old clothes." That the educational reformer Sarah Trimmer (1741–1810) objected to this practice illustrates that Lancaster's judgment was not wholly representative at the time.[71] When most poor Jews in London were pedlars and the popular image of the Jew was that of a pedlar, Lancaster found nothing offensive in punishing his students as ordinary Jews. Lancaster was not advocating and would have been horrified to advocate physical attacks on London Jews. Therein lies the ambiguity, the parameters of the antisemitism within which aggression is permitted and outside of which not permitted. What makes antisemitism different from innumerable other instances of insensitive majorities treating their minorities badly, as majority cultures are prone to do, is the long history, especially in a Christian society. That long history casts a dark shadow that is not easy to interpret.

CHAPTER 2

1656 AND THE ORIGINS
OF ANGLO-JEWISH WRITING

When Menasseh ben Israel (1604–57), arguably the first Anglo-Jewish writer, campaigned for the readmission of Jews to England in the middle of the seventeenth century, he provoked William Prynne (1600–69) to publish what is arguably the first modern antisemitic pamphlet.[1] At precisely the same time, James Harrington (1611–77) published *The Commonwealth of Oceana* (1656), which to some extent advances the philosemitic tradition of political writing that extends well into the nineteenth century. These three kinds of Jewish writing emerge in the 1650s, each one with its own rhetorical and argumentative orientation toward religion and politics. Menasseh wrote as an ambassador representing the interests of Jews to the English Protestant world, a role other Anglo-Jewish writers would play in the future. The militantly Protestant Prynne, whose sincerity was registered on his body scarred by legally sanctioned torture—his cheeks were branded and his ears had been removed for opposing the crown and the church in the 1630s—intervened forcefully with his pamphlet in the Whitehall debates of December 1655, turning public opinion—skeptical already about readmission—against the Jews.[2] Keeping alive the medieval absurdities about Jewish villainy to justify the expulsion in 1290, Prynne assumed a role that will be played later by the "Jew Bill" pamphleteers of 1753–54 and William Cobbett (1763–1835) in the early nineteenth century. Harrington addressed the readmission question by proposing that Ireland become a Jewish colony while he treated Judaism as Mosaic republicanism, a source of political wisdom rather than nefarious anti-Christian sins and heresies. Although

the Ireland idea resonated with hardly anyone, Jewish republicanism appealed to other writers, such as John Toland (1670–1722) and
Thomas Spence (1750–1814).

Although Jewish writers after Menasseh did not always play the
role of defender of the faith, they never wholly ignored the already
existing discourse about Jews and Judaism. The two competing traditions of Jewish representations, one mostly hostile, the other comparatively friendly, supplied Jews with the grammar, vocabulary, and
background assumptions they could hardly ignore. The power of
harmful stereotypes waxes and wanes over time but never disappears.
For example, late in the nineteenth century the American Emma
Lazarus in her play *Dance to Death* (1882) returned to a fourteenth-
century pogrom in the Rhineland to undermine still current stereotypes by revising dramatic patterns and character typology established
in (among other texts) Shakespeare's (mostly hostile) *Merchant of
Venice* (1598) and Lessing's (comparatively friendly) *Nathan the Wise*
(1779). New pogroms, such as the Russian massacres that started in
the 1880s, evoked the older ones for Jewish writers who must work
with, through, and against already existing Jewish representations,
narrative structures, and symbolic associations.

If the most troublesome text for Jews in medieval Christendom was
the New Testament, especially the Gospels,[3] from the eighteenth century the *Merchant of Venice* was the master text of Jewish representations, according to Michael Ragussis, popular with theatre audiences
and strongly present in the English imagination.[4] For eighteenth-
and nineteenth-century literature, a Jewish male literary character
had to answer to Shylock, just as Jessica haunted literary Jewesses.
Even when displaying character traits unlike the established pattern,
the anti-Shylock (Cumberland's Sheva, Edgeworth's Montenero)
and the anti-Jessica (Scott's Rebecca, Aguilar's Marie) betrayed their
Shakespearean origins. Whatever power these by no means harmless
stereotypes exerted outside the theatre and books is hard to measure,
but they had consequences for a minority like the Jews who protested
against Thomas Dibdin's *Family Quarrels* (1802) and effectively boy-
cotted Marlowe's *Jew of Malta*, which was playing during Passover
in 1818.[5] Vulnerable but not powerless, Jews fought back when they
could, at times effectively, as when Rachel Mordecai persuaded Maria
Edgeworth that the novelist's Jewish representations were harmfully
stereotypical.[6]

Although Edgeworth corrected what she perceived as an error,
non-Jewish writers represented Jews for all kinds of reasons, rarely to
benefit Jews. James Harrington developed his republican ideas based

on scripture not to assist Jews but because he was convinced that the Mosaic ideas were true. His suggestion about "planting" Ireland with Jews was in a single paragraph in the introduction and hardly constituted a major proposition.[7] Prynne, to be sure, launched his diatribe specifically to prevent Jewish readmission, but his pamphlets were also an exercise in religious and national definition: English Protestantism should not be anything like loathsome Judaism. Moreover, as suggested by Eliane Glaser, Prynne's laborious thoroughness in listing every single Jewish misdeed in various historical records was his way of establishing a common law case against Jewish readmission.[8] As Michael Ragussis shows in his recent study of the Georgian theatre, the extensive Jewish representations in eighteenth-century plays were part of the ethnic conflict by which normative Englishness was being defined. National identity was imagined, performed, and acted out on stage by means of stereotypical characters, even as the stereotypes were being challenged and revised.[9]

Just as some American Protestants today, animated by millenarianism, try to influence certain outcomes in Israeli politics, so the English Protestants from the seventeenth century onward understood Jews within an apocalyptic narrative of national restoration and conversion. The philosemitic millenarians, including Cromwell, conceived that treating Jews more humanely would lead them to become Protestants. Although a few Gentiles like Toland were content with an autonomous Jewish community, valuable for its unique differences, most Protestants wanted either to transform those differences or to keep them as far away from Britain as possible.

Although a secular skepticism about millenarianism prevails now among scholars who view the enterprise as social fantasy, only a small minority of seventeenth-century Europeans would have doubted the truth of scriptural prophecy; the debatable point was how to interpret the prophecies, not whether they contained a truth that had to be understood. Many if not most Jews at that time also eagerly expected the arrival of the Messiah, who turned out *not* to be Shabbatai Zevi (1626–76), to the grievous disappointment of millions.[10] Although Jewish messianism declined precipitously after Shabbatai's failure, Christian millenarianism enjoyed widespread popularity after 1789 because of the emancipation of Jews under French political control and Napoleon's conquest of the Holy Land, along with his institution of the Sanhedrin. For the sake of spiritual justification and national prestige, it was important that the New Jerusalem where the messianic events were to take place happened under English—not French—auspices.[11]

Even as Enlightenment rationalism redefined messianic transformation as social-political progress guided by liberalism and socialism, the "Jewish Question" mattered in countless ways but almost always in relation to how Gentiles defined themselves. Rather than genuine multicultural tolerance of Jews, there was ambivalence in a surprisingly large body of texts. One can speculate on why this was so—guilt over the 1290 expulsion, investment in the millenarian narrative, insecurity over the commercial empire, anxiety over secularism—but the sheer textual presence of Jewishness in the literary culture, from novels and poetry to popular songs, is remarkable, given the small number of actual English Jews.

JEWISH READMISSION AND NATIONAL IDENTITY

The works of Menasseh ben Israel illustrate the literary and cultural ambiguities of Jewish representations in England. His writing makes prominent issues that frequently arise in Jewish texts: language, identity, millenarianism/messianism, conversion, commerce, misrepresentations, and stereotypes. Although by the late nineteenth century Zionism replaces millenarianism as the overall emphasis becomes more secular, the other six issues still structure Jewish writing. A cosmopolitan European intellectual who used ten different languages, of which he published in five, Menasseh anchored his hybrid identity—Dutch, Portuguese, English—in the Jewish experiences of the Iberian New Christian community. The Spanish Inquisition had arrested, tortured, imprisoned, and confiscated the property of his father, leaving him in bad health and lifelong poverty. England—or rather the idea of England—represented something entirely unlike the typical seventeenth-century Jewish life: unprecedented religious freedom connected indirectly (but meaningfully) with messianic hope.[12]

The first title Menasseh published in English, *The Hope of Israel* (1650), was a translation by an English millenarian from the Latin translation rather than the Spanish original.[13] The other texts in English produced under Menasseh's name were pamphlets addressed to Cromwell and parliament for the readmission of Jews to England (1655), and *Vindiciae Judaeorum* (1656), a rebuttal of the antisemitic misrepresentations generated during the public debate on Jewish resettlement. Lobbying government officials and appealing to public opinion, Menasseh lived briefly in London (1655–57), a place he—from a Portuguese New Christian family—wanted to become a second, even more welcoming Amsterdam (his own city), a haven for Jews fleeing persecution. According to Todd M. Endelman, "Jewish efforts to gain readmission to England were part of a broader strategy of securing new places of refuge for persecuted New Christians."[14] With the Inquisition pursuing conversos in the New World and with the catastrophic massacres of Ashkenazi Jews in Poland and Russia (1648–58), Jewish messianic thinking, which pervades Menasseh's writing, was typical of seventeenth-century Judaism, reflected in the movement led by the false messiah Shabbatai Zevi.

Although Menasseh's slender purchase on an English identity rests with a short residence in London and several English publications, one of which was definitely translated, one probably translated, and the third might have been translated. Regardless, Menasseh has what Foucault called "author-function" because the printed words by his name were tied to "discursive practices" he put into print-culture circulation.[15] Writers at the time and historians later made him the "author" of Jewish readmission, even if those actual words were in translated English. From what does national identity come? Geography, language, religion, culture, and constitutional law—or a combination of the five? Jews historically—at least since 70 CE—experienced routinely in the Diaspora the insecurities of national identity, hiding their religion in Spain and Portugal, and being alternately tolerated and persecuted by Muslim and Christian rulers. Centuries-long residence in any particular place did not guarantee Jews security, as expulsions, starting with England's in 1290, were not uncommon in Europe. Menasseh promised political loyalty in exchange for religious and commercial freedom, but many Jews by the eighteenth century, according to Todd Endelman, even those who retained a strong Jewish identity, also adopted English cultural norms in the areas of clothing, leisure activities, and entertainment.[16] Cultural hybridization really begins with Menasseh's deploying English prose to argue the case for readmission. With *Humble Addresses* and the later *Vindiciae Judaeorum* Menasseh could have worked with translators, and he could have contributed to the Englishing of his ideas.

Menasseh positions himself as a petitioner to Cromwell and public opinion in the *Humble Addresses*, where he identifies the four "Motives for his coming into England," namely: (1) to worship freely in synagogue; (2) to advance the messianic agenda by inserting Jews where there were none; (3) to pursue commerce; (4) to join as the biblical Stranger the already existing learned and pious community of Christians.[17] All of these motives were matters of bitter controversy, as religious toleration in the commonwealth was not understood or practiced in universal terms, as only some versions of the millenarian narrative required universal Jewish dispersal, as London's merchants

fiercely opposed Jewish competition, and as numerous scholars saw
the Jewish foreigners as threats to Christian piety. These four empha-
ses reflected Menasseh's familiarity with liberal Protestants, with
whom he corresponded and spoke extensively in Amsterdam, and
whom he hoped would respond favorably to his appeal. He seems to
have underestimated the opposition to Jewish readmission, but he
was not alone—so too did Cromwell. It is doubtful that Menasseh
could have chosen other, better words to make his case, for the opposition, angrily expressed by the fanatical Prynne, forcefully expressed
by the London merchants, was not open to persuasion.

As Menasseh expands upon the four motives, he cannot extricate
himself from stereotypes, even as he tries to counter them. Assuming
that England would want an immigrant group that was commercially
successful, politically loyal, and genealogically "noble," Menasseh is
also dispelling fearful images of predatory economic practices and
hostility to Christians. The very phrase used to signify nobility—
limpieza de sangre (purity of blood)—evokes the horrors of Spain and
Portugal, where the impurity of Jewish descendants occasioned suspicion, torture, and death. As Yosef Kaplan observes, Menasseh here
seems to have internalized the norms of the antisemitic oppressors;
this also seems to be an example of what Sander Gilman called Jewish
self-hatred.[18] Menasseh's providential reading of Jewish commerce as
a compensation for the loss of Zion includes a rhetoric of innate qualities: God has given Jews a "natural instinct" for "merchandizing" so
they can "thrive in Riches and possessions." As a compensatory skill
to make survival in the Diaspora possible, commercial abilities can be
construed not only as a divine gift but also as a negatively stereotypical quality. Although Menasseh understandably presents political loyalty as a virtue for a people who have no home-country (at least until
the Messiah comes) to which they could return with their wealth
acquired in England, the very organic cohesiveness of the community
accents the foreignness of the Jews. We will not compete for political
and social honors outside our community, insists Menasseh, but the
very self-sufficiency of the Jews evokes an image of power and independence, "clannishness."[19]

The last part of the *Humble Addresses* counters the antisemitic
slanders that have survived their medieval origins: usury, ritual murder, and proselytism. Each one is carefully discussed, as usury is not
exclusively Jewish and most Jewish lenders require low not exorbitant interest; as ritual murder, which has been dismissed as fanci-
ful by authorities as powerful as the Pope, was even leveled against
Christians during the Roman Empire; and, finally, as Jews do not

seek but discourage converts, Christians have nothing to worry about from Jewish proselytism.[20] Menasseh's treatment of Christian prejudice is rational and idealistic, but also scriptural, as when he disputes the usury slander: "In our Law it is a greater sinne to rob or defraud a stranger, than if I did it to one of my own profession: because a Jew is bound to shew his charity to all men: for he hath a precept, not to abhorre an Idumean, nor an Egyptian; and that he shall love and protect a stranger that comes to live in his land."[21] Deliberately Menasseh throughout the *Humble Addresses* uses the biblical Stranger to signify both Jew and Christian, thus making generosity to Jews seem like a way of being true to the most basic Christian principles.

William Prynne, of course, was having none of this interfaith harmony, for his pamphlet, vehemently opposing readmission, was placed in the hands of the delegates at the last meeting of the Whitehall conference in December 1655. *A Short Demurrer to the Jewes Long Discontinued Remitter into England* appeals to the reader in two contradictory ways: it is wildly irrational in accepting as true the most improbable transgresssions ever attributed to Jews; however, it is also obsessively scholarly, with sources cited, dates given, trials annotated, culprits and victims named, and dead bodies enumerated. The rhetoric of persuasiveness in 1655 London was high scholarly, even in the aspect of thoroughness, for Prynne seems to have scoured every chronicle, history, and legal code for every single instance of Jewish crime and punishment. Perversely, Prynne has the honor— surely against his wishes—of inaugurating Anglo-Jewish historiography because no one before him had identified so many primary sources and "published, in full or part, hundreds of documents from the public records."[22]

Prynne's pedantic style is in the service of a simple argument against readmission: he claims—inaccurately, as it turns out[23]—that parliament legally banished the Jews from England in 1290 for their numerous misdeeds. This parliamentary act cannot and should not be undone, according to Prynne. On this issue Prynne challenges the finding of the Whitehall conference, whose lawyers could discover no legal obstacle to resettlement.[24] The constitutional issues aside, *A Short Demurrer to the Jewes Long Discontinued Remitter into England* acquaints mid-seventeenth-century Protestants with all the offenses that occasioned Jewish expulsion in the thirteenth century. His main points break down as follows: (1) Jews, who are evil, cannot and do not change, so that the passage of time or individual conversions to Christianity brings only illusory transformation of what is in fact immutable Jewishness; (2) Jews exercise their evil power

through money, discourse, and violence; (3) because Jewish power
is so hateful toward Christians and Christianity, there can be no safe
interaction with Jews, who should be isolated or expelled. Knowing
the London merchants opposed the Jews for economic reasons,
Prynne heavily stresses Jewish commercial evils: forgery, counterfeit-
ing, usury, extortion, and corrupting currency. He invariably juxta-
poses instances of ritual murder with illustrations of Jewish economic
power. After describing the child killings of William of Norwich and
other children at Gloucester and Bury St. Edmonds, Prynne remarks:
"What punishments were then inflicted on them [the Jews] for these
Murders, and Insolencies, I find not recorded; perchance they purchased their Peace with monies."[25] The power of Jewish money operates like Satan: "What a prevailing Engin the Jews money is, both to
scrue them into Christian Kingdoms, though the most bitter, inveterate, professed Enemies of Christ himself, Christians, and Christianity;
and how their money can induce even Christian Princes to perpe-
trate most unchristian, and antichristian actions; and enforced by
threats and violence, even converted Christian Jews to renounce their
Christianity, and apostastise to their former Jewish Errors which they
had quite renounced."[26]

Prynne turns even the most gruesome examples of Christian torture of Jews into illustrations of Jewish greed, such as the famous
episode of removing the teeth from a Bristol Jew whom the king targets for extra taxes,[27] or most remarkably the York Massacre of 1190.
One of the most shameful English pogroms illustrates, in Prynne's
narrative, the moral inadequacies of the Jews who rather than give
up all their wealth to Christians (impoverished by usury) and convert
to the true religion Christianity chose to "murder" their wives and
children and to destroy themselves and their valuables in a degrading
manner: "casting their golden Vessels and Jewels into Privies, that the
Christians might not be inriched by them, these murderers shutting
up themselves and the rest they had killed in the kings house, set it
on fire, and to burn both themselves and it."[28] Prynne's being able to
turn the mass suicide of the trapped Jews into ordinary murder, theft,
and vandalism suggests that no historical detail would threaten his
overall narrative of Jewish villainy and Christian innocence.

The only possible justification for allowing Jews to resettle would
be their eventual conversion, but Prynne repels that argument in two
ways, by insisting upon their unchanging evil nature, which makes
conversion impossible, and by pointing to the much greater probabil-
ity that Jews and their dangerous textuality (oral and written) would
turn Christians into Jews: "in this giddy, unsettled, apostatizing age,

wherein they are likelier to gain a thousand *English Proselytes to their Judaisme*, than we one Jewish convert to *Christianity*."[29] Not a time for letting down one's guard or welcoming the Stranger, Prynne urges increased vigilance against whatever might weaken Protestant faith at a historical moment he understands as perilous, "this giddy, unsettled, apostatizing age." Prynne was not the first nor the last writer to link Jews with modernity and its "giddy" freedom, its disorderliness in the wake of ruined certainties and devastated truths that once had been "settled," and its ideological warfare and doubtful outcomes. Scapegoating Jews was one way of alleviating the anxious effects of fundamental historical changes.

Four months after Prynne's lobbying against readmitting Jews to England, a chastened Menasseh ben Israel took up his pen in April, 1656, and wrote his most politically effective pamphlet, *Vindiciae Judaeorum*, which had no immediate effect, but became the Enlightenment's most eloquent rebuttal of the commonplace slanders against Jews and Judaism.[30] It is not certain whether Menasseh himself wrote this in English or it was translated into English. When Moses Mendelssohn appealed to German and European public opinion for Jewish emancipation and wanted to attack the prevailing prejudices and stereotypes, there was no better text available than the *Vindiciae Judaeorum*, which he translated into German and reissued in 1782.[31] Although it is a credit to Menasseh as a rhetorician that his pamphlet, created as a timely intervention in a political dispute, would become a useable "classic" well over a century later, it does not speak well of the Christian community that required such a pamphlet.

The *Humble Addresses* had concluded with his refutation of the three main defamations against Jews—usury, ritual murder, and proselytism—and the new pamphlet develops its first and longest section on the blood libel and usury. Dissecting the absurd logic of the blood libel consumes the pamphlet's first fifteen pages (about 40 percent of the pamphlet), as Menasseh combines incongruities—the Jewish prohibition from eating blood applies obviously to Christian blood—and commonsensical objections—killing a boy after circumcision defeats the purpose of gaining a Jewish adherent, if that were the purpose of circumcision in this case. He claims that the Christians were practicing what we now call displacement of the shameful things Christians themselves had been doing to Jews and other innocent victims: the Christians in the New World baptized and then killed the Amerindians; the Inquisition burned to death many innocents; Christians tortured and dispossessed many Jews, and not infrequently framed Jews for the murders they themselves committed. The accusation of desecrating the Communion wafer makes no sense in terms of the Jewish ban on any kind of idolatry and traffic with graven images. Jews are nowhere in Torah instructed to perform any of these nefarious deeds; rather, they are instructed not to murder, not to consume blood, not to acknowledge idols, and to love the Stranger. As for usury, Menasseh points out that the usurious rates in parts of Germany and Poland are required to compensate Jewish lenders for widespread nonpayment of Christian debts. "And so," Menasseh concludes this first section, "it hath been divers times; men mischieving the *Iewes* to excuse their own wickedness."[32]

The next four sections calmly explain how Judaism's religious practices—the daily prayers and policy of conversion—should not offend a reasonable Christian. He dutifully and considerately explains parts of the Aleinu prayer that might disturb a Christian, what the prayer against the "*minim*"—the "heretics"—is all about, and how the sincerity-guaranteeing act of circumcision for the handful of adult converts to Judaism should not worry Christians secure in their own faith. However, it seems evident that the real issues, if there is anything "real" in this discourse of hate and misrepresentation, are the blood libel and usury, the two issues with the most spectacular textual histories. The final point of confutation is that Jews, who are barred by scripture from stealing, have been invariably beneficial for the economies of which they have taken a commercial part. The final section concludes with a bitter observation that the failure of the Whitehall conference to grant readmission resulted in Jews moving to other places—Italy—where they would not advance the messianic narrative, which requires that Jews settle in England.[33]

Menasseh has worked with, through, and against already existing Jewish representations, narrative structures, and symbolic associations, blurring some of the differences between Christian millenarianism and Jewish messianism, validating Jewish commercial prowess, which he balances with Jewish ethical rigor. (It is ironic that the miserably poor scholar Menasseh grants some legitimacy to a stereotype he himself in no way resembles.) Although there is little reason to doubt Menasseh's messianic commitment, as Cecil Roth seems to do,[34] one can see the great advantage such a commitment carries in millenarian-intoxicated England.[35] Menasseh appeals to the prudence and wise public policy that would let in money-making foreigners, but he also speaks urgently of readmission as a form of the highest kind of piety in clearing an obstacle for the Messiah's arrival. The piety of welcoming the needy and persecuted Stranger, a rhetoric Menasseh employs more than a few times, appeals to us in a cosmopolitan register and creates a messianic tone without the super-naturalism. From Menasseh to Mendelssohn to Kant to Habermas to Levinas and Derrida: the trajectory is a way of reading and making meaning.[36] The fourth motive identified in the *Humble Addresses* highlights a rooted cosmopolitanism and the biblical injunction to love the Stranger:

> My sincere affection to this Common wealth, by reason of so many Worthy, Learned, and Pious men in this Nation, whose loving kind-nesse and Piety I have experience of: hoping to finde the like affec-tion in all the People generally; the more, because I always have, both by writing, and deeds, professed much inclination to this Common-wealth; and that I perswade my selfe they will be mindfull of that Command of the Lord our God, who so highly recommends unto all men the *love of strangers*; much more to those that professe their good affection to them. For this I desire all may be confident of, that I am not come to make any disturbance, or to move any disputes about mat-ters of Religion; but onely to live with my Nation in the feare of the Lord, under the shadow of your protection, whiles we expect with you the *hope of Israel* to be revealed.[37]

Behind this idealistic rhetoric is an actually existing network of per-sonal relationships, correspondence, and textual encounters between Jews and Christians. David S. Katz inquires how, after centuries of prejudice, would English Christians sufficiently de-demonize the imaginary Jew to entertain readmitting real Jews? The how is easier to answer than the why, as Katz describes Christian scholars like John Selden (1584–1654) who conducted sophisticated studies of Hebrew and Jewish history, Protestant Judaizers like the Traskites who adopted many Jewish customs, and of course millenarians who imagined a his-torical role for actually existing Jews.[38] However self-serving it often was, the philosemitism depicted by Katz was the context that enabled Menasseh to write and act as he did. Indeed, without that philosemi-tism, Menasseh would have looked elsewhere for a messianic haven, perhaps only an imaginary one of mystical, kabbalistic construction; or, of course, he could have followed his student Spinoza in detaching himself entirely from the messianic enterprise. Regardless, the point is that Anglo-Jewish writing in its origins is connected, for better or worse, with philosemitism, which was strong enough to bring about the Whitehall discussions of December 1655, but not strong enough to issue an invitation to Europe's Jews. Perhaps Richard H. Popkin is correct in suggesting that the Whitehall discussion foundered on the issue of whether to let in Caraites as well as Jews,[39] but the distinctively

English compromise that resulted in the absence of any legal declaration either for or against readmission allowed a de facto toleration of conversos already in London to worship openly and a modest settlement of Dutch Sephardic Jews—only eighty families by 1684.[40] As pointed out by Eliane Glaser, England was far more accepting of the many thousands of Huguenots who sought and received admission to the country at the same time.[41]

PHILOSEMITISM

To sketch a discernible shape of philosemitism at the time Menasseh was in London, one can look first at several texts addressing directly the readmission question, Henry Jessey's *A Narrative of the Late Proceedings at Whitehall, Concerning the Jews* (1656), and John Dury's *A Case of Conscience* (1656). Then I will take a brief look at James Harrington's *The Commonwealth of Oceana* (1656). Jessey (1603–63) and Dury (1596–1680) were part of the so-called Samuel Hartlib (1600–63) circle of reformers and philosemites who knew Menasseh and supported readmission. Although Jessey's *Narrative* strongly argues the case for readmission, Dury's pamphlet takes a narrow view of Jewish resettlement. Harrington speaks more obliquely on the readmission question but his treatise becomes the founding document of philosemitic political writing.

Jessey's *Narrative*, while providing a summary of what happened at the Whitehall conference in December 1655, characterizes the opposition to resettlement as unreasonable, hypocritical, and unchristian, and represents the 1290 expulsion as shameful and murderous. In response to the request, advocated by the "agent" for the Jews, "Rabbi Manasses ben Israel," that Jews be permitted to resettle on the terms of full religious freedom to worship in their synagogues, the assembled notables were disapproving: "The most did fear, that if they should come, many would be seduced and cheated by them, and little good would be unto them."[42] The fear of being seduced by Judaism itself, its alluring texts and arguments, as well as by Jews themselves, their physical persons and conversation, is something upon which Prynne expatiated extensively. Jessey attributes this fear in part to the more general fear of "subversion" because "so many here are soon carried aside to new opinions."[43] The "giddy" freedom of modernity makes Judaism an option, something in fact exercised by the so-called seventeenth-century "Judaizers" like the Traskites who adopted aspects of the Jewish religion. The London merchants claimed moral superiority to the Jews, but it was London merchants who were responsible for the drowning deaths of thousands of Jews in the thirteenth century.[44] Jessey undermines the accusation of Jewish commercial evil by pointing to the dubious morality of the self-serving and hypocritical London merchants themselves.

Jessey insists upon two major points: biblical doctrine clearly obligates Christians to deal "courteously with strangers, and persons in affliction," and Jews petitioning for readmission to England qualify as afflicted strangers. Citing a half dozen biblical passages, Jessey declares that the New and Old Testament alike command kindness to the Stranger, not the "cruel and inhuman injuries [that] have formerly been done in our nation against the Jews." Jessey points to the numerous sites of violence against contemporary Jews: in Poland, Lithuania, and Prussia by Swedes and Cossacks; in Jerusalem by the Turks; in France, Spain, Portugal, and the Indies by the Inquisition and the Church.[45] The pamphlet makes no excuses for the Whitehall conference, which has failed to advance the millenarian story of reconciliation that must occur before the Messiah arrives. According to David S. Katz, Jessy illustrates the overall closeness between Christian millenarianism and Jewish messianism because of shared kabbalistic texts, material support for the poor Jews of Jerusalem, and a social network that included the Sabbateans.[46]

If Jessey represents one pole of philosemitism that imagines the conversion of the Jews as taking place in the fullness of time, after Christians have repented of their disgraceful treatment of Jews, and have accepted Jews as equal partners in the messianic enterprise, another pole is represented by John Dury and his pamphlet *A Case of Conscience*, published in June, 1656 but written earlier in January. One of Oliver Cromwell's agents on the continent, the Scottish clergyman John Dury, born in Holland, studied in Leiden, was a pastor for a German congregation in Cassel. This Protestant cosmopolitan, who tried for decades to reunite the Protestants of Europe, thought so highly of Menasseh that he planned to name him as one of the three professors for the projected London college of Jewish studies.[47] As a leading figure in the Hartlib circle, Dury takes an unusually restrictive view of Jewish immigration. The constraints on readmission advised by Dury are so substantial that some have read the pamphlet as actually opposed to resettlement itself, but J. Minton Batten takes another position: "Dury's views certainly fell far short of present-day principles of toleration, but there is nothing in the pamphlet to justify the assertion that he 'wrote fiercely against the Jews.'"[48] Mordecai L. Wilensky explains that Dury, while in Cassel, translated the coercive decrees (1539, 1646) establishing the conditions for Jewish settlement in Hesse. Although Dury found the decrees too harsh and in fact counterproductive, he discovered an educational purpose in fashioning a more moderate set of English restrictions.[49] Because Dury was advocating Protestant unity with his patron, Landgrave William VI of Hesse, he probably found it easy to formulate his backing of the Jews in terms his powerful supporter would understand. Dury was distinctive in the Hartlib circle for strongly promoting unity—rather than doctrinal diversity—among Protestants, so that it would not have seemed a great burden to him to ask the Jews settling in England to conform to his set of restrictions: Jews would be prohibited from blaspheming Christ and making converts; they had to observe both the Jewish and Christian Sabbath; they had to listen without comment to Christian sermons, defend in public their Judaism, and discuss the Bible with Christians. Additionally, by "laws and special orders" Jews, who would be segregated from Gentiles and be required to conduct religious services in Hebrew, would be prevented from oppressing the Gentiles especially in the areas of usury and trade.[50]

Dury's *A Case of Conscience* also expresses compassion for the distressed Jews who deserve hospitality, citing the duty of a Christian to the biblical Stranger, and insists that inviting Jews to England should be motivated wholly by Christian love and not by commercial benefits. The conditions recommended by the pamphlet are intrusive, condescending, and coercive, closer in rhetoric to William Prynne rather than to his friend Henry Jessey. In the postscript Dury characterizes Menasseh's *Humble Addresses* as excessively demanding and offensive to Gentiles. Accepting as a truism that Jews naturally try to oppress Gentiles in trade and commerce, Dury seems to share Prynne's stereotypical perspective but in fact he does not, at least not entirely. Dury's pamphlet argues for moving the Jews toward a voluntary not a coercive conversion to Christianity; Prynne believed the Jews too evil to ever convert. In fact, Dury's rhetoric is not more negatively stereotypical than much of the German pro-emancipation rhetoric in the eighteenth and nineteenth century. German emancipation hinged on the re-education of Jews, their adoption of German culture and manners, and their acceptance of Bildung as a disciplinary and ethical project. Like the German emancipationists promoting Schiller and Goethe, Dury imagines the Jews becoming morally improved by their exposure to Christian and English ideas.

Remarkable is not that a writer from a dominant culture imagines an oppressed minority needs the transformative benefits of hegemonic education, or that philosemitism is always mixed with agendas extraneous or at best distantly related to Jews (Protestant unity,

Christian millenarianism, and national competition with the Dutch, Turks, Catholics, and Spanish). Remarkable is that the philosemitic writers also conceived of Judaism and Jews as being valuable more or less on their own terms, thus requiring ethical understanding. Henry Finch (1621), who addresses Jews in Hebrew on one page of his pamphlet, develops the New Jerusalem narrative of millenarian change almost exclusively with material from what he would call the Old Testament. It is not that he sees Jews as blameless, for they killed Jesus, "shamefully nayling him ypon the Crosse," but he also suggests that God has forgiven the Jews, or as he phrases it, has "winked" at the crucifixion.[51] The laboring-class Baptist Thomas Collier (1656) in his rebuttal of Prynne's pamphlet argues that the expulsion was reprehensible and evil, something demanding national repentance; readmission would constitute a form of "recompense" for the wrong of 1290.[52] Collier undermines the position of moral superiority assumed by most philosemitic writers when he links moral rectitude with national remembrance of guilt. In another pamphlet of 1656, "D.L." claims that the laws governing the relations between different nations require the application of the golden rule, so that not vexing the Stranger means allowing the Jews to resettle if they wish, even after their miserable treatment between 1066 and 1290.[53]

With rare and notable exceptions like Toland, the philosemitic writers supporting Jewish settlement and naturalization were also Christian supercessionists whose theology conceived of salvation as exclusively Christian, indeed Protestant; if Jews did not convert, their immortal souls were in peril. Nevertheless, as Richard H. Popkin argues, the Jewish-Christian dialogue under these inadequate philosemitic conditions paved the way for modern toleration as it was practiced in the Netherlands, the United States, and Britain.[54] In addition, the constrained, ambivalent toleration also produced a normative mixing—constrained and ambivalent—of Jewish and Christian texts and tropes evident in texts produced by Jews and Gentiles. The ways that Menasseh's Jewish messianism and the philosemitic millenarianism share a discourse illustrate what will become a pattern of similarity and difference repeated in the Georgian period as well. Another fundamental pattern of the seventeenth century endures well into the nineteenth: the persistence of negative stereotypes, even in Jewish and strongly philosemitic texts. The genial D. L. who dismisses the common antisemitic libels with cheerful rationalism, nevertheless also writes that Jews are "naturally addicted to trade and traffick."[55] But D.L. is merely echoing Menasseh's comments on Jewish commerce, upon which Dury greatly expands. Collier deflects the negative power of the stereotype by suggesting that Jewish commerce will bring cheaper consumer goods, even if a few Christian merchants might lose some business.[56] Aesthetically intensified by Shakespeare's powerful play, the stereotype of Jewish commercial greed and unnatural expertise will become the debilitating Shylock stereotype.

I want to conclude with James Harrington's *Oceana*, a text that opens up into the eighteenth century and a tradition of philosemitic economic and political writing. The major philosemitic aspect of *Oceana* is that in the context of 1656 and the readmission question, Harrington cites Jewish texts and history extensively to sketch models of constitutional and economic order. "Planting" a depopulated Ireland with Jews, a bad idea in more than a few ways (exploiting anti-Catholicism, using Jews to displace the native Irish, not permitting Jews to live in Scotland and England),[57] nevertheless counters some stereotypes: "Though the Jews be now altogether for merchandise, yet in the land of Canaan (since their exile from whence they have not been landlords) they were altogether for agriculture; and there is no cause why a man should doubt but, having a fruitful country and good ports too, they would be good at both." *Oceana* opts for Jewish autonomy—"allowing them their own rites and laws"—rather than a conversionist educational program.[58] Harrington's text tilts always toward using Jewishness as a model for Christians, in effect a conversionist Bildung for Gentiles, not the familiar philosemitic stance of abolishing Judaism with Christian "love." Although I am not disputing that Machiavelli is the master intertext for *Oceana*, as Pocock has stated,[59] it is striking that Harrington grants so much authority to the Mosaic republic as a divinely sanctioned model of governance.[60]

Especially in the opening section, "The Preliminaries, showing the Principles of Government," the primary constitutional model is from the Hebrew Bible. *Oceana* states that the very first "ancient prudence" of government "discovered unto mankind by God himself in the fabric of the commonwealth of Israel, and afterward picked out of his footsteps in nature and unanimously followed by the Greeks and Romans."[61] Harrington engages one of the most powerful tropes in Jewish representations—the polarity of Jerusalem and Athens, the Hebraic and the Hellenic—to establish the priority of Judaism. The Mosaic republic has a political and economic aspect, and Harrington distinctively argues for the determinative power of the economic. The commonwealth depends on people being their own landlords or holding land so that "no one man, or number of men...overbalance them." The agrarian law "fixing the balance in lands" was "first introduced by God himself, who divided the land of Canaan unto his people by lots, and is of such virtue that, wherever it hath held, that government hath not altered, except by consent"—as when Israel decided to have a king.[62] Oceana has biblical and classical authority for preferring government by law and reason rather than force and passion—"authority, not empire."[63] The commonwealth's tripartite division of power has biblical precedent, as does the idea of a natural aristocracy and the principle of "liberty of conscience," exemplified in the right of prophets to criticize the powerful.[64]

According to Susan Manly, who reads *Oceana* by highlighting the Jewish dimension, Harrington's emphasis on discussion and participation at the lowest levels, along with liberty of conscience moderates the aristocratic emphasis.[65] "For Harrington, the rightness of this system is clear because it is the system that had been laid down by Moses, as a contract with God. It is important for Harrington that ancient Israel was a theocracy, because he is keen to emphasize that the relationship between God and men was originally a civil compact expressed in a political society, not a Church, and through the mediation of democratically elected civil rulers, not a separate order of priests or clerics. God could thus be shown to communicate with men in their political nature, and, furthermore, could be appealed to as the founder of republicanism." Although God functions as king, "God's republic" has no king.[66] Out of Harrington come eighteenth- and nineteenth-century traditions of republicanism and land reform, while the aristocratic dimension, essential for the major commonwealthman theorist, has no influence on writers such as Thomas Spence and John Thelwall but considerably more influence on writers such as Toland and Coleridge. Harrington thus is the vehicle for transmitting biblically based political and economic thinking into the eighteenth and nineteenth century.

CHAPTER 3

THE PEDLAR

When the most common occupation of poor Jews in eighteenth- and early–nineteenth-century London was that of street pedlar, images of the Jewish old-clothes man were ubiquitous in British culture. In the Old Bailey trial *Proceedings* (also called *Sessions Paper*) and the numerous "Jew Songs" from the London theatre and in the collection *Universal Songster* (1825), the figure of the Jewish pedlar is commonplace. While the stereotype of the commercially dishonest foreigner is pervasive, a few songs are respectful of Jewish life, which is accepted as part of multiethnic London. Although I will draw upon some social history of the pedlar and Jewish London, making a few social-historical observations, my primary interest here is literary and more broadly cultural, for the Old Bailey *Proceedings*, a rich resource for the social historian, is an aesthetic and cultural text, readable not just for what it discloses about the actual life of people who once existed but also for what it reveals about the constitution of a discourse about Jewishness. The popular songs about Jews reflect not only London social realities but also cohere at a cultural level where stereotypes, ethnic competition, and national identity are worked out.

The pedlar figure in nineteenth-century literature appears in Wordsworth's *Ruined Cottage* (1797) and *Excursion* (1814), Maria Edgeworth's anti-antisemitic novel *Harrington* (1817), and the fictions (*Benjamin the Third* (1878), *Fishke the Lame* (1888), etc.) by Mendele Mocher Seforim (1835–1917)—Mendele the Bookpeddler—one of the first Yiddish storytellers, the so-called grandfather of Yiddish fiction. The associations of peddling, poetry, fiction, and Jewishness are explicitly integrated for Mendele but the same connections for Wordsworth and Edgeworth are mediated and indirect.

At least as early as the 1790s literary authors like the popular writer Charles Dibdin (1745–1814) associated the pedlar with the writer in *The Pedlar* (1796), where the persona of the commercial writer plays ironically with the parallels with the pedlar selling his wares. Literary texts as commodities designed to please the market—Dibdin dedicates the inexpensive book (18d) to "John Bull"—both embarrass and inspire Dibdin, who in the introductory verses declares: "A PEDLAR I—but, mark, no Jew— / I've conscience, and my wares are new."[1] Dibdin identifies Jewishness here with unscrupulous commercial transactions as well as a lack of originality and creativity, claiming for himself literary products that are the very symbolic opposite of "old clothes" and counterfeit coins. Similarly, Wordsworth's Pedlar is inside and outside of his society; estranged enough not only to wander and be connected enough to return back to the community; wise from bookish study, nature mysticism, and diverse human encounters, but also shrewd as a seller of commodities and a close observer of people and their needs. One Christian version of the diasporic Jew is similar to Wordsworth's Pedlar—and Shelley's Ahasuerus, Byron's Cain, and Romanticism's Wandering Jew. The old-clothes man assumes a sinister role in *Oliver Twist* where Fagin learns of Oliver's whereabouts from a Jewish pedlar who purchased from Mrs. Bedwin Oliver's old clothes (ch. 16). Also, when Fagin wants to hide from the legal authorities, he goes to Rag Fair in the East End, where he is known, welcomed, and accepted (ch. 26).

OLD BAILEY *PROCEEDINGS*

When poor Ashkenazim from Central and Eastern Europe settled in London, they took up the one occupation available for penniless immigrants: peddling cheap goods on the street. The Jewish community, anxious to prevent the politically inflammatory spectacle of Jewish begging and determined to care for its own poor, provided modest loans for novice pedlars, the poorest of whom would become one of the several thousand old-clothes men and women or one of the numerous pedlars who sold their goods in the countryside, mostly in the south and east of England. Old-clothes men, the most numerous class of pedlar, would acquire used clothing in the upper- and middle-class neighborhoods in the morning as they would have their pre-established and recognized territories or "walks" as they were called and in the later afternoon return to Rag Fair in the East End to sell or trade their garments to secondhand retailers, tailors, and other pedlars.[2] Until inexpensive clothing became mass-produced later in the nineteenth century, middling- and working-class people depended on secondhand clothes. For many decades the old-clothes enterprise was a "thriving and necessary business."[3] Country pedlars also served a valuable function, providing people in rural areas with difficult-to-obtain goods. Being a pedlar had its attractions for a new immigrant: little English was necessary, one had freedom to set one's own hours, and one could observe Shabbat and the festivals. Vulnerable to robbery, harassment, violent attacks, and harsh weather, the pedlar, like other poor people, was ill clothed, ill fed, and subject to disease. The pedlars, especially those who worked in the countryside, subjected their bodies to long hours of walking out of doors and not always finding shelter from the inclement weather. However, compared with the harshly anti-Jewish restrictions in Europe, English peddling offered opportunity and freedom.[4]

Because the Jewish poor could not afford the fees for getting an apprenticeship in the Jewish trades—pencil-making, glass cutting, engraving, watchmaking, jewelry, tailoring, hatmaking, shoemaking, pastry cooking, confectionery, pen and quill making—and also because the Jewish trades themselves were not especially thriving, the Jewish poor had few options.[5] Whether Jewish criminality was roughly proportional with other national groups is impossible to determine, but Jewish criminality, even before Dickens's *Oliver Twist* (1837–39), was vividly represented in the public discourse. Fairly or not, Jews were associated with receiving stolen goods and circulating bad coins. Quentin Bailey has pointed out recently that in the last two decades of the eighteenth century, parliament directed its attention to the perceived social dangers from pedlars, hawkers, hackney men, pawnbrokers, and chapmen, who were suspected of criminality, receiving and passing stolen goods and counterfeit currency; and in the 1790s, the street sellers were linked with Jacobinism as well. One proposal, pushed strongly by Patrick Colquhoun (1745–1820), was to license pedlars and hawkers, using the fees to finance a new police force, which then could watch over the suspect population. As capitalism and the state were becoming more rationalized, the pedlar was becoming a source of social anxiety.[6] Perhaps reflecting this anxiety, the number of Jews sentenced to death or transportation had several peaks, in the 1770s—sixty-five—and in the 1810s—eighty-nine—and then in the 1820s—ninety.[7] These numbers seem roughly comparable with those of the non-Jewish poor. According to Todd Endelman, the Jewish poor lived according to the traditional, pre-capitalistic norms of poor people and disdained "both the work ethic and the personal morality of respectable folk."[8] Jewish participation in crime, both organized and occasional, as well as gambling, prostitution, prizefighting, and nontraditional sexual arrangements was not insignificant. It is certainly a myth that the Jewish poor were all religious traditionalists. Many of the poor were religiously observant but many were not and were, like the wealthy and well educated, attracted to the novelties and pleasures of modernity.[9]

The poor one finds in the Old Bailey *Proceedings* are mediated by legal procedures and the formal literary structures of the court representations, which are *not* trial transcripts. Rather, the author/editor/shorthand transcriber selects for emphasis some speeches and dialogue and leaves other interrogations unreported or only summarized. Trials with special appeal in terms of scandal and notoriety get the cliffhanger treatment, with the trial divided in two: the reader will have to purchase the next issue of the *Proceedings* to find out what happens in the second half of the trial, as happened in the case of Lady Howard prosecuting a Jewish servant for perjury, the report on which was spread over two issues of the *Proceedings*.[10]

The *Proceedings*, which started in the late seventeenth century as cheap, popular entertainment, competing with newspapers, novels, chapbooks, and ballads for the audience eager to read about crime, evolved over the eighteenth century to become a court record, obligated to follow the norms of objectivity and accuracy. Although by the end of the eighteenth century the *Proceedings* downplays to some extent the sensationalistic, aiming for a professionally legal rather than common reader, it nevertheless functions aesthetically. Indeed, anxious authorities want the *Proceedings* to intimidate would-be criminals with clearly moralistic narratives of crime and forceful punishment, while liberal constitutionalists want a published record of evenhanded justice; in either case, the factual material gets shaped, framed, and structured by social intentions. The former would exclude stories of acquittals as encouragement to commit crime, but the latter considered such accounts as essential instruments for creating a legitimate justice system. That sodomy and rape trials were not represented in the *Proceedings* indicates the Georgian-period understanding of the power of represented crime: some crimes, which were too toxic to be contained by available narrative techniques, had to be passed over.[11]

As one reads through the Old Bailey *Proceedings*, whether Jews are victims, perpetrators, or witnesses to crime, one cannot help but notice the power of stereotypes, which can be explicit or assumed as a meaningful context. The outcomes of the trials are not wholly determined by prejudice against Jews, reflecting a cultural situation where antisemitism exerts considerable force but other discourses are in play as well, notably social class, the protection of property, and the ideal of impartial justice.

I will start with a not uncommon case of an old-clothes man being mugged in 1780. Four women rob Nathan Showell of his money, for which they are convicted—whipped and imprisoned six months—but he does not get his money back. Here is the victim's testimony:

I am an old clothes–man. I was going up St. Giles's, calling old clothes, at about one or two o'clock, on Thursday the week before our Easter; somebody called old clothes; I looked up and saw some girls, I thought they wanted to fool me. They called me again, and held an old coat out of the window and said they had some clothes to sell. I went up. All the four prisoners were in the room. As I was looking at the coat, three of them went out of the room and locked me and the little one, Alice Willoughby in; I threw down the coat and went to pull the door open; she struck me on the fingers with something, I do not know what. She said why would I not buy the coat; I said I would have nothing to do with the coat; I wanted to get out. I went to the door again and she ran against me, and got hold of my pocket. I had ten guineas and a half and some silver in my purse in my breeches pocket. She got her hand into my pocket; I clapped my hand into my pocket and got hold of the purse; she had hold of it at the same time; I held her hand. She cried out I have got it, upon which the other three came in directly; they pushed and pulled me about. The little one and Charlotte M'Cabe had hold of the purse together; I kept hold of it; the purse broke, and all the money dropped down; I picked up three guineas and a half myself; they picked up the rest. I had the money in the morning of a shop-keeper in rag-fair; I had laid none of it out. As soon as they had the money they all ran down, and I ran after them. I was almost distracted about my money. I could not tell where they were gone; some of the neighbours took notice of them, and told me where they were. I found the little one in the necessary [privy]; she said you Dutch bougre what do you want with me, do you want my life or my child's life. I said give me my money; she said you Dutch bougre I won't give you a farthing, I wish I had more of you, do you want my life or my child's life, she said again. She said what she would do to me if I did not go out. I was afraid and went away, and she went out. They saw some of the neighbours run after them, and then they ran into the house again. The woman of the house asked me what was the matter, I cried and took on so. She bid me look over my money, and see what I had lost. I took my money out to count it, then Green came up and took a guinea out of my hat and ran out. They all ran out again. The constable took them in the street, and searched them, but did not find any thing upon them. I did not get any of my money again.[12]

The robbery occurred in the West End where he was still purchasing second-hand clothes in the early afternoon. Being robbed
by four women, including a diminutive one, was not uncommon,
as the *Proceedings* record many women taking part in robberies
and other crimes. That he had so much cash on his person—over
ten and a half guineas—was a consequence of having sold clothing to a shopkeeper in the morning; ordinarily he would have to
carry enough cash to pay for the used clothing as he made his daily
"walk." The old-clothes man was an obvious target in routinely
carrying money. When the pedlar apprehends the woman who calls
him a "Dutch bougre," she accuses him of attempting her life or
that of her child. Assuming the maternal role shrewdly accesses
the enduring stereotype of Jew as violator of children, a stereotype
founded on the blood libel upon which Edgeworth's *Harrington*
focuses much attention. Establishing the time of the robbery he
says it was "a week before our Easter," meaning Passover, a locu-
tion suggesting routine explanations of Jewish holidays to curious
Christians. That three of them left the room so Nathan Showell
would be alone with "the little one, Alice Willoughby," suggests
an obvious sexual trap to separate the man from his money, a not
uncommon strategy one finds represented in numerous cases of
robbery. When the sexual trap is ineffective, they go to the back-up
plan of taking his money by force. The amount of money stolen
from Showell easily qualifies as a capital offense but the women's
crime was treated as a misdemeanor, perhaps because of the victim's
Jewishness but it is not easy to tell. In the trial report Showell's
Jewishness is represented but without giving him a foreign-sound-
ing speech or stage dialect; his English is indistinguishable from
the native-born English voices.

Some of those who testified at the Old Bailey were not nearly
as fluent as Nathan Showell; an old-clothes man Emanuel Myers,
for example, required an interpreter. Robbed of two shillings six
pence, Myers ordinarily conducted business by pointing and other
physical gestures. The judge's instructions to the jury included a
reminder to them of the ideal of equality before the law: "The sum,
Gentlemen, to be sure is trifling, but then the man is poor, from
whom that sum is taken, and he is to be protected in his property,
as well as people in a superior station." The defendants were convicted and sentenced to seven years transportation to America.[13]
Episodes like this might provoke one to commend the lack of antisemitism in the court system but another factor is the protection of
property above all else.

An interesting example of a Jewish pedlar who speaks understandable but not fluent English is the case of Daniel Levy, old-clothes man, robbed by Mary Marshall of 29 shillings 12 pence in 1784:

Are you a Jew?—Yes.

Do you know the prisoner at the bar?—Yes.

Did you meet with her in June last?—Yes.

Where?—On the second of June, I go out with old cloaths, I cannot speak very much English, you will not understand me because I have been no long in England.

Court. You speak English very well, Sir, where did you meet her?—I met her in Cross-lane, on Wednesday about eleven in the morning, she called me up stairs and wanted to sell me a great coat.

In whose house?—One Martin keeps the house, a woman, when I went up stairs the woman locked the door, and she said to me I do not believe you will buy the great coat, because it cost me twenty-four shillings, I said to the woman let us look at it, she said to me I do not believe you have so much money in your pocket, then I shewed the prisoner my money, I had thirty shillings in my pocket, I put my hand in my pocket again, and the woman shoved me against the wall by force, and took my money from me.

How did she take your money?—She put her hand in my pocket and took my money from me.

Did you make no struggle?—She threw over me with force and took my money.

Did she throw you down?—I was upon my feet.

Go on and tell your story?—Indeed I cannot, I cannot go on.

Was you on your feet?—Yes.

What did she do then?—She run down stairs, and locked herself in a closet somewhere.

What did you do?—I run below stairs, and said to the woman of the house, that woman has robbed me, the prisoner came out of the closet upon my making a noise, and said I took no money from you, then the prisoner and another women took hold of me and beat me, and threw a pail of water over me besides; the woman took the shilling's-worth of halfpence out of my money, and threw them out of the window, and said here is your money, a gentleman took my part and fetched an officer.

Mary Marshall was convicted of the robbery and sentenced to death for stealing less than 2 pounds, an appalling but ordinary event at the Old Bailey.[14] Levy represents a third kind of Jewish speaker, someone between the fluent Nathan Showell and the more linguistically awkward Emanuel Myers. Nowhere in the Old Bailey *Proceedings* is there an attempt to imitate nonstandard pronunciation, which the popular songs do obsessively. The abuse of Daniel Levy might have escalated further if someone had not taken his side: "A gentleman took my part and fetched an officer." Levy could not have prosecuted Marshall without some bystanders aligning themselves with Levy. Even the victim of crime must play a convincing role in the theatre of the street if he wishes for any measure of justice. The trial report is respectful of Levy whom it could, given the sexual overtones of the theft, make contemptible; there are no salacious sexual innuendoes, nothing to make Levy's foreignness an object of ridicule. In this case it seems that robbery and Jew-baiting are nearly equal motives, as the pail of water seems especially gratuitous. When Levy says that he "cannot go on" upon being asked to tell his story, one is not sure if the inarticulacy is from inadequate language resources or from painful humiliation or both. The report structures this climactic statement as poignant rather than mocking.

Jews of course were not exclusively the victims of crime. In June 1780 two Jewesses who get acquitted of stealing whale fins seem guilty from the report.[15] Another acquitted prisoner, who was caught carrying stolen property, seems lucky in the verdict; he gets characterized by the accuser in a way that as a matter of course brings in the defendant's Jewishness: "I said it was remarkable that a gentleman, and a Jew should be carrying a bundle on a sabbath day."[16] As Jews are living in proximity with the non-Jewish poor, the relations between the two are not always amicable, as is evident when a woman accused of stealing calls a witness who testifies against her a "Jew bitch."[17]

Jews were also constables and even thief-takers. Although Jewish constables were fairly common in the East End, even some of the court attorneys were surprised by that fact. There is this exchange in a trial of 1781:

> Nathan Lion sworn. I am a constable;—I am a Jew.
>
> Do Jews exercise the office of constable? (the officer of the court said customarily).[18]

In another case (1785) the famous attorney William Garrow (1760–1840) won an acquittal for four Christian men apparently guilty of breaking and entering. Garrow purchased his victory by savaging on the stand the Jewish thief-taker who apprehended the defendants. The attorney discredits Joseph Levy as untrustworthy because he cares only for the "blood money," and lacks respectability. His interrogation never allows the jury to forget Levy is a poor Jew. Here is a typical exchange:

Your other name is Cockey Barber, is not it?—Yes.

I want to know your flash name in short?—Joe Barber.

You are one of the traps belonging to Mr. Staples's office?—No.

Garrow is insinuating by "flash name" and "traps" that Levy's lack of respectability earns him no credibility. The barrister goes for the kill in the following exchange:

Mr. Garrow. Now, Master Levy, otherwise Joe the Barber, how long have you been engaged in this honourable business of thief-taking?—I cannot rightly tell.

Now guess a little, ever since you was convicted and pardoned, ha! Speak man; how long have you been a thief-taker?—Longer than you have been a Counsellor.

I know that, because during the eight years I attended as student, I remember you?—Very likely; I do not attend any office now.

How long have you been out of place?—I do not choose to answer that.

How many trials did you appear upon last Sessions?—Never a one, only one.

What, there was no blood money last Sessions?—If there were no thieves, how would you get a brief?

Did not Norris come to that house you have spoken of in Fashion-street, for the purpose of surrendering upon any charge that had been made against him, with respect to this place?—No, Sir.

Do you swear that?—I do.

What did he say going along?—He desired to speak to me and go to the Justice's.

Upon your oath, (God knows that is no great sanction) was you sworn with your hat on?—I was.

Now, Master Levy.—Well, Master Garrow.

Are you a Jew?—Yes.

How long is it since you said at the Sessions-house at Clerkenwell, that you was a Christian?—Never.

Did you never assert at the Sessions at Clerkenwell, that you was a Christian, and not a Jew?—No, never, Sir, because I never was christened.

Will you swear that this man was not extremely drunk at the time he entered into this conversation?—I will swear he had not drank any liquor, I would not let him have any thing.

> Had you said any thing to him about his weight?—Nothing at all.
>
> Perhaps you do not know that there is a reward for these men if they are convicted?—How should I know.
>
> What is the price of the blood of these men, if they are convicted?—I shall not tell you.[19]

Levy gets in a few good retorts—"If there were no thieves, how would you get a brief?"—but Garrow wins the contest easily.

Using antisemitism to win a conviction or acquittal does not always work, however. Everyone in court—sympathetic and hostile alike—identifies the key witness in a robbery as "the Jew" (1781). The defendants try to discredit Jacob Michael, a lemon hawker, by claiming the following: "The Jew said, if it was possible, for the sake of the reward, he would have our lives." The jury in this instance sided with "the Jew" rather than the two defendants, who were both sentenced to death.[20] Another case of drawing upon prejudice against Jews was ineffective: a counterfeiter was convicted and sentenced to death, even though the main witness against him was Jewish. The skilled defense attorney, William Garrow, verbally assaulted the witness, Asher Simon (or Simons), an old-clothes man, badgering him with repetitious questions, sarcasm—"honest Mr. Simon"—and hinting of criminality. Garrow cleverly has Asher Simon's English-born sister-in-law testify against Simon:

> How long have you known Asher Simons ?—He is my brother-in-law; he has been guilty of a great many bad actions, both in his own country and here.
>
> What countryman is he?—He comes from abroad?—I cannot tell the country.
>
> You are an Englishwoman?—Yes, he is a foreigner.

Garrow cannot elicit from the sister-in-law any specific "bad actions," other than to accuse him of lying to get money without identifying any specific episodes, but that was hardly the main point, which was to accent Simon's foreignness. After a tedious interrogation of the sister-in-law by the fumbling prosecuting attorney, Simon himself asks her what specifically can she say against him. She replies:

> I can only tell what people have said; he gave a man a kick, and the next morning he was dead, and it was very well known, he flew away for it. The jury sat, and if they had not brought it in manslaughter, he would have been hung.

Her testimony seems no more convincing now than it must have seemed to the jury, which convicted the defendant, siding with Simon. The defendant Thomas Dean himself could have been Jewish, and the sister-in-law likely was Jewish, but in the theatre of the trial there is only one Jew, Asher Simon, poor, greedy, untrustworthy, and foreign.[21]

The Henry Levi case of stealing a harness (1782) is interesting because from the report it seems that Levi, a journeyman barber, is innocent, and the report provides a glimpse into the social life of poor Jews. Usually the verdict follows understandably from the report but not here, where the evidence is overwhelmingly exculpatory. The court, however, for whatever reasons, thinks Levi is guilty and interrogates witnesses aggressively, identifying one Jewish witness as a criminal to be watched carefully. Levi is convicted, and sentenced to six months at hard labor in the House of Correction after being whipped. At one point in the trial Simons, a witness sympathetic to Levi, is interrogated by the court:

> What are you?—I am a jew by profession, and a chapman and dealer; I deal with master hackneymen for hammer-cloths and harness, and any thing in their way; I buy at sales; I deal in old cloaths besides. There was a man had them to sell, the harness was not there; I went to Henry Levi's house; I do not know whether he keeps the shop, it is his mother's house, and a barber's shop; one Levi is the master.

Simons, who assumes he has to identify himself as Jewish, first and foremost, is a chapman (hawker of ballads and cheap literature), dealer in harnesses and other horse equipment, and old-clothes man. During the trial we hear from Jewish barbers, masters and journeyman, and coach masters. There is nothing in their represented speech that identifies them as Jewish except the hostility between the court and the Jews—defendant and witnesses.

Some trial reports are too ambiguous to decipher anything but details that do not, however, fully cohere. Although Thomas Harwood was sentenced to seven years transportation for stealing a box with a servant's clothes inside—a box returned one day before the trial with almost all the clothes as well—it is not clear who stole the box or even if the box was ever really stolen. The servant's employer, an obnoxious antisemite, attacks the veracity and honesty of the constable, Joseph Levy, insinuating that Levy was part of a Jewish gang that stole the box. Levy, who finds himself caught between the accusations of the defendant Harwood and the testimony of Acquillard, the black servant's employer, appears to have the most credibility, but in this case one glimpses the ethnic tensions of multicultural London and its rough system of justice.[22]

A source of ambiguity is mental illness, which sometimes enters the trial reports. Perhaps because George III had his own difficulties with mental health, the court was usually sensitive to the extenuating circumstances of madness. Although Jacob Abrahams was sentenced to death for assaulting another man, the court registered his unstable mental status—"out of his senses"—and recommended mercy rather than punishment.[23] Another case in which a mentally ill Jew was prosecuted occasioned a remarkable demonstration of support by the Jewish community for John Glover—not his real name, which was Judah Bottibo—to plead for leniency; there was no disputing that the unfortunate man actually stole the ring for which he was arrested. After the supportive testimony of nine friends, relatives, and neighbors, Bottibo was acquitted by the jury, which was convinced that the community would care for the emotionally distressed man.[24] Occasionally the sacredness of property gives way to other concerns.

The trial reports are sometimes chillingly unambiguous, such as the trial of the three men who robbed and physically assaulted Lazarus Moses, an old-clothes man. The guilt of Moses's attackers was hardly in question, as the evidence was unambiguous about the physical assault, slightly less so on the robbery (not that it happened but who precisely took how much). Even the judge, surprised that the jury returned a verdict of acquittal after only fifteen minutes of deliberation, ordered one of the defendants to be retried for misdemeanor assault, and he threatened to prosecute the unindicted woman who lured the old-clothes man to the house where he was attacked. The particular defendant who prevented Moses from getting beaten to death received considerable praise from the judge and witnesses, who apparently did not find it morally problematic to be commending someone for committing violence just short of fatal severity. The extent of Moses's injuries was serious: cut by a knife, thrown down a flight of stairs, repeatedly struck by a stick on the head and elsewhere, he lost too much blood to stand on his own. Even one of the defendants admitted that they were at the very least having "fun" pulling Moses's beard as if he were a "nanny goat." The defendants suggested that they were just entertaining themselves by baiting the Jew, and maybe it got a little out of hand, but it was certainly not worth prosecution. The attorney for the three men who interrogated Moses made him appear greedy and duplicitous, not really needing an interpreter. The exchange with Moses reveals some things about the language practices of old-clothes men who did not know much English:

Court. Why would not you give your evidence in English?—I cannot hold a discourse but I can speak a few words.

What language did you speak to these people in the room?—The few words I did speak were in English, they would not let me speak, some few words I know but I cannot speak them plain, they spoke English to me, I understood them, they said give me money directly, how much money, have you any more, and I understood all that.

Mr. Sheridan, Prisoner's Counsel. How long is it since you forgot to speak English?—I have been only a year and a half here, I am an old man, I cannot take the language quick.

Did the woman or man speak very good Hebrew?—She said no more than clothes, come up.

In what language did she speak to you, that she had a petticoat and gown to sell?—In English.

In what language did she say, that in general, your people has plenty of money?—In English.

In what language did you reply that you had no more than five shillings in silver, and five pennyworth of halfpence?—In English.

Why will not you hold a conversation with me now in English, as well as you did with the prisoners?—In the bargaining for clothes, some words I knows.

The judge initiates the queries about Moses's language skills, but the attorney probably knows that a functional vocabulary for transacting the commerce in old-clothes would not have to be large; rather, he wants to insinuate that Moses, who is pretending to know less English, is trying to trick the court. The second suggestion the attorney makes through questioning is that Moses is testifying against the three men to get a reward. Even the judge gets involved, "Who was it told you you would get forty pounds, if you would go against the prisoners?" Moses replies, "Upon my oath I have not heard any thing of the kind from any body." The main issue should have been the nearly fatal beating Moses suffered but the trial report, permeated with antisemitism, makes that almost peripheral. Although the judge is disturbed enough by the jury verdict to retry one of the defendants—but only for a misdemeanor—he collaborated, consciously or not, with the defense attorney to make Moses an unsympathetic victim, a greedy trickster, a stereotypical Jew.

The discourse of antisemitism is prevalent in the case of Ann Callaghan, a servant for a Jewish family, which she robs at Easter, and for which she is convicted, receiving a whipping and two years hard labor at the house of correction. Although the court report makes no remark on the timing, Callaghan's dislike for her employers is obvious from her testimony: "I never had a farthing for my wages, I had not a gown till one was lent me to come here before your Majesty."[25] The miserliness of Callaghan's employers, whether true or not, is stereotypically available for her as a justification for her theft. The holiday of Christmas provides the context for the trial of Matthew MacDonald, who was caught stealing a jacket from a Jewish shop on Christmas Eve. Although convicted and whipped, he is released rather than harshly treated, largely because of his sad Christmas Eve story:

> I was fetched away from America by the mate of a ship; and they have left me here, destitute of friends and money; and I never tasted a mouthful of victuals that day, nor the day before, only a roll in the morning. I have no place to go to.

This Dickensian narrative is emotionally effective: "The Jury, the Under-sheriff, and several of the audience, gave the prisoner money."[26] As with the Easter timing of Callaghan's theft, the Christmas timing of this one brings out the sentiment for the starving MacDonald, hardly the first starving young man ever tried at the Old Bailey for stealing, but in this instance—taking a coat from a Jew on December 24—sympathy seems to be justified.

Another clash in court between the Irish and Jews hinges on the integrity of the sole witness, a Jew, to an alleged theft by an Irish boy of a handkerchief worth ten pence. In this case it seems that the Jewish witness is lying, but it is not entirely certain (especially because Bacherah the witness would have no financial motive to testify in court if he had actually received all the money from the defendant's mother). Conventional antisemitic tropes shape the discourse of the trial: the boy's mother claims that Bacherah the Jewish witness extracted repeated blackmail payments from her to keep him from testifying against her son; his persistent visits, his ever escalating demands for money, and his threats to harm a Christian boy evoke the image of the predatory Jew, preying on innocent Christians, especially innocent boys. After the mother's testimony receives confirmation from another witness, the court turns on Bacherah, threatening him with prosecution, but he makes an appeal to the judge: "My Lord, I hope you will send me to Woodstreet Compter, I shall be killed by the prisoners in Newgate, they do not like me." The court ultimately lets Bacherah go free with only a verbal reprimand, for the court presumably realized its interests were served better by keeping Bacherah, a professional witness or "snitch," alive and testifying against criminals rather than punishing him for lying on the witness stand.[27]

The *Proceedings* sometimes discloses fairly amicable relations between Jews and Gentiles, and even reasonable decisions by the court. A Jewish teenager, Henry Asser, confesses to stealing from his Gentile employer, who agrees to recommend leniency. The Jewish witnesses to the crime point to extenuating circumstances, while the Gentile shopkeeper in a largely Jewish neighborhood has good relations with the local people. Although the theft could have resulted in a capital sentence, the court refrained from issuing any penalty.[28] In another case the Gentile jury acquits a possibly guilty Jew in part because it was impressed by the Hebrew writing in the defendant's marriage contract (*ketubah*) displayed in court. A defendant's character witness brought into court the *ketubah* proving that the defendant was married to his wife, thus substantiating the man's respectability. Although the evidence that the defendants were knowingly receiving stolen goods was considerable, the jury, none of whom probably could read a word of Hebrew, issued an acquittal.[29] Here is perhaps the legacy of Protestant philosemitism and its esteem for Hebrew.

The report on the trial of Elias Abrahams who, for stealing a coat and few other things, received a sentence of seven years transportation, reveals his close association with unrespectable poor Gentiles as well as "girls of the town."[30] Not surprisingly numerous other trial reports disclose Jewish life with more than a little familiarity with prostitution and unconventional sexual arrangements.

In a perjury case a Jewish woman, Elizabeth "Bet" Cohan, testifies against another old-clothes woman who falsely (according to the court) accused a man of theft. As she is forced to defend herself, Bet Cohan several times affirms her religious identity—"I am a Jewess, I never deny being a Jew"—and rebuts the aspersions on her sexual character, denying that her husband was hanged, denying she had two children with him, and explaining her frequent visits to Newgate by claiming that "I knew that man's mother, she nursed me; I have been parted from my husband these seven years, I defy the world to say anything against me." It is quite possible Bet Cohan herself is lying about everything but she puts on a convincing performance that persuades the jury to convict her former friend of sixteen years acquaintance to seven years transportation.[31]

The ambiguities of respectability are illustrated by the cases in which Jewish men like Benjamin Solomon (1788) were robbed by prostitutes. Walking home on a Saturday night from the coffee house, he encounters Mary Anson:

> She took me to a house in Paul's Alley; it was dark and she desired me to give her a penny for a candle, which I did, and she brought a candle; then she asked me to give her something to drink, I put my hand in my pocket and gave her a shilling; then she asked me for something for supper, and I gave her another shilling; then it was time to go to bed, and she says to me, as you are so very generous and you look like a gentleman, I dare say we need not make any agreement, you will give me a compliment when we rise. She wanted me to go to bed first, I undressed myself, and going to put my breeches under my pillow, she snatched them from my hand and ran out of doors with them; I immediately arose from the bed, I thought I would put on the remainder of my cloaths; but before I could get my waistcoat on, entered the other prisoner, and demanded to know what I wanted there.
>
> Was that the first time you saw the prisoner Underhill?—Yes, but before I could give her an answer, she shewed me a place in an entry with a well in it, and she says, here you rascal, if you say a word about your property you shall be smothered alive in this place, and nobody shall ever know what became of you; a place, I suppose, where there was six or seven load of soil, not above a week before emptied from the necessaries; I then thought it the best policy to give her the best words that I possibly could to get away with my life; she then said to me, you have behaved very generously, and I suppose you can live like a gentleman; the property you have lost is no object to you, if you will never mention it any more, I will go and fetch you your breeches back again; she went out of doors and brought me my breeches; after I had made the greatest dispatch I could out of the house, I acquainted the patrol with what had happened....

Robbing a prostitute's client is an old practice but Solomon clearly is not too embarrassed to testify in court to persuade the jury to convict the prostitute—seven years transportation—but not the prostitute's accomplice, whom the judge targets for retrial after he learns that Solomon is a respectable dealer in linen drapery. For the court social class—and gender—trump (usually) religion and ethnicity. I never found a single court case involving a prostitute bringing charges against a man for violence or theft, when both were presumably common experiences.

Another case in which social class is prominent is the perjury trial of Esther Elias (1789). The sequence of events is as follows. Lady Juliana Howard's aunt, Lady Mary, died in 1787, after which Esther Elias's mother Leah claimed a debt of 190 pounds, which Lady Juliana refused to honor. Leah Elias sued Lady Juliana, who won the court case, during which Esther was the only witness. After Esther and her mother still pursued the debt, Lady Juliana had Leah jailed for failure to pay court costs for the failed suit; impoverished, Leah Elias could not pay the court costs and at the time of Esther's trial was still in jail. Esther then used an attorney to prosecute Lady Juliana for failing to pay the debt, for which Lady Juliana was arrested, spending an hour in custody before her own attorneys effected her release. The final step was the prosecution of Esther for perjury.

Split between two issues of the *Proceedings*, this trial of aristocratic scandal receives special treatment, given far more pages of testimony than other trials. Lady Howard hires William Garrow, one of the most skilled courtroom attorneys at the time, to prosecute the case. The report is an astonishing display of aristocratic power. Esther herself is allowed to speak only once and that is to utter an apology to Lady Howard, who has graciously asked the court to find a verdict of not guilty, even though the whole point of the case was to demonstrate that Esther had lied about her aunt owing money. The only thing Esther Elias says during the whole trial is that "I did not want to do any thing to affront her ladyship, nor ever meant to do it." The trial focuses principally on the dishonor suffered by Lady Howard by being arrested and detained for sixty minutes. That Esther's mother Leah had been in jail for months does not receive even a token gesture of sympathy, and that Esther herself had been incarcerated until the trial's conclusion is framed wholly by Lady Howard's pained annoyance at these women pestering her about money and provoking her with legal actions. At the start of the trial, the attorney makes sure that the Jewishness of Esther is the first thing the jury discovers about her by asking the court clerk how Esther took her oath. "Sworn on the Old Testament." Just to press the matter home, the attorney continues: "Of course that is for persons of the Jewish persuasion?" The clerk replies, "Yes."

Through interrogation of various witnesses, Garrow and associates establish the social crimes committed by Esther Elias: she did not acquaint her own attorney who brought the charges of nonpayment of a debt with the social position of Lady Howard; she personally witnessed the humiliating arrest of the aristocratic woman; she continued to press for payment of the debt even after the disrespectful and futile law suit.[32] The Eliases have not been deferential, for which they will be overwhelmed by the full weight of the law and social custom. Presumably after Esther's trial Lady Howard would have arranged to have Leah Elias released. It is worth noting that in terms of attorney and court costs, the legal proceedings would have amounted to much more than the 190 pounds claimed by the Eliases, whose Jewishness was not essential in this instance because Lady Howard would have crushed anyone. Another way to look at this trial is to see it as a mark of Jewish confidence when two poor women felt they had a chance to succeed in court against a powerful aristocrat. Of course they had no chance whatsoever, but it does not seem they were inhibited by their Jewish status.

THE "JEW SONGS"

If a song were especially popular in the theatre, it could get reprinted in three different formats, the inexpensive (1d) broadside with its several songs, the slightly more costly (usually 6d) chapbook with its usual thirty-two pages, and the often high-priced (18s) song-book or songster, with hundreds of songs, thick paper, elegant prints, and calf covers.[33] I will be discussing the so-called Jew song from a chapbook and the *Universal Songster*. A subgenre of song with great appeal in the Georgian period was the so-called Jew song, a kind of Jewish minstrel performance in which the voice of a Jew would be mimicked in a comic register. Just as the black-face minstrelsy would employ a supposedly authentic black dialect, so too the Jew songs would imitate what is presented as genuine Jewish speech. Originating probably in the interludes between the main play and the after-piece in the London theatres, the Georgian Jew song usually follows a structure of song stanzas interspersed with paragraphs of prosaic recitative.

A chapbook edited by Ann Lemoine, *Laugh When You Can; or, The Monstrous Droll Jester* (180?), advertizes prominently on its title page "The Benevolent Jew, As Recited At The Royalty Theatre." Located at Wellclose Square in the East End, the Royalty Theatre would have had numerous Jewish patrons, so that this particular song and chapbook seem aimed at the same audience that would have attended the Royalty. That her brother Henry Lemoine (1756–1812) collaborated with the Jewish printer and theological writer David Levi (1742–1801) provides another informative context for the chapbook and its intended audience. The coarse humor of chapbooks is well represented in *Laugh When You Can*, where one of the numerous vignettes takes off on *The Merchant of Venice*:

> When a certain Jew's daughter married without his consent, he roared like a Westphalian Polyphemus: thundering through all his

house, "Vat a dam bish, my own shile too; but she mos always fond of reading boedry; dam boedry—mut she shall never have a stiver of mine: I do now swear by Cot, I will cut off my own bosteriors mid a shilling."[34]

I will provide a more detailed reading of this piece in the fifth chapter, but for now I will point to the playing of a variation on *The Merchant of Venice* for the purpose of representing the tensions of assimilation to English culture. The Jewish speech is represented for comic effect, as is the usual manner in the Jew song. This angry Jew is not evil and frightening like Charles Macklin's Shylock but clownishly ineffectual and an object of ridicule.

The very title, "The Benevolent Jew," comes from the theatre, specifically Richard Cumberland's *The Jew; or, Benevolent Hebrew* (1794), which had a successful run in the London patent theatres and had numerous published editions (I will discuss this play in the next chapter). Exploiting the play's popularity, George Walker's novel *Theodore Cyphon* (1796) also featured a "Benevolent Jew." The identified author of the Jew song in Lemoine's comic chapbook is C.F. Barrett, about whom little is known other than he or she also published at least five gothic romances in chapbook form in the early nineteenth century.[35] Barrett's Jew song is brief enough to reproduce in its entirety:

Well, well, things went on pretty well at Shange too-day: stocks low in de morning, and I buys in, dat vas good, very good, den owing to some good news from de Continent—stocks got up in de afternoon, and I sold out—dat vas fery good again, fery good; aye, aye, though I says it, that should not say dere ish no one understands these monish matters betters than I do; 'tis true, I lives by taking advantage of de folies of mankind—bloods will be bloods say vat you will, and if I wa'n't to lend dem monish when dey want it, somebody else would: but I defy any one to say dat I ever took advantage of a fellow-creature in distress—no, no, I have experienced the frowns of fortune myself, and therefore can always feel for the miseries of the unfortunate.

Medley Air.
Tune—*Sailor's Journal.*
At nine years old my parents died,
  And to the wide world's pity left;
Oppress'd with grief I often sigh'd
  That fate had of my friends bereft me—
Became more calm, I vas inclin'd,
  For to *hold-up*, and try my fortune;

Wou'd to an orphan boy prove kind,
   And his hard fate for once more soften.

   Tune—*Father, Mother, and Suke.*
So I bought me some pencils my fortune to try,
Some sealing-wax too and pomatus;
And den went to de Shange 'mongst de merchants so gay;
And my goods for to buy did entreat 'em.
I soon sold them all and then went and bought more,
Kind fortune my dealings did prosper;
And I'm now sirs, content for I've money galore,
   To satisfy every want, sir;
Thus industry ever is crown'd with success,
   Be honest you're sure to do.
     For I made that my plan,
     I made that my plan,
To be honest and just to mankind, sirs,
     Altho' I'm a Jew.

   Tune—*Tom Bowling.*
Thus having, sirs, full oft experienced,
   Of life the ups and downs—
I sure must prove a brother feeling,
   For those on whom fortune frowns;
'Gainst the distress'd and truly needy,
   I ne'er will shut my door—
But both my hand and heart be ready
   For to relieve the poor.

In various countries I have been,
   But none I like so well,
As England, where the King and Queen,
   All others doth excel:
Their subjects, they are good and kind,
   This is the place for me:
So long may GEORGE o'er England reign,
   The Land of Liberty![36]

The prosaic recitative establishes the linguistic markers of stereotypical Jewish speech. Although the theatre and popular songs customarily mocked all kinds, not just Jewish linguistic difference in the areas of accents and pronunciation, rarely is a performance of Jewish speech allowed to appear in standard English; rather, the effect of a supposedly authentic speech is generated by certain consonantal substitutions: p's for b's, v's for w's, f's for v's, d's for th's, sh's for s's and ch's, c's for g's; often too the preposition "with" is rendered as "mit." Barrett's text sounds most intensively stereotypical in the prosaic section that introduces the song and that establishes the premises of his character: he makes money on the Exchange where he follows the basic capitalist rule of selling high and buying low, but he does not break any laws or violate ethical norms. The capitalist system itself has a brutality the speaker does not disguise, for he economically exploits "follies" and misfortune, but the moral fault, assuming there is one, is systemic not particular to any individual, and surely not a characteristically Jewish quality. The proverbial citation, "bloods will be bloods," perhaps alludes to Macbeth's grim observation, "They say blood will have blood" (*Macbeth* 3.4.122), suggesting the murderous nature of economic competition. The speaker tries to balance the predatory qualities of his means of earning money with references to his ethic of restraint—he never takes advantage of anyone who is truly needy and in distress.

The rags to riches story includes being orphaned at nine and moving up the economic ladder from hawking pencils to buying and selling stocks. Swearing by honesty and hard work, he compassionately aids the poor, with whom he identifies, having been poor himself. The concluding stanza cements his link with the English audience by affirming his patriotic loyalty to the ruling monarch. With each of the three stanzas sung according to familiar tunes, the song at the melodic level diminishes the Jewish difference initially established so strongly in terms of his stereotypical speech and wealth. If indeed pedlars were suspected of Jacobin sympathies, this song certainly counters that suspicion, but the song is loyalist not just in the narrow political sense; rather, the speaker is performing his commitment to Englishness from his position as somewhat foreign.

Turning now to Jew songs published for a wealthier audience than for Lemoine's chapbook, one finds a large number of such songs in the *Universal Songster* (1825–26), an anthology of popular songs culled from Shakespeare and the contemporary theatre. According to Anthony Bennett, "Theatre songs are probably the most important ingredient in the songsters, many of which consist of songs from the latest productions."[37] The full title of the three-volume collection was *Universal Songster; or, Museum of Mirth: Forming the Most Complete, Extensive, and Valuable Collection of Ancient and Modern Songs in the English Language: with a Copious and Classified Index. 29 woodcuts by George and Robert Cruikshank, engraved by J. J. Marshall.*[38] The *Universal Songster*, reprinted several times in the nineteenth century (1832 and 1878 by George Routledge, 1834 by Jones & Co.), was produced initially by one of London's most prolific publishers, John

Fairburn of Ludgate-Hill, who began his publishing enterprise in the 1790s. The original price for the deluxe three volumes was apparently 1 pound and 16 shillings, but an advertisement of 1848 lists a new copy for 18 shillings. The Cruikshank prints would have attracted customers as well, perhaps explaining why Routledge issued a reprint of the *Songster* right after Cruikshank's death in 1878. Fairburn did not specialize in the high-end audience, to be sure, for he published numerous broadsides and cheap publications aimed for a popular audience, including radical and pornographic texts, according to Iain McCalman in his study of nineteenth-century "unrespectable" radicalism.[39] As publishers could make healthy profits from selling a relatively small quantity of very expensive books, perhaps Fairburn, Jones, and Routledge conceived of the *Songster* as fulfilling those commercial expectations.[40] Reflecting its publisher, the *Songster* has a mixture of art-songs from Shakespeare and Byron as well as many more comic and satirical songs with coarse humor characteristic of the "illegitimate" theatre.

John Fairburn or whoever he hired as editor constructed a consumer-oriented classification system for its categories of the 5,000 songs: ancient, amatory, bacchanalian, comic, Dibdin's (over 250 songs!), Irish, Jews, Masonic, Military, Naval, Scotch, Sentimental, Sporting, Welsh, Yorkshire, and Provincial, and of course miscellaneous. There are six times as many Irish songs as Jewish, and four times as many Scotch as Jewish, and twice as many Jewish as Welsh. The Irish and Jewish songs are filled with crude ethnic stereotypes, but the Scotch and Welsh are not. Reflecting the influence of abolitionist discourse, most representations of blacks portray them as innocent victims whose represented speech is not in dialect. The songs accent Jewish difference with negative stereotypes of the greedy Shylock who is dishonest in business dealings with the innocent Gentiles. Of the fifty-two "Jew songs" in the *Universal Songster*, twenty-one or 40 percent depend on harshly negative stereotypes about pork-loving, hook-nosed, immoral, criminal, commercially predatory Jews. About 30 percent of the songs, even when stereotypical, focus on sentimental or humorous situations that do not severely scapegoat Jews, and their relative mildness leads me to classify them as moderately stereotypical; let there be no mistake, however, that they are not friendly to Jews, and one could just as easily classify most of them with the antisemitic songs. Another 30 percent of the songs depart from the stereotypes to the point where the Jewish characters, despite their odd dialect, share qualities with the culturally constructed English. It would be going too far to call them sympathetic but the songs include Jews in the London cityscape with a mixture of acceptance and disdain. My label for this last class of song is ambivalent.

I want to look at a song representing each class.

First, a not untypical negative song entitled "The Jew in Grain; or, The Doctrine of an Israelite," depicts a Jewish speaker who proudly confesses his dishonesty in business and his love of pork. Here is the first stanza:

> I once was but a pedler, and my shop was in my box,
>   So sure as I'm a smouch, and my name is Mordecai;
> And I cheated all the world, in spite of whipping-posts or stocks,
>   For I never sticks for trifles when dere's monies in the way.
> I had good gold rings of copper gilt, and so I got my bread,
> With sealing-wax of brick-dust, and pencils without lead,
>   In my pick-pack, nick-nack, shimcrack, tick-tack, tink lum tee,
>   And de shining chink to clink is de moosick still for me.[41]

In a song like this the Jewish pedlar lacks the morality of an ordinary Christian. Immune to correction by legal punishments or social shame, the pedlar cheats the world by manipulating appearances, experiencing pleasure only in the moments of profiting from exploitation of obtuse Gentiles who exchange good money for shoddy goods. A recurrent theme of the most negative songs is that Jews lack a soul and the natural emotions because they are rendered inhuman by their maniacal love of financial gain and their contempt for Gentiles. Barrett's "Benevolent Jew" counters each one of these standard stereotypical points. The obsessive focus on eating pork serves several functions: it indicates that Jews cannot control their appetites, that they are no better than Christians who eat non-kosher food, that the Jewish religion is a sham that is not really observed, and that Jews secretly desire what the Christians highly value. A moderately stereotypical song would be "The Cook and the Old Clothes Man." In this song Mo the old-clothes man sings of his misadventure with a Gentile cook whom he was romancing when the "great Irish footman came blustering in" and treated the amorous Mo rather roughly:

> He took me right up like a piece of a rag,
>   Clothes sale, &c. [clo, clo clo]
> And popp'd me head foremost plump into my bag,
>   Clothes sale, &c.
> And a mud-cart, just passing, the unfeeling soul
> Threw me in, vere I looked like a toad in a hole,
>   O dear, vat a row!
>   Vith my clothes sale, &c.

> The men took me out, and my Becky came by,
>   Vith her clothes sale, &c.
> And hearing the tale broke my head very nigh,
>   Clothes sale, &c.
> So, our peoples, beware of great fat tempting cooks,
> And ven you puy pargains, remember the cooks,
>   For I do I know,
>   Vith my clothes sale, &c.[42]

Sexual humor, a staple of plebeian culture, draws its energy here from the humiliation of the amorous Jew at the hands of the stronger Irishman. The audience enjoys the spectacle of a pedlar trying to romance one of the women with whom he does commercial business, even eating the cooked meat she gives him, which he calls "trypher"— that is, treyf, food that is not kosher. Although this song surely has a stereotypical old-clothes man—an amorous, treyf-eating Jew—it also represents some of his daily difficulties, such as harassment on the street: "As I valk the boys teaze me about pits of pork, / Vich they say, though they lie, that they've stuck on a fork, / But on I do go, / Vith my clothes sale, &c." In fact, it is the cook who invites him for an intimate conversation; he does not initiate the encounter. In the Old Bailey *Proceedings*, as we have seen, there are several unfortunate encounters of actual old-clothes men with both women and men. The Irish footman humiliates him, certainly, but he is not severely injured as some of the actual Jews represented in the Old Bailey reports were, and the comic turn of events is reenforced when his wife witnesses his humiliation. Mo is depicted as weak and ineffectual, a schlemiel, but altogether human. The harshly negative songs drain the Jew of any humanity at all. For the ambivalent song, "The Happy Jew" by a Miss Bryant is interesting for its focus on the Jewish family. I'll reproduce the whole song:

> My father he kept a clothes-shop and a stand,
> His name it vas Moses, of Israel's land;
> My mother vas Rachael, the daughter of Ben,
> Who kept a big stall down in Rosemary-Lane.
> And I vas their son, a sweet Hebrew boy,
> Till my father he died, and I lost every joy,
> For he left me no money, and died in a smash,
> But soon found the method of raising the cash.
>
> Spoken.] Yes, for vhile de other little boys were dirting their fardens at pitch-in-the-hole, I vas at home, mending a *hole* in my jacket, or dirting de brass buttons, to take de flats in by passing them for

old farthings: and den, vat did I do? Vhy, I bought a penn'orth of Prummagem pall with 'em, and making a bad shilling look vite, I passed it at the chandler's shop, and so, like a true-hearted Jew, I made a good shilling out of an old button, and sung—

  Tol de rol, &c.

Ven a poy, I was clever at brushing the clothes,
At *barking*, and leading each fool by the nose;
But, growing up pigger, 'twas soon time to think
How to take in the flats, and to handle the chink;
Which I did, spite of all de queer tricks they might show,
Though they bid me eat pork, and dey christened me Mo!
But I peat all the boys, and I *licked* all the men;
And then, laughing, I bid them call out "*pork*" agen.

Spoken.] Oh! how pleasant it is to see me and my little dear vife drinking our coffee every night, and frying the flat fish, to make a good supper for the children—and to see 'em all coming home:—there's Sammy sells slippers in St. Paul's-Churchyard—Joey cries heart-cakes in Cheapside—Becky sells oranges at the Mansion-house—and little Isaac carries about *Dutch* sealing-wax, made in Duke's Place—vhile I sings

  Tol de rol, &c.

With every trinket I vishes to meet,
And I cries my old clothes round each London street,
Vhile down all the areas I bawls—"Clo's a shange!"
Though I oft get my nose, dears, bit off as I range,
Though they calls me a Jew, sure I know what I am
I'm *Yedchin* born, and I don't vant to sham,
Though pray what's the matter with Christian or Jew?—
I only want money, and so do they too.

Spoken.] But, pless my heart, when *Shaboth* comes I doesn't care, for I dresses myself like a gentleman, in my pest clothes—go to Shool—say my prayers—come home—eat all the *cold roast*, with my dear *ulca* wife and the pretty children—then go and beg some orders from the performers, who owe me all the money, and in the evening take my vife and the pretty shildren to the boxes, where nobody can tell we are Jews till they look at the tips of our noses—and sing

  Tol de rol, &c.[43]

This song has sympathetic as well as negative representations: Mo as a child learns how to pass bad currency "like a true-hearted Jew" and at the theatre his family's noses publicly disclose their Jewishness, but the song humanizes Mo in several ways. First, his zeal to make money is contextualized by the sudden death of his father. Second, we see his physical courage in fighting and defeating first the boys and then the older men. Third, the song depicts details of family life, from coffee-drinking to Shabbat dinner and attending synagogue to going to the theatre in their best clothes. Moreover, the following couplet, "Though pray what's the matter with Christian or Jew?— / I only want money, and so do they too," concisely captures the song's position that Jews and Christians are similarly materialistic and imperfect, that is, with material and spiritual needs, family loyalties, and a difficult life of weekly labor that is necessary. Neither this nor any of the other songs, even the most negative, suggests that Jews should convert to Christianity. The song does not mock Mo's pride in being Jewish, which is taken as a sign of integrity. It would be going much too far to suggest that the song implies a multicultural tolerance and full acceptance of difference, but it shows ambivalence, a sense of Anglo-Christian superiority and Anglo-Jewish inferiority, to be sure, but also a grudging acknowledgment of the Jewish place in multiethnic London.

THE PEDLARS OF EDGEWORTH'S *HARRINGTON*

Turning from the popular urban culture of the Old Bailey court and the ethnic songs, one also finds the Jewish pedlar and old-clothes man in Coleridge, Southey, Dickens, Edgeworth, and arguably Wordsworth as well. In one of his *Table Talk* pronouncements, Coleridge contrasted the sublime lyricism of the biblical Isaiah with the ugly street cries and unpleasant appearance of the London old-clothes man. Using the biblical "Hebrew" to denigrate the contemporary "Jew" was a commonplace rhetoric before and after Coleridge. So much prestige became attached to the Hebrew label that American Jews tended to call themselves Hebrews well into the twentieth century, as the word Jew had such bad connotations. Coleridge being Coleridge, he confronted an old-clothes man who effectively defended himself and corrected Coleridge's prejudiced perception.[44] In Robert Southey's essays on traveling through England there are several harsh criticisms of Jewish pedlars for aesthetic reasons: their speech is ugly and loud, their dress is peculiar, and their style of selling is too aggressive.[45] In the sixth chapter of *Sketches by Boz* (1833–36) Dickens records how much he disliked "the red-headed and red-whiskered Jews who forcibly haul you into their squalid houses, and thrust you into a suit of clothes whether you will or not."[46] The aesthetic judgments against the pedlars are barely disguised affirmations of national and class identity: the Jewish pedlars are ugly because of their "un-English" appearance, speech, and style of interaction. Turning the middle-class customer into a victim of aggressive Jewish salesmanship is a way of registering discomfort with the absence of Jewish begging: these poor people did not seek assistance in an obsequious manner, thereby depriving the would-be alms-giver of a spiritual experience.

The two Jewish pedlars in Maria Edgeworth's *Harrington*, Simon the Jew and his son Jacob, play central roles in the main character's development from frightened, neurotic, sickly antisemitic child to morally mature adult who has overcome his early affliction. His nurse Fowler had frightened the vulnerable boy by associating the image of Simon the old-clothes man with predatory behavior, drawing upon the tradition of the blood libel and child-killing. As an older boy and adolescent, Harrington learns to overcome his prejudice and recognize the moral worth of Jacob, Simon's son, who sells school supplies to the students. The image of the Jewish pedlar, one realizes, disturbed not just impressionable young boys but grown up English writers like Coleridge, Southey, and Dickens. Edgeworth's Harrington overcomes his prejudice largely by seeing the Jewish pedlar as a good and honest businessman. The domestic and religious life of Simon and Jacob is not touched upon, whereas the popular songs treat the Jewish pedlar in a much fuller and multidimensional way. The ambivalent and moderately stereotypical songs to which I alluded earlier also undermine prejudice like Edgeworth's well-meaning, Enlightenment fiction, but they do so without trying to fulfill a philosophical goal and without calling attention to their moral virtue.

In the first chapter of *Harrington*, the protagonist's traumatic encounter with Simon the Jew, the old-clothes man, begins with the lamplighter illuminating the street to reveal "the face and figure of an old man with a long white beard and a dark visage, who, holding a great bag slung over one shoulder, walked slowly on straight forwards, repeating in a low, abrupt, mysterious tone, the cry of '*Old clothes!—Old clothes!—Old clothes!*' I could not understand the words he said, but as he looked up at our balcony my maid nodded to him; he stood still, and at the same instant she seized upon me, exclaiming, 'Time for you to come off to bed, Master Harrington.'"[47]

It is easy to pass over this part and move to the manufactured nightmare instigated by Fowler the maid, but it is meaningful in several ways: the phallic beard, the dark face, the large bag all suggest a sexual subtext that is reinforced by the maid who appears to be communicating with the pedlar. From this imagined sexual coupling Harrington is excluded and pushed off to bed. The words, "old clothes," do not mean anything to the boy, so that it seems the pedlar and the maid are communicating something from which he is barred.

Harrington, who does not want to be left out, puts up a fight: "I resisted, and, clinging to the rails, began kicking and roaring." Precisely at this point the maid delivers her traumatic threat: if he does not go calmly to bed, she will " 'call Simon the Jew there,' pointing to him, 'and he shall come up and carry you away in his great bag.' " Harrington feels assaulted by Simon's gaze: "The old man's eyes were upon me; to my fancy the look of his eyes and his whole face had changed in an instant. I was struck with terror—my hands let go their grasp" (70).

Edgeworth narrates Harrington's trauma with a subtext of castration and Oedipal exclusion. The maid supplies the appropriate cultural reference: she tells Harrington that the Jews "had been known to steal poor children for the purpose of killing, crucifying, and sacrificing them at their secret feasts and midnight abominations" (70). Her narrative of the blood libel, Jews killing Christian boys after circumcising them, reinforces the earlier experience of being threatened by Simon and his sexuality. Edgeworth cannily has Fowler access antisemitic mythology casually, without thought, unreflectively, for it accurately locates the status of such myths in the popular culture.

Insofar as Edgeworth identifies with her characters, there is Fowler herself with whom she has similarities: she too told unthinkingly antisemitic tales until the American Rachel Mordecai initiated a correspondence during which Edgeworth realized the full extent to which her Jewish characters possessed uniformly stereotypical qualities.[48] The novel's narrator mythologizes Edgeworth's own experience in terms of history: "In our enlightened days, in the present improved state of education, it may appear incredible that any nursery-maid could be so wicked as to relate…such tales" (71). Equally rhetorical and historically precise, the category "our enlightened days" neglects the persistence of the medieval myths like the blood libel. One of the most notorious blood libels, the Hugh of Lincoln episode, memorialized by Chaucer in the *Prioress's Tale*, led to the deaths of eighteen Jews. The plaque commemorating Hugh's death was not removed from Lincoln Cathedral until 1959.[49] That Jewish ritual murder was not universally disbelieved in Edgeworth's enlightened days is evident by Wordsworth's 1820 publication of a translated *Prioress's Tale* by Chaucer: the first edition presented Wordsworth's modernized *Tale* without comment, but after some readers expressed outrage at the *Tale's* publication, the second (1827) and subsequent editions included a note indicating the Prioress's "fierce bigotry."[50]

Neither the *British Review* nor the *Eclectic Review* found anything to praise in Wordsworth's version of the *Prioress's Tale*; the former review found it "horrible" in its facts, "disgusting" as a narrative, and "odiously profane in its language," while the latter review called it an "ill-chosen" remnant of medieval "credulity" that serves no purpose "transplanted into modern poetry."[51] Although both reviews wanted Wordsworth to exclude it from subsequent editions of his poetry, Wordsworth kept the *Prioress's Tale* in all his editions. If Wordsworth were modernizing all or most of *Canterbury Tales*, then one could justify the inclusion of such a poem, but the *Prioress's Tale* is the only part of *Canterbury Tales* he ever published, at a time when many English and European Christians found the blood libel, at least as it applied to medieval Jews, wholly credible. Even Hazlitt, whose sensitivity to Jewish oppression was among the most well known at the time, found the *Prioress's Tale* aesthetically compelling, but he never seems to have reflected on the ethical issues of Wordsworth's modernization of it.[52]

Edgeworth's Harrington suffers from castration anxiety as a result of his nursemaid's tale—the Jew with the long beard and "terrible eyes" carries a big bag with the "mangled limbs of children" (72). Even after Fowler the nurse discloses the fictionality of the story about Simon the Jew, her purpose to only frighten him "into being a good boy," his imagination has become a source of perverse pleasure, as the intensities of hysteria have addicted him to terror, not unlike the avid reader of gothic page-turners. Indeed, Harrington/Edgeworth employs the word hysteria, which is one of the many indications that Harrington has been feminized by his antisemitic fright.[53] Harrington's father vows to make sure his son's fear of Jews will be overcome so that he will not become a "Miss Molly," the term for homosexual (87). The novel's subtext here is that fiction is never innocent of offense and violence. A disavowal—"just kidding!"—does not undo the damage, as Edgeworth herself discovered how much harm her previous representations of Jews had caused.[54] In a bizarre turn of the plot, Harrington's family pays Simon not to cry "old clothes" near their house because of its effect on their son, but the publicity of the payment provokes others to seek a similar arrangement. Some of the Jews who sought payment were "good Christian beggars, dressed up and daubed for the purpose of looking as frightful and as like the traditionary representations and vulgar notions of a malicious, revengeful, ominous-looking Shylock as ever whetted his knife. The figures were well got up; the tone, accent, and action suited to the parts to be played; the stage effect perfect" (79). These faux

Jews perform the role of old-clothes man with Shakespeare's Shylock as the ideal to be imitated—or rather Charles Macklin's version of Shylock. Edgeworth's awareness of the theatricality of antisemitism governs the absurd parade of old-clothes men performing the role of Shylock to get paid to leave Harrington's neighborhood. Edgeworth also makes sure that the decisive first meeting of Harrington and Berenice, *la belle juive* of the novel, takes place in the theatre during a performance of Charles Macklin's *Merchant of Venice*. Performative theatricality does not make the antisemitism any less toxic but it makes it susceptible to retrospective analysis.

The second Jewish pedlar in the novel is Jacob, Simon's son, the "Jew boy" who replaces the Scotch pedlar serving Harrington's school (ch. 3). Harrington finds that he hates young Jacob, whose very presence torments Harrington so much that the sadistic and cruel harassment that he and his friend Mowbray inflict on Jacob appear fully justified (91). Edgeworth's insight into racial hatred is that it works in terms of self-defense: the bigot feels he is protecting himself, and at the unconscious level, he is protecting himself from castration. The school boys finally decide to choose Jacob as their pedlar rather than someone else because of the logic of the market: Jacob is honest, fair, and offers the lowest prices, as opposed to Jacob's unreliable rival. Jacob's Jewishness means less to the boys than commercial honesty. Representing liberal capitalism, Edgeworth's Jacob with his economic utility illustrates one of the reasons for integrating Jews into English society. From torturing Jacob because of his Jewishness to defending and accepting him, Harrington undergoes a moral education Edgeworth intends to be socially representative.

When Harrington as a young man heading to Oxford meets Jacob who acquaints him with information about Moses Mendelssohn, Harrington attends especially to the "nervous disease" suffered by Mendelssohn, something the two share (103–04). As Mendelssohn's nervous disease always became most acute when he had to battle with public bullies who taunted him to convert to Christianity, the novel cleverly illustrates the destructive nature of racial and religious prejudice, and its capacity to make bodies ill. The nervous disease makes Harrington not just feminized but also Jewish.

The pedlar also functions within the novel as a marker of Jewish status, pedlar being the lowest rung of the hierarchy, with the Ashkenazi Israel Lyons the Hebrew teacher and rabbi next, and at the top the aristocratic Sephardi merchant, Montenero. The learning, culture, and manners of Lyons attract Harrington's notice but the chief characteristic distancing him from the pedlar is the Cambridge rabbi's "carelessness about money matters" (107). Lyons displays an aristocratic attitude toward money: "His disregard on all occasions of pecuniary interest gave me a conviction of his liberal spirit" (107). The pedlar of course cannot afford to be careless of his pecuniary interest; were he to do so, he could starve to death, whereas within the value structure assumed by the novel there is no moral taint from possessing or consuming wealth. The principal meaning of *Bildung* as it applied to Jews before and during "emancipation" in Europe was to provide a process drawing people away from things traditionally Jewish—rabbinic interpretation, Yiddish, Hebrew, making money—and toward what was considered the humanistic national culture. As a knowledgeable reader of literature and a collector of art, Montenero has displayed the benefits of *Bildung* to balance against his materialistic role in acquiring money through trade. It is not difficult to find parallels between the Jewish and Irish situations, for the Catholic Gaelic and Hiberno-English speakers possessed within the Anglocentric structure of values a scorned foreignness that could be worked through by a program of *Bildung*. Although the negative stereotypes are not the same for the Irish and Jewish Others, *Bildung* will work effectively in either case.[55]

Yet another function of the pedlar within the novel is as victimized scapegoat. Simon the Jew's son Jacob suffers at the hands of Mowbray, the novel's evil aristocrat, but Jacob has his protectors too, namely Harrington and Montenero. Montenero, who is rich enough to settle in a variety of countries, can be scorned and verbally attacked but he is too powerful to be scapegoated, that is, until the Gordon riots, when he and his house are saved by the Widow Levy, an Irish pedlar of oranges. In Edgeworth's novel the scapegoating of Jews is concentrated into the victimizing of the pedlar, the most vulnerable Jew. The violence introduced by Mowbray finally turns against him by the novel's conclusion, thus balancing the novel's moral equilibrium.

Although it does not seem at first that Edgeworth would have identified with a Jewish old-clothes man, there is a chain of connections: Montenero vindicates the worth of Jews in general because of his ethical conduct and his aesthetic taste. He illustrates by example that Jews are not wholly materialistic and interested solely in acquiring wealth. During the Gordon riots (ch. 15), the wealthy Montenero family is saved from mob violence by the Widow Levy who rewards Montenero's ethical conduct (the episode allegorizes the saving of the Edgeworth estate by Catholics loyal to the Edgeworths during the 1798 Rebellion); in purchasing in order to destroy the antisemitic painting sought by the aristocratic Mowbrays (ch. 11) and to contrast with the vulgarity of the nouveaux riches Coates family from the City, Montenero displays his taste. Similarly, the Edgeworths occupied an Irish Big House but justified their social position by good works and ethical culture. Simon and his son Jacob both conduct themselves ethically in the novel but they lack Montenero's wealth, education, and cultural capital. Without money and *Bildung*, the Edgeworths would be in a position similar to that of Simon and Jacob. At a literary level, the Jewish pedlars would be similar to the professional writers of Grub Street, selling pre-owned words and narratives, recycling torn and tattered stories, mending old and damaged characters and plots. Here is a letter from Maria Edgeworth to her aunt Mary Sneyd (October 20, 1802):

> I wish I could send you in a frank a print which caught my eye in a shop window in Bond Street. At the bottom of it was written Belinda, or else indeed I never should have guessed that it had any relation to Belinda. The print is in a ladies memorandum book and if it was in your hands it would infallibly put you in a passion—that is into as great a passion as you can be put. Lady Delacour is a fat vulgar housekeeper and Belinda a stick worse a hundred times than sprawling Virginia. In many booksellers shops at Bruges, Ghent and Brussels we found the translation of Belinda by Miss Edgewortz as they call her and print her. I have not yet had time to see whether it is well or ill translated.

Edgeworth sees how her text gets represented in a commercial context, as a commodity, how her characters are misrepresented and made "vulgar," how her own name is misspelled and made foreign sounding; she becomes afraid to read the translation. Her sense of being genteel threatened by the visible commodification of her art, she comments on a Miss Clerke, "the granddaughter to the poor king of Corsica," and her popular novel *Ianthe*; she is happy for *Ianthe*'s popularity in a "republican country." To her aunt she remarks: "You will I am sure be glad of this for when the Granddaughter of a king has spirit enough to write for her bread she deserves to be read."[56] Edgeworth is positioning herself within commodity culture, affirming her gentility and justifying her writing for money. As described by Marilyn Butler, Edgeworth was the most commercially successful fiction writer of her day before the greater success of Scott's *Waverley* series.[57] To write only for money and to write from a social position lacking genteel status would be similar to being a pedlar hawking commodities in the street. Edgeworth's discomfort is from seeing the public existence, open to anyone's eyes, of her writing, out of her own control, circulating in the market, handled like common currency passed from one person to the next.

The most ideologically disruptive figure in *Harrington* is in the fifteenth chapter, the remarkable Orange Woman who saves the Montenero family from the Gordon rioters. The widow Levy is a working-class Irish Catholic with close connections with the anti-Catholic rioters. She is a hawker of oranges, an occupation at the time dominated by Jews. Orange of course is the symbolic color of the Irish Protestant Loyalists, and her name Levy is recognizably Jewish. As in a Freudian dream, she condenses the contradictory signifiers associated with ethnic and religious conflict; as a mediating figure the widow Levy effects a nonviolent resolution of what seemed inevitably violent.[58]

FROM WORDSWORTH
TO MENDELE THE BOOKPEDDLER

Finally, I want to turn to the curious figure of Wordsworth's Pedlar, a central character in *The Ruined Cottage* and a major character as the Wanderer in *The Excursion*. According to Quentin Bailey, "The *Ruined Cottage* is a radical poem not because of its socioeconomic analysis but because of its implicit critique of the kinds of control advocated by the Parliamentary Select Committee."[59] As is apparent from the manuscript evidence and his own testimony in the Fenwick notes, Wordsworth identified himself with the character of the pedlar, who was largely based on a Scottish pedlar known as the Intellectual Pedlar, James Patrick.[60] He goes so far to suggest a vocational inclination to the pedlar style of life: "Had I been born in a class which would have deprived me of what is called a liberal education, it is not unlikely that being strong in body, I should have taken to a way of life such as that in which my pedlar passed the greater part of his days." Whereas books were the passion of his friend Robert Southey, Wordsworth's own passion was "wandering."[61] While critics have pointed to the parallel of peddling household goods and peddling poetry, the figurative connection with Jewishness has gone unremarked. First, the epithet "wandering" has long been attached to Jews at least from the middle ages if not earlier and in the Romantic period, the Wandering Jew enjoyed numerous textual realizations. Wordsworth's Pedlar assumes the role not out of the economic necessity that motivated the poor Jewish immigrants but because he could not control his wandering thoughts as a school teacher, his initial job. The parallel would be Wordsworth's turning down the possibility of a clergyman's position for the more unsettled position as poet. The actual wandering of real Jews was anything but Romantic, as Jews were expelled from various places and as poverty and discrimination ordinarily motivated the wandering. Nevertheless, at a figurative level for Wordsworth, Jews are wanderers. Although in the late eighteenth century most Jewish pedlars who traveled the country routes worked the south and east of England, Jewish pedlars also traveled everywhere, including the north of England. At a time when the cultural associations of peddling were predominantly Jewish, Wordsworth chooses as his philosophical spokesman a country pedlar who is religiously pious, passionately committed to texts, and although he is a part of the community, he is also markedly different from that community. Another striking thing about the Pedlar and Wordsworth: Dorothy Wordsworth's journal records the many complaints of the poet who labored so painfully over the Pedlar. It is as though the poet's actual body were undergoing the pains of invention and composition, thus cementing the bond between the writer and his fictional pedlar.[62]

In MS. B (1798) the site of the poem's action, the ruined cottage, is a place to be used by "The wandering gypsey in a stormy night" for storing his "moveables."[63] The pedlar is not a gipsy but the parallels between the two wanderers with their movables are obvious. Similarly, the Wordsworth of the 1790s was a wanderer in his own right until the final settling down in Grasmere. The discursive and dialogic form of *The Ruined Cottage* and the later *Excursion* dramatizes the face-to-face encounter of a pedlar with his customers. Face-to-face defines the physical proximity of the narrative exchange, which is a form of linguistic and communicative production appropriate for the moral economy of Wordsworth's writing. Aware of the modernity he wanted to resist, Wordsworth structures his storytelling in the oral tradition, always under threat by the print culture and what the print culture comes to represent.

Symptomatic of the oral/print difference are the two different ways Wordsworth concludes the narrative of Margaret, Robert, and the Pedlar. In MS. B (1798) the poem ends with the Pedlar's final speech on Margaret's death and the ruined dwelling where she once lived: "Last human tenant of these ruined walls." The Pedlar has the last word, the last speech, and the reader must wrestle with all the implications and emotional disturbances of this tragic tale. MS. D (1799), on the other hand, concludes differently, shifting the focus to the reader's reaction, which the poem tries to shape and control. After the Pedlar's moving speech, the poem continues for another forty-five more lines by the narrator and Pedlar who address some

of the philosophical implications of the story and who provide a justification for nature and ultimately God's justice. The second and
more metaphysical conclusion, which is the one carried over into the
Excursion, follows print-culture conventions more faithfully than the
conventions of the ballad and oral storytelling. Ballads end abruptly
and harshly, as does MS. B, but MS. D and *The Excursion* hold the
reader's hand and provide a comforting hug of reassurance.

Storytelling, according to Walter Benjamin's essay on Leskóv and
the storyteller, is coming to an end along with the artisanal mode of
production upon which oral culture depends. The decline of storytelling is accompanied by the devaluation of experience itself, which
is becoming increasingly impervious to communication. Exchanging
experiences "mouth-to-mouth" and "face-to-face"—as God spoke to
Moses, according to the Hebrew Bible (Num. 12.8; Deut. 34.10)—
was the characteristic mode of narration for the medieval traveler.
Like Wordsworth's *Ruined Cottage*, where the Pedlar's seasonal visits and chance encounters with the narrator structure and punctu-
ate Margaret's story, storytelling in general, according to Benjamin,
reflects the storyteller's personality and the circumstances of hearing
it and retelling it.[64] An oral story is always retold and capable of end-
less retellings and multiple interpretations. The storyteller assumes
sufficient time and discursive space characteristic of a hand-produc-
tion economy; also assumed is a body of "wisdom," a body of knowledge gained through trial and error and passed on through tradition,
somewhat akin to Aristotle's phronesis. The storyteller embodies
this wisdom in his person: the "storyteller is the figure in which the
righteous man encounters himself."[65] Storytellers traditionally sympathize with "rascals and crooks," suggesting that the wisdom of oral
culture cannot be ascribed to the ideology of the powerful. Rather,
because no one feels wholly capable of playing the role of the righteous man, this role "keeps changing hands. Now it is the tramp, now
the haggling Jewish peddler, now the man of limited intelligence who
steps in to play this part."[66]

Conservative critics like Francis Jeffrey considered it ludicrous that
a pedlar could embody wisdom as a righteous man, but Wordsworth
intellectually wrestles with the tension between social class and wisdom in *The Excursion*, finally arriving at a conventional identification
of wisdom with the Church of England, but not before he had stirred
up many interesting possibilities. If for Wordsworth his Intellectual
Pedlar is the radical antithesis of print-culture commercialism, the
Jewish pedlar in popular culture is the most representative type
of raw, egoistic, materialistic commercialism. The Jewishness of

Wordsworth's pedlar is less in the parallels already pointed out than in the negation of a negative stereotype. Wordsworth's Pedlar is otherworldly, not materialistic, not greedy, not selfish but committed to the welfare of the community and its highest values.

The Jewish pedlar to which Benjamin alludes is perhaps one of the "rascals and crooks" the storyteller sympathetically represents, but Leskóv certainly represented Jews in some of his fiction, and the Russian towns and villages of the nineteenth century had significant Jewish communities. A story Benjamin would certainly have known is "Fish Soup Without Fish," an ironic Christmas story where the wealthy rabbi Solomon, who is given a counterfeit five ruble note by Christians at a card game, passes this note to a poor, unmarried Christian mother wholly neglected by her own community. Following the rabbi's instructions, she takes one ruble for herself to pay for her child's baptism and returns the other four rubles to the rabbi, for whom she has to work for three weeks. The rabbi, by appearing to be generous to a needy Christian, polishes his public image, but in reality he has tricked the Christians into accepting counterfeit money. The story is nothing but morally ambiguous: a Jew stereotypically passes bad money, but the Christians started it; he helps a woman with the baptism but he also gets his laundry cleaned for three weeks—and the whole winter, it turns out, as the woman becomes so grateful; the story contrasts money earned from labor and money earned from money and property—gambling, fraud, rent; "The Jews get all the money that the lazy, sorry Christian population manages somehow to earn."[67] If the story is rough on the Jews, it is also rough on the Christians, who are not better, only different. As Jewish representation (rather than history, which is another matter entirely), Leskóv shows Jews and Christians as moral equals and socially symbiotic, something one would have expected Benjamin to have noticed.

Benjamin's interest in Leskóv and storytelling might have led him to take up the Yiddish fiction of S.Y. Abramovitsh (1835–1917), a contemporary of Leskóv's (1831–95), not quite in the same neighborhood (Jewish Belarus versus eastern Russia) but in the same general area. Abramovitsh's fiction, especially *Fishke the Lame*, illustrates Benjamin's ideas on storytelling even better than Leskóv. The signatures of oral storytelling—the dialogic face-to-face, the frame tale structure, the physical setting and circumstances of the telling becoming a distracting source of story itself, the context of traditional wisdom, the parade of misfits, conmen, rogues, and thieves, and the drama of the righteous man in search of redemption—are all here in Mendele the Bookseller's delightful narrative. Suffering hunger pangs and a brutally hot sun during the Tisha B'Av fast, Mendele meets up with fellow bookseller Reb Alter who is also driving his horse-drawn cart to a small Russian village. To pass the time and distract themselves from their physical state, Mendele tells the story of Fishke the Lame, a schlemiel figure who actually turns up later and relates his story *in propria persona* after a few adventures. Fishke's attachment to his abusive, unfaithful wife is comic as cuckold stories always are, but Fishke's dependence, self-delusions, and masochistic passivity also express, good or bad (mostly bad) Fishke's sad identity, the extreme price he must pay for being innocent and virtuous rather than a brute among the brutal. Robbed, beaten, tricked, tortured, betrayed, Fishke somehow survives to tell the tale.

This beautiful story also has Benjaminian touches, such as the ridicule of pretentious writers who fancy themselves above the materialism of the literary market. Mendele the Bookpeddler proudly locates himself as a fellow "pauper" within the network of print-culture institutions: "because if we aren't richly deserving of being called paupers, then whoever is? And if book peddlers qualify, well why not the rest of the bookmen? That's to say, all of the *Publishers* and *Printers* and *Editors* after their kind; as also their servitors after theirs, in the way of *Journeymen printers* and *'Prentice typesetters* and *in Galley-proof readers* and *Fair copyists* and *Journalists,* and *Correspondents.*"[68] With less sentimentality than Benjamin, Mendele realizes oral storytelling as a part of print-culture commercialism just as much as the most stylized novel. The oral is remediated, as it has been for centuries, with no loss of authenticity.[69]

CONCLUSION

It usually took several generations for the families of Jewish pedlars in England to move out of poverty but they enjoyed, if that is the right word, a rich life in the print culture where they played out their stereotypical role as comic or menacing Shylocks, reflecting the eighteenth-century treatment of Shakespeare's character (Granville's comic and Macklin's menacing Shylock). The "benevolent" Jew figure moderated the negative stereotypes to some extent, as would be reflected in the Jew songs in the *Universal Songster*. It is not easy to hear something like a real Jewish voice not wholly distorted by hostile stereotyping until one turns to the Bailey trial reports where Jewish defendants and victims enter the public discourse. The figure of Jewish wandering, highly idealized, masked the actual social existence of real Jewish pedlars who rarely if ever found literary treatment except perhaps in the Old Bailey *Proceedings* where one glimpses some of the experiences of the pedlars, whose voices we hear. The criminal justice system ironically was one of the most reliable counters to the *at best* ambivalent literary culture. It was not until perhaps Mendele the Bookpeddler's Yiddish tales that Jewish pedlars were given a voice, a worldview, and a literary dignity worthy of them. It is ironic that Walter Benjamin ignored the Jewish storytellers whose work fit so well into his conceptual framework. Mendele also provides a retrospective understanding of Wordsworth's quarrel with modernity through his pedlar tales.

CHAPTER 4

THE MONEYLENDER

*From the cradle, the Jew directs his unvaried walk to the market;
and when, after his insipid round in the regions of huckstery and
barter, he descends at length into the grave, we see him rise again,
like a true type of the insect below, in the same form, and with
the same grovelling propensities, which before excited our pity and
contempt.*

An Essay on the Commercial Habits of the Jews *(1809).*[1]

*Our greatest enemies cannot deny this truth, "That the human
character is intirely the effect of education." This, which in all civilized countries forms the future man, has the same influence on the
Jew as the Gypsy, and if found defective both will alike be triflers
and fall into insignificancy.*

Levy Alexander, Memoirs of the Life and Commercial
Connections, Public and Private, of the Late Benj Goldsmid,
Esq, of Roehampton *(1808).*[2]

The emancipation debate in eighteenth- and nineteenth-century Europe pivoted on the questions of commercial morality and
national characteristics. If Jews were judged harshly for their economic practices of usury and hard dealing, as indeed they were by
most of the hypocritical and morally obtuse Christian world, then the
issue became one of nature or nurture: could Jews be educated away
from their odiously money-obsessed culture or were Jews, as a nation
or race, innately avaricious? Was the answer liberalizing *Bildung* or
harsh measures to punish, control, contain, and if necessary expel
the immoral Jews? That the Jewish commercial morality was no

worse than that of the Gentiles among whom they did business was a minority opinion that failed to push the debate away from the two customary positions. In literature and popular culture the figure of the Jewish moneylender symbolized what was wrong with Jews.

Although in the ancient Near East lending money at interest was commonplace—"in the second millennium B. C. E., Babylonian law permitted 20 percent interest on money and 33 1/3 percent on grain"—the practice of interest-bearing loans generates social and moral anxiety reflected in many traditions, including the Jewish, Greek, Roman, Christian, and Islamic. The Torah proof texts are Exodus 22:24, Leviticus 25:35–37, and Deuteronomy 23: 20–21. "Ezekiel (18:13) condemns it bitterly, and the Psalmist (15:5) praises the person who has never lent on interest." According to Rabbi Plaut, the interest prohibition did not apply to non-Jews because foreign traders who engaged in commerce sought profits, not social relationships.[3] Rabbinic writings were even more exacting in condemning the taking of interest, as Rabbi Akiba argues that even a "good deed" can be usurious if it is done within the context of an interest-bearing loan, and in the Talmud (Makkot 24a), moral perfection is attributed to the man who does not lend on interest "even to a Gentile."[4] In terms of actual social practices, however, Jews loaned to other Jews exacting interest but disguised it as "investment" for the sake of fidelity to religious law.[5] For providing some understanding of the tormented, long, and complicated history of Jews, moneylending, and usury, one cannot do better than turning to Jonathan Karp's study of Jewish commerce. The contrast between the Christian merchant Antonio, who lends money "gratis," and the Jewish moneylender Shylock, who takes interest, reflects the West's ambivalence about making money, rooted in traditional church teachings and ancient Greek thought and politics. Both the church and Hellenic culture looked unfavorably on trade and commerce.[6] Derek J. Penslar also shows how Greek, Roman, and Christian traditions were hostile to commerce and trade.[7] The historian J.G.A. Pocock's influential thesis concerning seventeenth- and eighteenth-century Britain—that the central ideological conflict is between republican virtue based in aristocratic land ownership and the amoral power of commerce—helps explain the difficult position in which Jewish bankers and merchants found themselves because Christian Europe prohibited Jewish ownership of land and excluded Jews from the guilds and skilled trades as well.[8] Although the received wisdom is that Jews were forced into usury because all other options were closed, Karp reminds us that early modern Europe had numerous Jewish merchants while the Christians monopolized the business of credit.[9] In the eleventh and twelfth centuries, Jews had been pushed out of commerce and forced into moneylending, but there was a flourishing Jewish commerce between 1450 and 1650 by New Christians and Sephardic Jews.[10] Simone Luzzatto in 1638 published an influential apology for Venetian Jewish commerce, which strongly influenced Menasseh. James Harrington, the Machiavellian republican, however, saw commerce as fatal to *"virtu"*—the force counter to arbitrary *"fortuna"*—such as civic action, creative adaptation to unexpected circumstances, military prowess, and courage. Like Milton, Harrington favored the landowners and their political enterprise over the monarch's court and the moneyed interests. Although Jews usually aligned with monarchies for protection, early modern thinkers such as Luzzatto, Menasseh, and Spinoza favored a republic.[11]

The Jews face a double bind: as moneylenders or merchants, they are both rewarded by governments for providing necessary economic services that promote overall prosperity, and racially stigmatized as inhumanly corrupted by the immoral activities of making money. Appalling hypocrisy permitted an ideology of clean and dirty money, as though taxes, rents, and sinecures were moral and natural, and finance and commercial capital were immoral and unnatural. Christian merchants and bankers suffered from the scorn and political opposition of snobbish aristocrats, but Jews were much more harshly stigmatized: "The image of Shylock has dominated popular conceptions of the Jews' economic identity in early modern Europe."[12]

Although Shakespeare did not invent the racist stereotype of the Jewish usurer, he gave that figure an aesthetic embodiment with enormous power. Even if actors like Edmund Kean (1789–1833) made Shylock somewhat sympathetic and readers like William Hazlitt (1778–1830) emphasized that the moneylender was a victim, not just a victimizer, there is no mystery why loan-sharks are still called Shylocks. Some parts of *The Merchant of Venice* cannot be accented to make Shylock look good. In answer to Bassanio's question why Shylock is whetting his knife "so earnestly," he declares: "To cut the forefeiture from that bankrupt there" (4.1.121–22). A Jew with a knife anticipating with great pleasure the prospect of extracting murderously a pound of Christian flesh—commonly read as castration (James Shapiro),[13] as well as ritual murder, evoking the victims of Isaac and Christ (Janet Adelman)[14]—cannot be seen innocently. The play's plain sense—to follow the rabbinic interpretive mode of *peshat*—contrasts a generous merchant, Antonio, and a greedy, murderous moneylender, Shylock, and then in the trial scene a merciful legal scholar, Portia, and a vindictive Jew. Just as rabbinic interpretation is not limited to the plain sense, so too Shakespeare's readers who do not want the play to be so brutally moralistic, especially against a vulnerable minority, have found hermeneutic strategies around these stark binaries. As with other texts, when the plain sense is unacceptable—stoning adulteresses, exterminating war captives—the humane option is to find other meanings. Nevertheless there is a danger in being so hermeneutically clever that one forgets what has to be remembered, and in this case I follow Matthew Biberman, who insists that "antisemitism is a central component of modern European culture, and not simply an extremist appendage."[15] Biberman's approach to *The Merchant of Venice* recognizes that Shylock, as the "Jew-Devil," is emasculated in Act 4 to become the "Jew-Sissy," a prototypical feminized Jew who has countless manifestations over the centuries.[16]

Antonio the merchant is generous to Bassanio but to Shylock and his Jewish community the rhetoric of abuse, hatred, and dehumanization prevails. To Shylock Antonio replies: "I am as like to call thee [dog] so again, / To spit on thee again, to spurn thee too" (1.3.121–22). Abuse, hatred, and dehumanization, as well as animal and other subhuman metaphors characterize a Romantic-era pamphlet directed against Jewish emancipation, several decades before emancipation became a realistic political goal. The anonymous author of *An Essay on the Commercial Habits of the Jews*, an abolitionist and a defender of Irish Catholics, argues that Jews have brought oppression upon themselves by clinging to their religion, refusing to assimilate, and pursuing fraudulent, dishonest business practices. Jews "flock" to cities where "the poorer herds" of pedlars "rally round the wealthy" to form their conspiratorial community using a secret language unknown to Christians, plotting ways to cheat the Gentiles: "like the monsters of the deep, they wanton in the storm, and thrive upon the miseries of their fellow-creatures" by dominating the system of funding war. The actual physical layout of the streets in the East End where Jews live reflects Jewish characteristics: "The number of intricate lanes and alleys near Whitechapel, and other parts of the town, entirely occupied by these miscreants and their associates, render them formidable to the officers of justice; and at the same time impervious to the public eye. These depositories of filth and iniquity, the approach of morning sends them in herds over the whole face of the capital."[17] The pedlar herds seem to come from nowhere, escape the surveillance of legal authorities, and threaten the truly human precincts of the city with their animalistic presence. The author goes to botany for another metaphor, as he compares Jews with plants that "may be classed among the number of those exotics, which, from mere baseness of constitution, take root in every soil, although known to be indigenous to none."[18] As an invasive species of plant Jews are weeds that should be eradicated. Similarly, the author takes an entomological turn in the following passage: "From the cradle, the Jew directs his unvaried walk to the market; and when, after his insipid round in the regions of huckstery and barter, he descends at length into the grave, we see him rise again, like a true type of the insect below, in the same form, and with the same grovelling propensities, which before excited our pity and contempt."[19] About a century before Kafka's *Metamorphosis*, this text uses the insect to signify the uncreative, monotonous, spiritually impoverished, and wholly materialistic existence of the commercial Jew. The author does not want to consider Jewish oppression as something that deserves amelioration; it is not a worthy liberal cause because Jews have chosen their social existence with all its disabilities and their social interests are limited entirely to selfish economic gain.[20] Moreover, the lamentable "general spirit of engrossing" that characterizes the "present age" derives its "thirst for gain" from the same insects, herd, and weeds the pamphlet has been criticizing from the first paragraph. Jews are guilty of immoral commercial practices as well as infecting the whole culture with their destructive immorality. While Jews themselves have not enslaved Africans and plundered "America, Asia and Africa," the Jewish "spirit" has animated these efforts nevertheless.[21]

The two main reasons for opposing Jewish emancipation are that Jews would dominate the economy even more than they now do and they would destroy what remains of the Christian culture and its distinctive morality. Christians mixing with Jews would not be beneficial because it is more likely that Christians would become Jews—or lose their Christian faith—than the other way around. For reasons the author does not explain, he assumes that religious error has more appeal than religious truth.[22] The author sounds like William Prynne of the seventeenth century, whose spiritual ancestor he (or possibly she) certainly is. The pamphlet concentrates its attack on Jewish merchants, pedlars, stockbrokers, and bankers, not really distinguishing between good and bad forms of commercial activity, as all Jewish business is "fraud and deception."[23] This gloomy and perverse essay might be representative of more than marginal currents of thinking at the time because unlike Prynne's essay it contains no stories of ritual murder and host desecration and it assumes a center of moral and political gravity that favors abolition of slavery, political rights for Irish Catholics, and moral criteria for European relations with other countries. One reason for this kind of liberal antisemitism is *The Merchant of Venice*, its extraordinary popularity in the eighteenth century, especially the harsh interpretation of Shylock given by Charles Macklin at a time of ethnic conflict and the Jew Bill controversy.

Prior to Macklin's version there was George Granville's *Jew of Venice* (1701), which enjoyed its own popularity in the first half of the century (thirty-six performances from 1701 to 1748).[24] Taking more liberties with Shakespeare's text than did Macklin, Granville added a masque about Prometheus for a new scene set at the dinner at Bassanio's. Also in this version Shylock is not forced to convert to Christianity, perhaps reflecting a theological latitudinarianism or simply the playwright's carelessness. There is a cynicism about all commercial activity articulated by Gratiano: "Jew, Turk and Christian differ but in Creed; / 'In ways of Wickedness, they're all agreed: / 'None upward clears the Road. They part and cavil, / 'But all jog on—unerring, to the Devil" (2.1).[25] Shylock, who is also more crudely drawn, grotesquely makes a toast to money at Bassanio's dinner party, whereas everyone else commends love and friendship: "My Money is my Mistress! Here's to / Interest upon Interest" (2.1).[26] The Masque, which might seem gratuitous and unrelated to Shakespeare's themes, is fascinating: Peleus and Thetis love each other but Jupiter, who desires Thetis, prevents their union. Prometheus utters a prophecy that the offspring of Thetis will be greater than the father. After hearing this, Jupiter withdraws his intention to have Thetis, so the couple can be free to produce Achilles. Out of gratitude to Prometheus, Jupiter liberates Prometheus from his Mount Caucasus torture and punishment.[27] Everyone is happy: a perfect symbolic analogue of an idealized Glorious Revolution: the sovereign power, subject to certain limitations, is flexible and listens to reason; the new order, in which constitutional monarchy prevails over arbitrary authority, entails a progressive order in which sons are stronger than fathers. The new moderate order is all about love and friendship. Shylock is a comic not a tragic villain because he does not participate in the network of reciprocity, the fraternal exchange. Caring more for money than for friendship, he embodies a possessive individualism that threatens this new order. Granville's version mutes the antisemitism of Shakespeare's version to some extent, most dramatically in sparing Shylock the Christian conversion. Jessica's own problematic features—her disloyalty, her stealing from her father, her excessive sexuality—are also muted for she travels from Shylock's narrow world to the wider loving world of Belmont.

Characteristic of Jewish history, Granville's relatively innocuous play—at least for Jews—was followed by a malicious play, turning the Jewish moneylender into one of theatre's most memorable villains.

John Gross is surely right that "Shylock would not have held the stage for four hundred years if he were a mere stereotype,"[28] but Shylock *is* stereotypical, if a complexly intriguing one. Like a dream symbol in the classical Freudian interpretation, Shylock condenses powerful and ancient prejudices to produce something uniquely energetic and provocative.

In the English theatre the first major counter to Macklin's Shylock is Richard Cumberland's moneylender, Sheva, in the popular play, *The Jew* (1794). For modern readers this clumsy, sentimental play is far inferior to Gotthold Lessing's *Nathan the Wise* (1779), but as Michael Ragussis has argued, Cumberland's Sheva at the time performed important cultural work and had an "immense impact" on public opinion.[29] The figure of the revisionary Benevolent Jew requires close attention as one of the important manifestations of philosemitism.

The contexts for the theatrical Benevolent Hebrew (the subtitle for the first American edition)[30] are textual and political events in Germany and France reflecting on and promoting forms of Jewish emancipation: Lessing's play *Die Juden* (1757), C.W. Von Dohm's *Concerning the Amelioration [Verbesserung] of the Civil Status of the Jews* (1781), Abbé Grégoire's *An Essay on the Physical, Moral and Political Reformation of the Jews* (1789), and French Jewish emancipation (1791). With liberal European opinion already siding with emancipation, Cumberland is not risking too much with his own version of the anti-Shylock. As the play is not well known, I will briefly summarize it and Lessing's *Nathan the Wise*, from which Cumberland takes much.

Lessing's play situates the protagonist Nathan and his adopted daughter Recha in twelfth-century Jerusalem. The Christian Templar, Conrade, who had been recently pardoned by the ruler Saladin, happens to save Recha from a fire and he falls in love with her. Conrade befriends Nathan but the Christian leader in Jerusalem declares to the Templar that capital punishment fits the crime of having converted a Christian child to Judaism, as Nathan is alleged to have done with Recha. In the play's most famous scene of the three rings, obviously a revision of Shakespeare's three caskets, Nathan answers the Sultan's question about which monotheistic religion God prefers: one can never know which religion God favors, so that it is best to treat each faith as though it were God's beloved. Conrade the Templar refrains from killing Nathan and seeks the hand of Recha in marriage. In a series of recognition and reversal scenes, the audience discovers (1) that Recha is not a Jewess but has been raised to respect all the monotheistic religions; (2) that Recha is actually Conrade's sister; (3) that the parents of Recha and Conrade are a German Christian woman and a Muslim, Assad, the brother of the Sultan. The backstory is that Nathan adopted the abandoned Recha only after his own family had been slaughtered by Christian crusaders.[31]

Cumberland's play revises eighteenth-century romantic comedy with some assistance from Shakespeare and Lessing. The plot revolves around a young couple, Frederic Bertram and Eliza Ratcliffe, who have clandestinely married, but family disapproval and poverty are obstacles to their happiness. Sheva the moneylender, whose life was saved twice by a Ratcliffe—from the Inquisition by the father in Spain and from a London mob by the son—uses his wealth to bring the Bertrams and Ratcliffes together so that the young couple can reconcile with their families. Frederic Bertram, who in the first act is a Jew-baiting antisemite, undergoes an education in cultural awareness over the course of the play. Charles Ratcliffe, from a decayed aristocratic family, protects Sheva from the London mob from a sense of honor and fairness.[32] The two acts of Sheva's being saved by Ratcliffes repeat Lessing's lifesaving episodes, Nathan and much later Conrade the Templar rescuing Recha. As Nathan is the principal agent by which the conflicts of the play are resolved, so too Sheva. Cumberland restructures entirely the "bond" between Shylock and Antonio to signify the mutual ties of indebtedness between Sheva and the Ratcliffes. Whereas Shylock hates Christians, Sheva loves them and practices extreme forms of self-denial to assist them, incurring the complaints of his ill-fed Jewish servants. Sheva plays the role of the merciful and wise Portia, distributing justice to the families by means of his money and kind words. The eloping couple here, which is Christian, does not rob and humiliate the moneylender as do Jessica and Lorenzo, but provide the occasion for Jewish philanthropy. Both Shakespeare and Lessing develop emphatically the themes of miscegenation and cross-ethnic sexual unions, but Cumberland steers his play away from those issues. Sheva is the grandfatherly presence, entirely without masculine desire, nor does he have any children: "I am a solitary being, a waif on the world's wide common."[33] To Shylock's rage and urgent needs, emotional and material, Sheva contrasts his own sublimated sentimentality, drained of any personal craving. The play has no indication whatsoever that Sheva considers London's Jewish community, exceedingly poor as it actually was at the time, worthy of his philanthropic efforts, but in his final speech he condemns using wealth to build a "synagogue or any other costly pile"—nothing vain with his name on it, not public works, only charity to individuals—building "my hospital in the human heart."[34] Synagogues and hospitals, apparently not worth constructing, as they would be used by Jews rather than "human" individuals. The philosemitic play has a Benevolent Jew who cares nothing about other Jews but everything about the "human"—Christian—heart. A very different kind of philosemitic play, Thomas Wade's *The Jew of Arragon* (1830), which I will discuss in the next chapter, constructs community loyalties and philanthropy very differently. Cumberland's play shows that even when some stereotypes are undermined, new ones take their place, perhaps almost as harmful.

In the Romantic era there were several other attempts to counter the ill effects of the Shylock figure. A few years after Cumberland's play there was an "apology" for Shylock, but Richard Hole's essay is equivocal at best. The tone is captured in the introduction: "Justice would authorize, and humanity applaud us for rescuing a culprit from the gallows, who merely deserved a whipping."[35] Shylock—and Jews along with him—come in for a thorough whipping in this so-called apology. The essay never questions the moral and theological superiority of Christianity and its "mild precepts,"[36] but it seeks, through a series of counterfactual experiments in trying to see *The Merchant of Venice* through Jewish eyes, to sensitize the well-meaning Christian to feel sorry for poor Shylock. These counterfactual experiments are really parodies of Shakespeare's *Merchant* and Jewish perceptions. It is not fair, according to Hole, to use the higher Christian morality to judge the cruel, vindictive, usurious Jews who do not know any better. The highest kind of Christian morality elevates one's perspective to permit pity for unfortunate Hebrews. A moderate cultural relativism is the form that philosemitism takes in this essay, although there is never any doubt as to the superiority of the Christian culture. Apparently being whipped is better than being hanged.

My reading of Richard Hole's essay is somewhat harsher than that of Judith W. Page, who gives an incomparable account of the Romantic Shylock in the third chapter of her book, *Imperfect Sympathies* (2004).[37] The Romantic revisions of Macklin's Shylock by Kean and Hazlitt turned the scapegoating comedy into a tragedy that enabled audiences to sympathize with Shylock's position as a victim who became a victimizer. According to Page, "Hazlitt sees Shylock's mistreatment as the reason for his bitterness and revenge rather than an innate evil." Moreover, "Hazlitt argues that Shylock's enemies stifle his potential humanity."[38] Kean and Hazlitt also prepared the ground for an essay like George Farren's, which is very different from the begrudging concessions to Shylock and Jews by Richard Hole.

An Essay on Shakespeare's Character of Shylock (1833), which does not take Christianity as the center of moral and historical gravity, makes nuanced comments on the play and its context. The play, according to Farren, is about the passion of revenge, which is not characteristically Jewish; rather, Shakespeare clothes Shylock "with all the delusive impressions which might serve to palliate, if not to justify, his acts." Farren acknowledges Shylock's desire to murder Antonio, but suggests that Shylock would kill Antonio as *kashrut* instructs Jewish butchers, with a minimum of pain. Without sarcasm, Farren commends the "laws of Moses," which "are in themselves beautiful; *cruelty* is *no* where inculcated, nor indeed can the people professing the Jewish faith be justly charged with the practice of that vice."[39] With Farren, who even imagines Shylock sparing Antonio pain if he could kill him, one is in a very different cultural space than the one inhabited by Macklin's hateful Jew. It is Kean's and Farren's Shylock that one will now see in the theatres and on the cinema screens, for now it takes an effort of the historical imagination to see the play in its antisemitic context; the Bard, the author of our secular scripture, has to be protected from racism.

It will be instructive at this point to look closely at two actual Jewish moneylenders at the high end and low end of English society, Benjamin Goldsmid, the prominent banker who made loans to the British government, and John King, who in some respects conforms to the negative stereotypes of the Shylock, but who in other respects does not. Goldsmid's suicide occasioned a text by the Jewish artisan Levy Alexander that is in some ways a defense of the wealthy banker but in other ways critical, reflecting the cultural ambivalence about Jewish moneylenders. John King's writing and career are contradictory and fascinating in their own ways. Just as the Old Bailey *Proceedings* provided a voice to counter the many stereotypical pedlars, so King and his many masks and roles supply something new.

THE GOLDSMID TRAGEDY

Only several months after the April suicide of Benjamin Goldsmid, Levy Alexander published in July of 1808 his biographical sketch that had several aims: to counter the negative publicity on the well-known financier but without whitewashing the narrative; to present what will be taken as an accurate picture of the life of a wealthy Jew engaged in high finance, a figure strongly stereotyped in English satires and plays. Standing behind these stereotypes is Shakespeare's Shylock, especially the villain so effectively portrayed by Macklin. Alexander addresses the negative stereotypes directly on several occasions. When he emphasizes the revival of Jewish learning in France, Germany, and Italy and the high level of cultural achievement reached by some Jews in Prussia, he contrasts these accomplishments of what the Germans call *Bildung* with the English view of Jews, "little known but by their contrivances in traffic."[40] Explaining that Jews out of necessity became the brokers and bankers and not the farmers of the world, making use of standard Enlightenment historical analysis, Alexander draws out the philosophical basis for his argument: "Our greatest enemies cannot deny this truth, 'That the human character is intirely the effect of education.' This, which in all civilized countries forms the future man, has the same influence on the Jew as the Gypsy, and if found defective both will alike be triflers and fall into insignificancy."[41] Denying any innate Jewish qualities, positive or negative, Alexander rules out racial science. Alexander's bringing together Jews and gypsies not only reminds one of the Nazi taxonomies but also illustrates his efforts to counter the racial logic of inalterable and biologically determined qualities. He argues that if the Jews who engaged in commerce and finance display unattractively "covetous" and "rapacious" characteristics, one can point to the utter dependence Jews have on "precarious profits."[42]

Alexander's narrative includes episodes whose effect is to counter the Shylock image of the economic Jew. The biographical sketch begins, for example, with a story to illustrate Goldsmid's anguished feelings upon being separated from his Gentile lover. His family, which enforced the break up, keeps Goldsmid out of England and on a continental tour until his former lover is safely married off. The story is structured to bring out Goldsmid's emotional pain to illustrate that he is a man of feeling. The narrative turns the continental tour, which strategically kept Benjamin out of England, into a story of cosmopolitan education, the training of a broad-minded philanthropist who soaks up wisdom from Jewish sages in Paris and Berlin. Schemes for improving the lives of the Jewish poor are represented as being prominent in his thinking. After returning to England to marry a Jewish heiress, he becomes associated not with making money, which he did with great efficiency, but with constructing his estate at Roehampton, which becomes a symbol of Jewish acculturation: the mansion houses elegant art; the 150 acres of very expensive land are farmed and cultivated; he entertains the most powerful politicians and businessmen in the nation. In short, he has become a tasteful and patriotic English gentleman initiating bold philanthropic schemes to help both the Jewish community and the English nation, as well as celebrating national military victories with ostentatious grandeur. He exhibits the virtues as well as some of the vices of aristocratic gentlemen. Alexander's extended portrait of the extramarital sexual exploits with courtesans and mistresses of the Jewish financiers depicts a sexuality that conforms to residual aristocratic norms but violates the emergent Evangelical, bourgeois norms. That Alexander spent 35 pages of a book only 144 pages long on sexual activities the knowledge of which Goldsmid tries to keep from his wife suggests that the author was either playing up something sensationalistic that would attract readers or demonstrating to wealthy men that he could expose their intrigues if he were not adequately compensated. It was not uncommon at the time to use the threat of published scandal as a way to blackmail the rich and powerful. Alexander's turn to the genre of scandal is curious to say the least and seems to contradict his other rhetorical choices.

It is important for Alexander's overall rhetorical strategy to dispel the idea that Benjamin killed himself because of a financial disaster or something morally disgraceful. The narrative insists that Goldsmid was depressed, in the language of the time, a "melancholic." The financial speculator who commits suicide because of economic ruin was an enduring nineteenth-century convention, tragically played out two years later by Benjamin's brother Abraham who indeed killed himself when his financial empire was troubled. Alexander's narrative of Benjamin Goldsmid is designed to show the powerful financier was not a Shylock but a man of feeling, a cosmopolitan man of culture and art, a philanthropist, a patriotic and loyal Englishman, and although foreign born and untitled, a man living the aristocratic life.

For Alexander, poetry and art signify value that transcends economic and merely material interests. Describing the Roehampton mansion Alexander declares that Goldsmid had "great taste and critical sagacity, though brought up to business" and that he "spared no expense in literary pursuits and improvement of mind."[43] The huge library and extensive paintings indicate semiotically Goldsmid's affiliation with the values of art rather than Mammon. Moreover, Alexander sprinkles his book with short extracts from Sterne, Pope, Milton, Chaucer, and others to provide a texture of proverbial wisdom that is also distinctively English, one of the many ways he fashions his authorial identity for the Jewish community and the English nation, claiming insider-status within both communities.

Mark L. Schoenfield's recent essay on Abraham Goldsmid and his suicide two years after his brother Benjamin took his own life provides a valuable commentary on how the Jewish financiers functioned

in the new age of paper money and credit after the Bank of England
stopped cash payments on its currency in 1797. With gold no longer
backing up the pound in the same way that it had, the British money
system depended on the good opinion of the market and the public.
As Jewish financiers helped stabilize the currency and credit markets,
the Goldsmids performed a public role as patriotic servants of the
nation, their loyalty demonstrated by giving large parties and maintaining friendships with the Prince Regent and Lord Nelson. That
the Goldsmids seemed to be like magicians in their ability to keep the
complex financial system functioning at a high level drew upon antisemitic myths about Jewish alchemy and sorcery, as became evident
when William Cobbett in *Paper Against Gold* (1810) scapegoated the
Goldsmids as greedy and corrupt Shylocks.[44] The Goldsmids cultivated an elite cultural image that bolstered their Englishness and
national loyalty, but in the view of Cobbett and other antisemites,
the display of cultural status was a mask to hide nefarious exploitation
and financial trickery.

As I turn to John King, a moneylender occupying a far lower level
of status and social associations, one will notice some continuity
between the two figures, like the libertine sexuality, but mostly the
contrasts predominate. Unrespectable political radical and criminal
associate King tried to stay one step ahead of the legal system that
pursued him, who was at no time an "insider."

THE MONEYLENDER AND THE PHILOSOPHER:
JOHN "JEW" KING AND WILLIAM GODWIN[45]

On the surface they could not have been more different: William
Godwin (1756–1836), from a middle-class Dissenting background,
and John King (1753–1824), from a poor Sephardic Jewish background; the one a philosophical radical who made his living from
literature, as author and bookseller, and the other an "unrespectable"
radical who published his writing, but who made his living on the
border between legal and illegal money transactions; the one wrote
a decisive pamphlet critical of the treason trial proceedings (*Cursory
Strictures* in 1794), and the other gave money to support the treason
trial defendants and their families.[46] Their main area of congruence
was as political radicals who were both writers, Londoners, and of the
same generation. Perhaps then it is not so surprising that Godwin and
King knew each other very well, often dining together or having tea at
King's house or calling on one another. King makes his first appearance in Godwin's diary on December 1, 1793: "Sup at Jennings's,

with Thomas [Holcroft (1745–1809)] and King."[47] The first of many times that Godwin dined at King's is recorded on January 22, 1795, and the last recorded dinner party at King's that Godwin attended was in March 1807. Not only does King appear over 130 times in the diary; the diary also records that Godwin meets separately with King's wife, Lady Lanesborough, and her two adult children; Godwin also meets King's son Charles and daughter Sophia, who criticizes Godwin in print. Godwin on December 24, 1812 writes to Nicholas Byrne, reactionary editor-owner of the *Morning Post*; Byrne was at that time the father of three children by Charlotte King, John King's eldest daughter; Byrne and Charlotte King finally married in 1815 after the death of Byrne's first wife.

The Godwin-King relationship is intriguing both for biographical reasons, showing a side of Godwin that has not received much attention, and for literary reasons. Biographically, Godwin learned through King of experiences from which his puritanical background had shielded him: gambling, prostitution, blackmail, risky financial transactions, and criminality. In addition, one of the women in whom Godwin was interested, both before and after his wife's death, was Mary Robinson (1758–1800), who had been intimate with John King in 1773–74 when he was a young man; they later became bitter enemies, but King's eldest daughter, Charlotte, used Mary Robinson for a literary role model.[48] Along with Francis Place (1771–1854), John King helped restructure Godwin's woeful financial indebtedness in 1812.[49] Godwin owed King a literary debt as well, and perhaps a philosophical one. The diary records Godwin reading one of King's political essays in January 1795, and it turns out that Godwin and King were writing on political topics in the same year, 1783. King's *Thoughts on the Difficulties and Distresses in which the Peace of 1783, has involved the People of England* invites comparison to writings by Godwin on Charles James Fox (1749–1806), Edmund Burke (1729–97), and the American Revolution. Another similarity is worth considering: just as King distanced himself from Thomas Paine (1737–1809) and violent revolution in a series of speeches and public letters between 1792 and 1795, so too did Godwin distance himself from the London Corresponding Society (1792–99) and John Thelwall (1764–1834). The single text that bears the most evidence of King's influence is Godwin's 1799 novel *St. Leon*, but there is another useful comparison in the area of religion and theology. King's religion, a Jewish mixture of the deistic and messianic, is both like and unlike Godwin's deism inflected in a Christian direction. Although King's final publication tries to reconcile his deistic

ideas with the divine origin of scripture in a manner wholly foreign to
Godwin's secular approach, it would probably be safe to assume that
the two men discussed religion more than a few times in their more
than one hundred meetings.

PERSONAL RELATIONSHIP

The exchange of letters related in C. Kegan Paul's biography of
Godwin suggests a somewhat anxious Godwin intrigued by but wary
of King. Godwin justifies attending the King dinner parties in terms
of a philosopher's duty to "study man," but he reacts angrily in 1796
when King invites him to testify in court as a character witness, as
though the dinners Godwin had enjoyed were bribes. King shrugs off
Godwin's outraged letter and invites him again to dinner.[50] Godwin
indeed accepted that dinner invitation and many more after that.
Although Godwin himself never described those dinners, other writers have done so, including the poet and drama critic John Taylor
(1757–1832), who fondly remembers those occasions. Taylor has
nothing but praise for Lady Lanesborough and King, whom he knew
for forty years. Despite hearing many criticisms of King's character,
Taylor insists that he "never observed any thing in his conduct, or ever
heard him utter a sentiment, that could be injurious to his reputation.
He was hospitable and attentive. He was fond of having men of talent
at this table, and seemed capable of comprehending and of enjoying
whatever fell from them." Regulars at these parties were Dr. Wolcot–
Peter Pindar (1738–1819); Mrs. Grattan, sister of Lord Falkland
(1766–96); and Charles Carey (1768–1809), the Lord's brother. The
entertainment was music and cards, but there was not excessive gambling. There were rumors that King and Lady Lanesborough were not
actually married, but Taylor is convinced that they were, especially
because King had legal access to the Lanesborough money. Thomas
Holcroft and Godwin were also regulars, according to Taylor, who
describes Holcroft as noticeably argumentative and unfriendly to any
opposition to his ideas; in contrast, Godwin was quiet. King enjoyed
talking to them both,[51] but he apparently liked Godwin much better
than he did Holcroft, because in his *Letters from France* (1802), which
does not mention Godwin at all, he harshly criticizes for intellectual
pretension Holcroft and the Helen Maria Williams (1761?–1827)
circle of Parisian expatriates. Calling Godwin's friend Holcroft intol-
erant, "dogmatic, virulent, and splenetic," King declares a preference
for moderate monarchy to the kind of government he imagines would
ensue under a Holcroftian plan: "that barbarism and rudeness which

would revert with Holcroft's system, to that frigid and chearless torpor that reduces life to inanity, and to that intolerable inequality which would level learning with ignorance and modesty with impudence. I dread all extremes, particularly such as would follow the innovations of visionary and frantic impostors."[52] King's self-description as politically moderate must be taken with a grain of salt, but the irritation over the perceived self-importance of the Holcroft-Williams group sounds genuine, as we know that King's own politics accented practical action over theorizing.

King seems to be characterizing Godwin's own political perspective when he discusses Thomas Paine's in a moving section of *Letters from France*. Apologizing for his earlier public attack on Paine in the 1790s—"I am ashamed of my error"—King notes how isolated Paine has become and pays an emotional tribute to his integrity, protesting against his abandonment by England, France, and the United States. "Payne fondly hoped, and not unreasonably, that changes might be effected by conviction, by unanimous agreement, without bloodshed or coercion: but as they [Paine's writings] exposed state impostures, and asserted the rights of nature, they excited irritation."[53] Nonviolent, uncoerced consensus achieved by rational discussion sounds much more like Godwin than Paine, although it is possible that King interpreted Paine's opposition to killing the royal family in 1793 in Godwinian terms. Intentionally or not, King has written Godwin into the text without mentioning his name.

Although their paths do not seem to have crossed in 1781–84, the respective publications of Godwin and Godwin compare and contrast interestingly. Both ambitious young writers in London, both from outsider social groups, both oriented to the reformist political currents, Godwin takes the more traditional Grub Street path, while King becomes an author by trying to blackmail the famous actress Mary Robinson by threatening to publish their correspondence of 1773. King himself had wanted to represent "Perdita" Robinson in the high-stakes negotiations with her former lover, the Prince of Wales, but that role was taken by her then lover, Lord Malden—ineffectively—and by her subsequent lover, Charles James Fox, successfully. It is uncertain just how intimate King and Robinson had been in 1773, but at the least the unhappy newlywed had been flirtatious and the letters were embarrassing enough for her and Lord Malden to suppress, if a price could be negotiated. King would have preferred the blackmail payment rather than his first publication, but *Letters from Perdita to a certain Israelite* made King a published author in 1781, when Godwin was still a year away from becoming a

Londoner.[54] Always attracted to the aristocratic and fashionable life
of London, King played a notorious role in a world that accepted
him only as "Jew" King the moneylender. His second publication,
*Thoughts on the Difficulties and Distresses in which the Peace of 1783,
has involved the People of England* (1783),[55] a pamphlet protesting government policies, uses boldly Wilkesite rhetoric from his self-identified
position as a Jewish moneylender. As the historian Todd Endelman
remarks, King's pamphlet is "one of the earliest occasions that a Jew
anywhere in Europe sought to participate in national political life in
pursuit of goals unrelated to Jewish communal needs."[56] Godwin's
early publications, in contrast, were three novels (*Imogen, Damon
and Delia,* and *Italian Letters*), a book of sermons, a biography of
Pitt the elder, and several pamphlets for the Foxite Whigs. Regardless
of how well or poorly Godwin executed these texts, all of them were
of conventional genres that required the submergence of the author's
personality, whereas King's two publications were idiosyncratic, fore-
grounding the author's identity as moneylender and Jew.

Their early political writings provide a contrast in styles and political ideology, but there are some important similarities, notably their
common anti-imperialism. Godwin's biography of William Pitt,
Lord Chatham, which ignores completely the Jew Bill controversy
of 1753 that falls within the frame of Pitt's political career, harshly
criticizes the commercial motives for the colonial wars, but admires
the appeals to patriotism and republican virtue by which Pitt is able
to rally Britons to a less than noble cause. Godwin's position is highly
nuanced for a political biography of one of the few heroic politicians
of the eighteenth century. The antithesis of the corrupt Walpole,
Pitt revived a republican idealism by means of wars that were brutal,
mercenary, and ultimately unjustifiable. Godwin stresses the idealism at the expense of pacifist anti-imperialism, which is nevertheless
forthrightly expressed: "It would be absurd to institute an enquiry
into which party [the French or the British] was in the right, when
the object of both was certainly not right, but convenience. It would
appear still more absurd, when we reflected, that the Indians were
the true proprietors; and that we, on each side, were indeed no better, than robbers, fallen out about the spoil, that they had made upon
the innocent and defenceless passenger."[57] His relativizing the morality of Pitt's colonial wars and diminishing their grandeur is a bold
move for a novice author such as Godwin. He will not knock Pitt off
the republican pedestal, however, for the biography has many passages like the following: "Lately, the nation seemed to be made up
of isolated individuals, where each man was left, by his uninterested

neighbour, to the defence of his own person and property. Now, they were formed into an unconquerable army of brothers, and their exertions concentered by the ardent spirit of patriotism."[58] What Godwin admires in Pitt, his patriotism and republican virtue, his community building around the idea of a common good, he also criticizes as nationalistic war; nationalism is better than mere pursuit of gain— but even better would be a common good more truly virtuous.

In King's political essay *Thoughts on the Difficulties and Distresses* there is a similar anti-imperialism. The essay has four parts: an introductory letter to Charles James Fox, and three sections on the condition of England at the time of the 1783 peace treaty, the English in the East Indies, and what America means for the English. *Thoughts* harshly condemns Charles James Fox, a leader in the government coalition, for his character and policies at a time when Godwin was defending Fox's controversial India Bill, the Rockingham Whigs, and Fox himself. The rest of the essay depicts an England suffering from economic distress and depopulation, while the East India Company with government support plunders India; moreover, America has become a magnet for the English industrious middle class, which cannot find economic opportunity in the United Kingdom. According to King, Fox is a self-indulgent aristocratic gambler who cares nothing about the economic distress of the middle classes and who hypocritically scapegoats Jewish moneylenders to obfuscate his own irresponsibility. King feared that, unless government acted boldly and quickly, Britain would continue to lose population to the United States.[59] He appeals to republican virtue, but his emphasis on commerce and trade suggests an un-Godwinian liberalism. King argues: "Perhaps if a virtuous industry was to be encouraged, such men as you would be banished from the land; but as a spirit of universal gambling has taken [the] place of industrious and virtuous merit, both in political and common life, I think you must remain conspicuous and of the highest importance."[60] Sarcasm and satire like this interlard the whole essay, whose rhetoric seems more intended to harm Fox than persuade him toward new policies. The letter to Fox, animated with a gleeful hostility and delight in doing verbal combat with a powerful statesman, also attends to material deprivations suffered by the British because of the war against American independence. King's anti-imperialistic rhetoric is at least as pointed as Godwin's. He laments the seizure of India: "When I approach this country [the East Indies], even in imagination, my cheeks feel a glowing shame at the degraded name and character of an Englishman; my fancy sees the sun-burnt coast swarming with the mournful spirits of the oppressed and famished natives, imprecating vengeance on their sordid inhuman tormentors; myriads of pale spectres, starved by artificial famine, shock my busy fancy; and the once peaceful plains, hallowed by a venerable religion and learning, seem strewed with unhappy victims." Praising the revolt of the natives of Hindustan against the "unnatural" invasion of their land, he condemns the invading "peculators and criminals" and "European monsters."[61]

Godwin rarely allows himself the pleasures of satire, for he is committed to the stance of the disinterested philosopher. He also has little to say at any time in his career in favor of trade and commerce, as he believes both are inherently antagonistic to republican virtue. Their respective positions on Fox's India Bill are instructive: Godwin praises the principle of replacing the arbitrary will of the East India Company with a publicly accountable board within government, but King objects on anti-imperialist grounds to the idea of government legitimating the theft and domination of another country.[62] Yet it would be naive to think that King's sexual competitiveness over Mary Robinson had nothing to do with his zeal in attacking Fox, just as it would be naive to think that Godwin's long deference to Fox had nothing to do with direct and indirect patronage.[63]

While their earliest writings are notable for their differences, King might have influenced Godwin in his dispute with Thelwall in 1795. Godwin's diary of 1795 records that on January 23, when he dined at King's, he also read "King versus Paine," probably an allusion to the John King dispute with Thomas Paine that was played out in print between 1792 and 1795. Twice in January he dines at King's, where Thelwall is also a guest.[64] The next month Godwin reads "King on the Peace," probably referring to King's 1783 *Thoughts on the Difficulties and Distresses*.[65] The year in which King and Godwin interacted the most was 1795—with forty-seven separate days of contact—which makes more plausible King's influence on *Considerations on Lord Grenville's and Mr. Pitt's Bills*, which includes the controversial criticism of Thelwall and the London Corresponding Society (LCS). Complicating the matter of influence is that what King published in newspapers and a pamphlet against Paine was probably not what he was saying to friends and associates in and close to the LCS, because in fact King was clandestinely supporting the most uncompromising elements of the Society. His public declarations on revolution in relation to Paine, most recently published in the March 10, 1795 issue of the anti-Pitt *Morning Post*, identified himself with the political Girondins and distinguished between violent and constitutional reformism, aligning Paine with mob bloodshed, and not recanting this grotesquely unfair charge until his 1802 *Letters from France*. King attacked Paine to distance himself from what the government and its collaborative press represented as extreme forms of radicalism, which were targets for harsh legal repression. As co-owner of the reformist *Argus* (1789–92), King was a target along with his partner, the radical physician Sampson Perry.[66] Perry responded to the government pressure differently: he scorned the various indictments, fled to Paris, joined the revolution, which imprisoned him for fourteen months as a "foreigner," then returned to London, where he was kept in Newgate Prison from 1795 to 1801. He died in debtor's prison in 1823.[67] Godwin's conceptual framework in his *Considerations* is similarly Girondin, as the essay triangulates just as King's does between state coercion, democratic coercion, and politically rational discourse.[68] Both the government's repressive legislation and the mass demonstrations organized by the LCS, Godwin argues, substitute ready-made constructions of ideology for the private judgment of the individual.

A member of the LCS who knew both Godwin and King fervently disliked the latter. Francis Place's outright loathing of King contrasts with Godwin's more positive perspective. A longtime friend of Godwin and an indispensable leader of London "respectable" radicalism, Place first became acquainted with King through his friend John Ashley in the LCS. To illustrate just how strongly Place detested King, he claims that in the late 1790s, when he was so poor he lacked food to eat, he would not take any assistance from "Jew King" because "to have accepted any thing from him would have been downright baseness."[69] Invited to the King dinners with other LCS members, Place represents himself as singularly distrustful of King, who is described as purchasing and storing pikes for a future revolution, and as looking forward to a French invasion in the late 1790s. Registering his moral disapproval of King's money transactions, Place concedes that the moneylender is intelligent and shrewd. Place becomes acquainted with George, the eldest of the three illegitimate sons King is said to have, and the son's harsh account of his father functions as a truth-telling narrative.[70] It is not surprising that Place, the "respectable" radical, disliked King, who frequented the radical underground. The historian Iain McCalman disputes Place's assertion that King's involvement in political radicalism was exclusively mercenary. King was genuinely attracted to a politics of enthusiasm, drawn to the violently prophetic rhetoric of Joanna Southcott (1750–1814) and Thomas Spence (1750–1814), who imagined "Jehovah's vengeance" against injustice and oppression. McCalman

concludes that "there is no doubting [King's] sincere belief in millenarian modes of thought."[71] In McCalman's portrait King backs
financially uncompromising muckraking newspapers like the *British
Guardian* (ca. 1811) and the *Independent Whig* (1812–17)—which
criticized Place more than a few times—and he bankrolls successful
efforts to blackmail and pressure vulnerable members of the social
and political establishment. King joined with working-class radical
Irish Catholics Davenport Sedley and Patrick William Duffin, angry
outsiders who shared his resentment at the Protestant English elite.
According to McCalman, "Many of King's victims and all of Sedley's
were wealthy and influential members of the English ruling classes,
especially ministers, government officials, and members of the Royal
Family and their courtiers. In this respect the interests of Sedley,
King and Duffin as professional criminals intersected with their
political radicalism."[72] King was also associated with political causes
that had respectable cachet, such as Sir Francis Burdett's imprisonment in 1810, and that had broad, even if somewhat disreputable,
public support; such as Colonel Wardle's campaign against the Duke
of York in 1809 exposing the duke's mistress, Mary Anne Clarke,
who sold government commissions; and such as the Old Price riots
at the reconstructed Covent Garden Theatre, to conclude which the
manager, John P. Kemble, was ignominiously forced to apologize,
withdraw the new private boxes, and moderate the higher prices.
There is no avoiding the fact, however, that King associated regularly
with criminals who blackmailed the Prince of Wales, the Dukes of
Cumberland and York, Prime Minister Spencer Percival, "senior law
officers, government and admiralty officials, and a variety of distinguished families."[73]

There is no evidence that Godwin shared Place's revulsion against
King's morals and politics, and one assumes Godwin knew as much
about the moneylender as did Place. It is risky, perhaps, to infer too
much from the laconic diary entries of Godwin, but in 1795, after
numerous dinners, suppers, and teas at King's house, he also simply
visits King, as on August 31, when King is not at home, or on October
16, when he meets King, or October 20, when King joins him at the
theatre.[74] On March 14 and April 4, 1796, as well as many other times,
he calls on King but dines elsewhere, clearly suggesting that they had
a friendly relationship not wholly dependent on King's ability to provide Godwin with food and guests with whom to converse.[75] He also
socializes with King at other people's houses, for example with Maria
Reveley—known as Maria Gisborne to Percy and Mary Shelley—on
May 14, 1796.[76] In 1797, when Godwin and Wollstonecraft begin

their sexual relationship, Godwin still dines at King's and socializes with him.[77] King's two daughters, Charlotte and Sophia, poets and novelists, visit Godwin in February and April of 1798. In May 1800 he is meeting "Miss King"—which one Godwin does not say, but it is probably Sophia, whose anti-Godwinian *Cordelia* he is reading in June 1800 when they meet. They meet again in September, when he also writes to her.[78] Even though the diary records the last time Godwin dined at King's as 1807, it also notes that he met Lady Lanesborough and her two adult children in 1808 and 1820,[79] and we know that King helped settle Godwin's financial affairs in 1812. Lady Lanesborough, according to William St Clair, involved herself to some extent in the maternity hospital arrangements for both Mary Wollstonecraft and Mary Jane Claremont.[80] (Both Percy Bysshe Shelley and Lord Byron knew King, with whom they had financial dealings.)[81] Godwin never seems to have been at King's house at the same time as Francis Place and the working-class radicals from the LCS. It is impossible to infer much from the lack of social meetings in the ten years after King's last dinner party in 1807—King and Lady Lanesborough emigrated for good to Florence, Italy, in 1817. It is unlikely, however, that Godwin acquired a sudden moral revulsion against a man he had known well for over ten years.

JOHN KING AND ST. LEON

Second only to *Caleb Williams* in popularity, Godwin's novel *St. Leon* enjoyed four separate editions (December 1799, February 1800, 1816, and 1831).[82] King's impact on Godwin's 1799 novel is of two kinds. Aspects of King's life and business seem to be reflected in what happens to the eponymous hero St. Leon, and the various Jewish allusions of the novel are probably linked to King also, the only Jew Godwin knew well. The aspects of King's life that appear to be suggested in the novel include the gambling and gallantry to which the young St. Leon is drawn after the demoralizing defeat of the French aristocracy at the battle of Pavia. Godwin treats the ostentatious display of wealth and the risky, imprudent expenditure of money as a displaced heroism that has been thwarted (75). King used to lend money at high rates of interest to young aristocrats and gentry who squandered their inheritance in gambling and whoring. As a guest at numerous dinner parties at King's house, Godwin would have become acquainted with some of these reckless young men and could have heard stories from King himself. King's own analysis of the irresponsible gambling of Charles James Fox in 1783 linked individual failure to a general class weakness. The Prince of Wales, a notorious gambler and wasteful spender, went through thousands of pounds as quickly as it was passed to him by a generous government. St. Leon's love of the high life is suspended after he falls in love with the Wollstonecraftian Marguerite, who persuades her young husband that domesticity in provincial retirement is superior to the splendors of Paris. After a number of happy years, St. Leon has to return to Paris to settle his son in the university, but he quickly falls back into his old Parisian habits, eventually gambling away the entire family fortune and bringing his family to ruin.

The experience of the St. Leon family, leaving France in disgrace for an exile in Switzerland, is similar to what happened to John King, who had to leave England in 1783 to avoid an indictment for perjury. He and Lady Lanesborough settled in Paris and northern Italy, not returning until the statute of limitations ran out in 1789. In 1798 King suffered the indignity of bankruptcy and the publication of parts of his diary, provocatively mutilated in order to discredit his attempts to live the life of a gentleman. The *Authentic Memoirs*, as the text was entitled, portrayed King as a low criminal who could only pretend to be a gentleman; moreover, he was a Jew, and invariably whenever King is represented in public discourse he is depicted as John "Jew" King.[83] Similarly, St. Leon tries to make all kinds of identity changes, but none of them is effective and his guilt as a gambler and an alchemist always haunts him.

After St. Leon accepts the dubious gift of alchemy from the nameless stranger (the Wandering Jew), the abrupt rise from poverty by means of his magical powers casts public suspicion on the legitimacy of his wealth and status. Similarly, the rapid transformation of Jacob Rey, the shoeblack, into John King, the husband of the Irish aristocrat Lady Lanesborough, was challenged in ways similar to what happened to St. Leon. "Jew" King was not allowed to forget his origins as a poor Jew, no matter how far he had moved away from those origins, and St. Leon, no matter where and how he lives, cannot evade the disgraceful origins—figuratively Jewish—of his wealth and longevity.

The Jewish allusions in *St. Leon* are pervasive and help frame the novel in the form of the inscription from Congreve: "Ferdinand Mendez Pinto was but a type of thee, thou liar of the first magnitude" (47). The topos of Pinto (1510?–83) as a proverbial liar came from the reputation of his popular *Peregrinação*, translated into English as the *Travels* in the seventeenth century.[84] Godwin's preface explains Pinto thus: "Becoming a fugitive from his country at a very immature age, he travelled through many parts of Africa and Asia for twenty-one years, and, by his own account, encountered a surprising number of distressful adventures" (52–53 n. 2). Citing the French edition, the most complete if still imperfect translation,[85] Godwin evidently had given considerable thought to Pinto, whose experiences with the Jesuits, the Inquisition, and the New Christians parallel those of St. Leon. "Marranos," literally "pigs," were Jews who conformed outwardly as Christians but who practiced a form of Judaism in private. "New Christians," formerly Jews, were converts to Christianity who were suspected of practicing Judaism out of the public eye. The Inquisition targeted New Christians, whom they would torture to test the sincerity of their conversion. Pinto himself might have been a New Christian, as the Mendes family was well known as New Christian and Pinto's departure from Portugal coincides with Inquisition attention to *conversos*.[86] While working on the Pinto material, Godwin could have inquired about details of Sephardic life from his friend John King, the former Jacob Rey, also famous for stretching the truth, especially in a courtroom.

In chapter 8 of the novel there is a peculiar sequence of events that seem to allegorize the expulsion of the Jews from England in 1290.[87] After a devastating storm ruins the Swiss area where St. Leon and family live modestly, the community irrationally turns against him, scapegoating him like a hated and feared outsider. The expulsion of St. Leon from Switzerland is so excessive and unmotivated it resembles the expulsion of Jews from England—and elsewhere. "I was forbidden, under pain of perpetual imprisonment, to return to the territories of the republic, and I had no friend to solicit in my behalf. In Constance [where he emigrated] I was utterly a stranger" (139). His property is confiscated without compensation, a fate suffered by Jews more than a few times, including in 1290 England. Although St. Leon eventually gets compensated (155), his victimization has all the appearance of a Jewish victimization, without the word Jew manifesting itself.

This is hardly the only time St. Leon is linked to Jews. The nameless stranger who passes on the "fatal secret" of eternal life and alchemy to St. Leon suggests the Wandering Jew myth. Moreover, Europe's most famous alchemist, Cagliostro (1743–95), had died recently (1795) in an Inquisition prison cell in Italy; when he was in London in the 1780s he associated closely with Lord George Gordon (1751–93), the most famous European convert to Judaism, who died in a Newgate Prison cell.[88] In chapter 17, St. Leon's son Charles leaves and rejects St. Leon because of the public consequences of the fatal secret; the

son cannot defend the father openly because the father has to conceal
the scandalous details of how he has become wealthy. As William
Brewer points out, the parallel evoked is Shakespeare's Jessica leaving Shylock. St. Leon says: "My son! my son!—wealth! wealth!—my
wife!—my son!" (213), just as Shylock cries: "My daughter! O my ducats! O my daughter!" (2.8.15).[89] Alchemy itself, producing gold from
other elements, was associated traditionally with magical Kabbalah,
as well as with Jews corrupting the currency. Creating wealth *ex
nihilo* conforms to the cultural fantasy of usury and interest-bearing
loans, money produced not from labor but from trickery and fraud.
Marguerite, usually the voice of moral clarity in the novel, distin-
guishes between legitimate and illegitimate wealth. "The ordinary
wealth of the world is something real and substantial, and can neither
be created nor dissipated with a breath" (225). The anxiety provoked
by alchemy is the anxiety over representations and appearances; as the
Constance magistrate tells St. Leon, "The devil can assume the form
of an angel" (236).

The stereotypically "loyal" black servant Hector (chapters 22–27)
becomes unwittingly the catalyst for mob violence against St. Leon,
as the Italian peasants scapegoat Godwin's hero in ways that call to
mind a pogrom. St. Leon narrates: "'Villain, renegado, accursed of
God!' I heard from every side; 'did not you bewitch my cow? did not
you enchant my child? have not you killed my daughter? Down with
him! exterminate him! do not suffer him to live!'" (289). St. Leon
tries to use reason to persuade the mob not to attack, but his effort is
fruitless, as the novel stages an allegory of inveterate prejudice resist-
ing the power of rational discourse. St. Leon's excessive grief over
the death of Hector in the fire started by the mob melodramatically
illustrates the indebted master's guilt and gratitude, but it also is
the philosopher's lament in seeing the futility of investing so much
intellectual capital in the enterprise of rationalism (294). Antisemitic
violence and prejudice operate semiotically as a synecdoche for what
Godwinian reason has to overcome.

The chapters that take place in sixteenth-century Spain include a
zealous Inquisition that imprisons and attempts to execute St. Leon,
who escapes at the last minute to the home of a Jew, a New Christian.
The novel draws a parallel between the Inquisition and Pitt's repression (334), which would make the harassed English "Jacobins" figurative Jews. About to be executed in an auto da fé, St. Leon during a
moment of confusion runs away to a Jew's house, where he has a tense
confrontation with Mordecai, who could have turned him over to
the Inquisition while St. Leon was sleeping, but who ultimately helps

him. St. Leon himself is uncertain whether Mordecai's assistance was motivated by a sense of moral duty or by knowledge of the promised monetary reward, but the novel suggests the former rather than the latter. As St. Leon holds hostage a five-year-old girl, Mordecai says to him: "We poor Jews, hunted on the face of the earth, the abhorrence and execration of mankind, have nothing but family affections to support us under our multiplied disgraces; and family affections are entwined with our existence, the fondest and best-loved part of ourselves. The God of Abraham bless you, my child!" (340). The Spanish chapters reproduce and weaken the stereotype of the mercenary Jew, who is also the victim of injustice. As St. Leon leaves Spain, he adopts the disguise of an Oriental merchant—an Armenian—yet another identification with a Jew-like character; as persecuted Christians in the Ottoman Empire, as merchants, and as scholars—Byron himself studied at the Armenian monastery in Venice—Armenians were an ill-treated nation like the Jews (350).

The concluding Hungarian chapters carry forward the Jewish motifs in several ways. St. Leon's attempts to improve society in his role as corn merchant prove ineffective, as the masses turn against him as a duplicitous middleman and profiteer. The gothic antihero, Bethlem Gabor, a tormented soul in whom St. Leon finds a mirror for his own anguish, has lost his entire family in a brutal act of political violence, a trauma that hints at pogroms—not unknown in that part of Europe—and evokes one of the famous literary episodes of family extermination, the story of Lessing's Nathan, who lost his family to religious hatred.[90] Gabor is St. Leon's double. The identification with Gabor is especially interesting because of Gabor's strikingly un-English appearance: Gabor's face suggests blackness—thick and large lips, "dun or black" complexion; in addition to the grotesque absence of three fingers, a facial scar, and the loss of his right eye, Gabor is monstrous, scarred, marked by political violence indelibly (382). Another dimension of the Hungarian chapters is the explicitly religious themes, as the novel relativizes religious commitment in a satirical way not unlike what Grimmelshausen did with the Thirty Years War in the magnificent novel *Simplicissimus* (1668). St. Leon starts out in Muslim territory, then finds himself in Christian, and finally in the midst of a Catholic/Protestant battle. Virtue and rationality reside in none of these religions. As the worldly-wise St. Leon remarks on his son's commitment to the Catholic cause: "I could not entirely enter into this sentiment of his, and indeed regarded it as an infatuation and delusion," and indeed he deemed the religious wars wasteful and loathsome (424).

Perhaps Godwin would have allowed his imagination to make the numerous identifications with Jews in *St. Leon* without knowing John King, but I find it probable that their close relationship and numerous discussions made those identifications powerful and compelling.

RELIGIOUS VIEWS

Finally, I wish to examine briefly their religious views, which for both men involved deism. "I am an unbeliever," Godwin bluntly declares in his unpublished 1818 essay *Of Religion*,[91] but his views were more nuanced and many-sided than a simple opposition to the Christian faith would suggest. Although from 1788 Godwin ceased reading scripture as divinely revealed, Coleridge was later able to nudge him toward acknowledging divinity, however vaguely understood. Because a key issue for Godwin was miracles, the area of inquiry where skepticism overwhelmed faith, he turned to the famous debunker of miracles, the English deist who was imprisoned for his writings, Thomas Woolston (1670–1732). Both *Political Justice* (book 1, chapter 5) and *The Genius of Christianity Unveiled* (essay 8) cite Woolston approvingly. King's favorite deist, William Wollaston (1659–1724), was theologically moderate and did not invite the controversy that Woolston deliberately provoked. (The similarity of their names is simply happenstance.) King cites Wollaston, famous for *The Religion of Nature Delineated* (1724), for the rhetorical purpose of demonstrating that there is no absolute difference between the monotheisms, and that Christianity and Judaism share a great deal. Godwin uses his Woolston to demolish the validity of miracles, though Woolston was not really a deist but an orthodox Christian committed to free speech and an allegorical approach to scriptures. From a working-class background, he used a popular style that appealed to an urban audience,[92] whereas Wollaston's approach was highly learned and scholarly, with each page densely packed with Greek and Hebrew quotations. That Wollaston was an accomplished Hebraist might have been one of the reasons King liked him so much. In several works King gives extended quotations from Wollaston, most interestingly in his 1817 introduction to a new edition of David Levi's *Dissertations on the Prophecies of The Old Testament*. King reproduces a prayer from Wollaston's *The Religion of Nature Delineated* for the exemplary purpose of showing a form of devotion to God that is consistent with reason, without mention of Jesus or Moses or anything supernatural.[93]

If from 1788 Godwin's deistic position was nuanced sometimes toward atheism and sometimes toward theism, King's theology never wandered far from Judaism. Whether or not King and Lady Lanesborough actually married, there seems to be little evidence that he ever converted to Christianity, as would have been customary for an Anglican marriage. However, according to the historian Endelman, "It was not unheard-of for an Anglican clergyman to perform the marriage ceremony for a Jew and a Christian without requiring the Jew to undergo baptism."[94] Although he equivocated sometimes in court, where he once declared that "he had considered himself a member of the Church of England since he had been old enough to judge such matters for himself," King in fact never joined the church or left Judaism.[95] By 1798 he refers to Judaism as "my faith," which he defends—making use of Wollaston—while criticizing Christian complacency, hypocrisy, and antisemitism.[96] King's understanding of Judaism and deism perhaps reflects his knowledge of Moses Mendelssohn's *Jerusalem* (1783), as it would have been summarized and discussed in journals like the *Analytical Review* and the *Monthly Magazine*. By removing entirely any supernatural agency in his progressive model of perfectibility, Godwin retained the goal of a heaven on earth—equality, peace, a long healthy life, the rule of mind over matter—without any supernatural elements. King, however, did not always rule out supernatural agency, as even when he conflicted with Joanna Southcott and some of her millenarian followers, he shared some of the same points of reference in biblical prophecy.[97] Moreover, in his sponsoring and introducing David Levi's work in 1817, King assumes the credibility of some traditional notions of divinely messianic agency.

The 1817 publication of David Levi's work on the Hebrew Bible's prophecies, however, reflects another dimension of his thinking that does not fit with the deism—King's attraction to millenarian currents in politics and religion. That the French Revolution stirred messianic and millenarian discourses is a commonplace, and neither King nor Godwin was immune to this particular aspect of the Zeitgeist. Godwin rigorously secularized his own millenarian tendencies, but King only imperfectly secularized his. A hero in the Jewish community, David Levi (1742–1801) waged a battle in books and pamphlets with English Christians of various religious denominations, including Joseph Priestley, over the correct interpretation of "Old Testament" prophecy.[98] Having divorced his Jewish wife and abandoned his three young children for an Irish aristocrat, entertaining and working mostly with Christians, involved with radical politics that only indirectly affected Jews, King had drifted away from a Jewish community to which he was returning in 1817 with the Levi book and its dedication to the English chief rabbi.

CONCLUSION

In Godwin's writing on religion he will concede that parts of the Hebrew Bible are extraordinarily valuable as literature (preface to *Bible Stories* in 1802), but his years of conversing with King never swayed him from viewing Judaism as a fundamentally flawed religion. The one area in which King might have had some influence is Godwin's sensitivity to the suffering of Jews as a persecuted minority. Caleb Williams famously disguises himself as a Jew in London, where he is hiding from Falkland's detection, and St. Leon, as I have already described, provides numerous stagings of the persecuted Jew, both explicit and symbolic. As an apostate Calvinist Christian in a strongly Protestant nation, Godwin felt he had to conceal his genuine religious opinions for fear of being persecuted, perhaps forgetting he was already viewed as an infidel and a hopelessly radical Jacobin by public opinion anyway; the care with which he "hid" his irreligion was perhaps not as necessary as he thought it was. His letter to his daughter Mary, who would edit his religious writings, alludes to his imagined victimization by a bigoted mob: "Yet this book will draw on me the misconstruction of multitudes. They will regard me with aversion and abhorrence. They will pursue me with execrations. Many of them would tear my poor remains from the grave, and treat them with every imaginable indignity. Many, if I were to return once more to the earth, would willingly give their suffrage that I should perish at the stake."[99] Not for the first time does Godwin's imagination generate the auto da fé where irrational society victimizes the heretic.

When John King reflected on his troubles with government, courts, and various libels, he saw himself in terms of a literary character: "Like Caleb Williams, I am destined a living elucidation of the author's principle, an instance of one man's being harassed and crushed by suspicion, while under an impervious duplicity, another like Falkland may murder with impunity."[100] William Godwin feels like a Jew and "Jew" King feels like Caleb Williams: the philosopher and the moneylender have perhaps learned from one another.

CHAPTER 5

THE JEW'S DAUGHTER

*When a certain Jew's daughter married without his consent, he
roared like a Westphalian Polyphemus: thundering through all his
house, "Vat a dam bish, my own shile too; but she mos always fond
of reading boedry; dam boedry—mut she shall never have a stiver
of mine: I do now swear by Cot, I will cut off my own bosteriors
mid a shilling."*[1]

The above quotation is from a London chapbook of the 1790s entitled *Laugh When You Can; or The Monstrous Droll Jester* edited by
the Huguenot, Ann Lemoine, who was part of James Lackington's
lower-middle-class literary circle that included her brother Henry
(1756–1812), a fellow writer, and Jewish artisan writers such as David
Levi (1740–99), a hat-maker, and Levi Alexander (d. 1834?) a printer.
Lackington himself (1746–1815), coming from a laboring-class background, made a spectacular fortune from publishing cheap literature,
taking advantage of the Donaldson decision of the House of Lords
in 1774 that abolished perpetual copyright at least until the revisions
of 1808 ended the so-called copyright window.[2] The paragraph from
the chapbook links the Jew's daughter with poetry, a metonym for
national and European culture outside the parameters of Jewishness.
Poetry, which here also entails enlightenment and the polite manners produced by the self-forming activities and discipline of what the
Germans called *Bildung*, is antithetical to money, specifically Jewish
money. The stage-Jew dialect, pervasive in English representations
throughout the eighteenth and much of the nineteenth centuries,
marks this particular Ashkenazic German Shylock as someone lacking *Bildung*. The stereotypical rich Jew, angry with his Jessica, has a

cultured daughter whom he cannot control and who is marrying for
love rather than money. The Polyphemus allusion illustrates the shift
of power between father and daughter, as the Odysseus-like daughter
knowledgeably manipulates the English norms with which she grew
up but which are foreign to the father. The father's cry of desperation,
threatening to cut off his posteriors, redundantly codes him with castration and Shylock. Here it is not Lorenzo and Christianity that have
stolen the Jewish daughter; it is poetry. — culture

The vignette about "boetry" brings up two aspects of *Bildung*, the
self-formation and education from culture and enlightenment: it is a
site for the emancipatory activities of the daughter to free herself from
what are perceived as the restrictions of patriarchal norms and traditions; it is a sign of what the father lacks and can never have, marking
him as foreign, morally deficient, and intellectually damaged. I will
deal first with the father, and then the daughter.

Mocking the rich Jew who is a philistine, the term popularized by
Matthew Arnold, and also who cannot control his rebellious daughter
starts with *The Merchant of Venice* and continues into the eighteenth
century. From Walter Scott's miserly Isaac and saintly Rebecca in
Ivanhoe (1819) to Phillip Roth's Ben and Brenda Patimkin ("Goodbye
Columbus" 1959), one sees a continual pattern of representation by
both Gentile and Jewish writers. Jews who lack *Bildung* and its visible
effects are contemptible. The process of making money and the taint
of commerce damage the Jew fundamentally, even irreversibly. That
the rich Jew without culture needs reforming is a topic of discourse
during German Jewry's long march to emancipation from the 1780s
to 1871. In the German context, all Jews, not just the rich, were
seen as degenerate, having been disfigured by centuries of oppression, usury, and commerce. Although a small minority like Moses
Mendelssohn (1729–86) and Wilhelm von Humboldt (1767–1835)
favored immediate emancipation, and a larger minority opposed any
kind of emancipation, the prevailing opinion for a century was that
emancipation had to be conditional, or as expressed by David Sorkin,
"a quid pro quo in which Jews were to be regenerated in exchange
for rights."[3]

Although Jewish emancipation in Germany was understood to be
provisional, Jews themselves like Moses Mendelssohn and the leaders of the Jewish Enlightenment (*Haskalah*) critically engaged and
took from European culture what was consistent with their interpretation of the Jewish tradition. Many *maskilim* (followers of Jewish
Enlightenment) found no reason to relax ritual observance of the

commandments in Jewish law. In England where Jews were not as
legally restricted and for whom emancipation was not a political issue
until 1830, Anglo-Jewry needed no prodding by liberal Christians to
embrace the modern English world. Anglo-Jewry, despite the implications of the comic paragraph from Lemoine's chapbook, largely
embraced Englishness, including the prevailing manners, theatre, and
popular entertainments. Visiting rabbis from the continent, according to the historian Todd M. Endelman, would complain about the
low level of Jewish learning and overall religious observance among
the English Jews.[4] Long before emancipation Jews from all social
strata adopted versions of Englishness without ceasing to be Jewish.[5]
Despite vigorous and well-financed efforts by Evangelicals, few Jews
converted to Christianity but many Jews attended the theatre and
cheered on prize-fighters like Daniel Mendoza (1764–1836) who
were national champions.

Although Jews accepted Englishness, the ambivalent English did
not rush to accept the Jews. In ways strikingly similar to the 1655–56
debates over readmitting Jews to England (see ch. 2), the nineteenth-
century opponents of Jewish emancipation had either self-interested
commercial reasons or fundamental religious reasons like the High
Churchmen in the House of Lords who repeatedly blocked emancipation until 1858 for parliament and 1871 for the universities. For the
nineteenth-century anti-emancipationists, it would not matter if Jews
took up *Bildung*, certainly not to the Christian businessmen and merchants, nor to the Anglican bishops who rejected outright the notion
of a secular state and secular university. In the eighteenth century
English Jews, with no prodding from philosemitic Protestants and
with no hopes whatsoever for emancipation, embraced *Bildung*, which
was described by Moses Mendelssohn as *Kultur* with *Aufklaerung*—
culture with enlightenment.[6] As narrated by the historian David B.
Ruderman, English Jews joined Masonic lodges, debated Christian
Hebraists and theologians in English, translated Restoration plays
into Hebrew, engaged Newton's ideas in Hebrew treatises, and published translations from the Talmud for English readers.[7] Jewish
artisans like David Levi and Levi Alexander, as I mentioned earlier,
wrote, published and socialized in an English context that was mixed
socially and religiously. Jewish intellectuals were fully engaged with
the philosophical and literary currents of the times, for Anglo-Jewry
was not reluctant to make English culture its own.

The archetypal story of cultural assimilation and the Jew's daughter
is of course that of Shylock and Jessica, who elopes, converts, and robs

her father. As read by recent critics Lisa Lampert and Janet Adelman, Shakespeare's Jessica is an ambivalent character. The commerce that the play takes for granted entails the danger of miscegenation with the exotic woman, who in turn threatens national identity.[8] Jessica is associated with an excessive and tragic sexuality: the shameful cross-dressing (2.6), the exchange of her mother's ring for the symbolically sexual monkey (3.1), the troubled duet with Lorenzo in which a trio of sad heroines—Thisbe, Dido, and Medea—figuratively link love with violence, childlessness, and death (5.1).[9] Her hope of not being racially Jewish, as Lampert points out, hinges on her mother's adultery with a Gentile, and the various cuckold jokes with Jessica, who has already displayed extraordinary agency for a woman, make her presence in Belmont problematic, for as Adelman suggests, Belmont highlights purity—having expelled all the foreign suitors—while Venice accepts aliens.[10] Unhappy with Jews, uneasy with Christians, Jessica does not fit well in either world.[11] As a converted Jew whose very identity is impure and mixed she is defensive among the Christians whom she tries to reassure of her Christian loyalty by revealing insider's information about her father (3.2). Her not responding to beautiful music is perhaps a racialized characteristic attributed to Jews who lack the aesthetic receptivity of Christians (5.1.67).

About three centuries after Shakespeare invented Shylock and Jessica, the great Jewish painter from Galicia Maurycy Gottlieb (1856–79) in *Shylock and Jessica* (1876) depicts the pair right at the point Shylock is about to leave for Bassanio's party and was giving her the keys. A tragically sad Shylock looks endearingly at his daughter, whose gaze is toward the viewer. Although Ezra Mendelson sees Jessica here as a "faithless, conniving daughter," as well as "deceitful," with "long fingers reach[ing] out for the key to her father's treasures,"[12] I read the painting differently. I see a Shylock who has no illusions and who knows his daughter is going to betray him for the Christian world. Jessica, unable to look her father in the eyes, knows that she is leaving but without a gleeful sense of anticipated freedom. The painting expresses a tragic sadness that is not readily apparent in Shakespeare's Act 2, Scene 5. The contrast between the very old Shylock—Shakespeare's Shylock is not emphatically old—and the beautiful Jessica could not be more absolute, as she embodies the force of new life, which is carrying her away from her physically depleted father. This revisionary treatment of Shakespeare's Shylock and Jessica—revisionary at least as I am reading it—is one of numerous other revisionary treatments of the father/daughter pair that this chapter will be examining.

WOMAN AND JEWESS AS MEDIATORS

In the nineteenth century women writers and the figure of the woman play the role of mediator between the Jewish and British worlds, for both *Bildung* as a site of cultural self-formation and religion as a site of piety and spirituality provide paths for acculturation and discursive positions from which to influence public opinion. As described by Michael Ragussis, Michael Galchinsky, Cynthia Scheinberg, Judith Page, and Nadia Valman, while Christian conversionist discourse in fiction, drama and religious tracts targeted the Jewess as the weak link in Judaism, imagining the Jew's daughter to be like Shakespeare's Jessica, eager to escape her oppressive father, Anglo-Jewish women writers countered with affirmations of Jewish domesticity and public virtue. Conversionist texts imagined a Jewish woman, oppressed by patriarchal Judaism, who would welcome the opportunity to develop her repressed spirituality and thwarted subjectivity by living as a Protestant Christian. Ragussis and Valman, who describe the many conversionist texts popular in the first seventy years of the nineteenth century, also explain the role they play in British cultural life in terms of working out national identity. Conversionist themes, tropes, and narrative structures migrate to other forms of literary discourse. The "revisionist" novel of conversion secularizes, according to Ragussis, the conversionist themes developed in the Evangelical texts, ultimately reversing and overturning the dominant imperative that Jews become Christians by tracing national guilt to the oppression of Jews. It is the Christians not the Jews who need a new identity in literary texts like *Harrington* (1817), *Ivanhoe* (1819), *The Jew of Arragon* (1830), and *The Vale of Cedars* (1835/1850).[13] Valman registers the powerful influence of the Evangelical texts of conversion throughout the nineteenth century, even when conversion is secularized. *Bildung*, especially under the sign of feminine spirituality and sentimentality, propels the literary Jewess, whether authored by a Jew or Gentile, toward a redemptive role.[14] While Ragussis and Valman stress the secularizing of religious themes, the other three critics return the focus to religious identity. Galchinsky shows how nineteenth-century Anglo-Jewish women writers such as the Moss sisters and Grace Aguilar countered the Christian conversionists with Jewish history and domesticity, and modestly expanded the normative gender roles. Scheinberg shows how Jewishness functions ambivalently in Christian poetry and how Jewish poets function discursively in a Christian-dominant context.[15] Finally, Page illustrates how Jewish voices, routinely overlooked like Judith Montefiore and Emma Lyon, reconfigure the established frame of reference in relation to how the Romantic poets represent Jews and Judaism, and permit the creation of critical counternarratives.[16]

In addition to the women authors usually discussed in the context of Jewish representations, I focus considerable attention on two unlikely writers, Sophia and Charlotte King, daughters of John King the moneylender. Both poets and novelists, they married outside the Jewish community and rarely thematized Jewish themes; nevertheless, they earn a place in this study in part not only for the light they shed on John King their father but also because of the intrinsic interest of their writing, a poetry of sensibility central to Romanticism, and gothic fiction with more sensationalistic sex and violence than in Matthew Lewis's work. Their writing reflects their unconventional lives that are Jewish by birth and upbringing. For the King sisters being a respectable Christian woman is a performance, a theatrical role each one played well enough to marry wealthy, successful, respectable Christian men. That their writing, especially Charlotte's, was commercially successful suggests that they understood well the literary conventions and cultural codes, although in many respects they were anything but insiders.

This chapter has three main sections, the first, "Mixed Identities: The False Jewess," is on the Jewess who is not Jewish, one of the key types in the literature about Jews. The second section, "Conversion and Resistance," focuses on a wide range of conversionist and counterconversionist literature in which the Jewess plays a central role. The final section, "The King Sisters: 'Lovely Little Jessica,'" explores the literary careers of the King sisters and their troubled relationship with their father.

MIXED IDENTITIES: THE FALSE JEWESS

One of the most curious figures is the false Jewess who appears to be Jewish but who turns out to be otherwise. The Jewesses I will be discussing include Lessing's Recha, Edgeworth's Berenice, and Scribe's Rachel. Although this type continues throughout the century, in heroines like Emma Lazarus's Liebhaid von Orb, *The Dance to Death* (1882) is later than the time frame I have chosen for the book.

The text that inaugurated this literary type is probably Lessing's *Nathan the Wise*, whose Recha seems Jewish to all the characters in the play but who has multiple identities: born to a Christian mother in a Christian nation (Germany), she is assumed to be Christian; with a Muslim father, however, she is in fact a product of a interfaith and cross-ethnic union; and her adoptive father, Nathan, presents her in public as a Jewess but in private he educates her as a universalist. By the play's end the audience discovers her various identities, but in the play's beginning she seems to be quite simply a Jewess. As a revisionary Jessica, Recha loves a Christian, the Templar, but she is not rebelling against her father, who has taught her tolerance of other faiths. As Jessica hoped for a Christian father, Recha discovers her biological father to be a Muslim, but her emotional loyalty is entirely with Nathan. "But is it only blood that makes the father? Only blood?" (5.7), she declares after finding out her real paternity.[17] Lessing's play strongly leans to the nurture rather than the nature side of the character determination question, far more strongly than Shakespeare's play, which equivocates on the status of a converted Jewess (5.1.67) and which uses racial discourse with Portia's suitors (2.7) and Jessica's skin color (2.4).

As the Templar falls in love with Recha almost immediately, as soon as he sees her, provoking him to question his Templar vows of chastity, Lessing's Recha follows Shakespeare's pattern of attributing to the young Jewess a powerful allure. As Recha and the Templar turn out to be siblings, the erotic charge between them becomes awkward; although their inconvenient sexual love has to be renounced and forgotten, Recha has established her identity as a *belle juive* in the Jessica tradition. As a daughter Recha plays a revisionary role not just as a loyal child but as an adoptive offspring who tragically compensates for the father's family, a wife and seven sons, slaughtered by the child's own Christian tribe. Jessica makes up for the loss of Shylock's wife Leah, which becomes poignantly clear when Jessica trades her mother's ring for the monkey. Within a scapegoating comedy, Jessica's betrayal is just one more justified blow to the villain's pride, but within the Romantic tragedy organized by Hazlitt, Kean, and Farren, her treachery is brutally painful. In terms of social status, Recha begins as the Jew's daughter and ends as such, her social position changing only in terms of acquiring additional affiliations with her Christian brother and her Muslim uncle and aunt. Her actual religion, such as it is, does not seem affected because she was educated to respect all monotheisms, and she fulfills her mediating role because she is connected intimately with all three. As a symbol of *Aufklaerung* universalism and religious toleration, Recha is at least as worthy as Nathan.

The second false Jewess I want to discuss is Maria Edgeworth's Berenice Montenero, who functions Jewishly for most of *Harrington* (1817) until the last chapter that discloses her mother as a Protestant

Christian, in whose religion her Jewish father raised her. It is not until the seventh chapter that the reader meets Berenice, appropriately enough in a London theatre for Charles Macklin's production of *The Merchant of Venice*. This justly famous scene of the novel is doubly theatrical, for the hero Harrington observes the drama of Berenice's tormented reactions to the antisemitic drama on stage. In addition, the novel's reader also observes Harrington, thus making three levels of sympathetic encounter. Before the reader knows the identity of Berenice, other characters call her "Miss Berry" with a dark, East-Indian skin complexion. Harrington, who eagerly anticipates the aesthetic transport of watching Macklin play Shylock, is distracted by a closer, more erotically entrancing drama of Miss Berry's anguish a few theatre seats away. Not too unlike the counterfactual game of imaginative experience set up in Richard Hole's essay on Shylock, Harrington sees Shakespeare's play through "Jewish" eyes. When "Miss Berry" the Jewess notices that Harrington has detected her trying to hide from public view, as the audience's feelings of hatred are being directed at Macklin's Shylock, the staged performance of Jewishness, "a sudden and deep colour spread over her face and mounted to her temples."[18] It is not unlike Harrington, who has been playing the voyeur and continues to do so even after this initial embarrassment, having seen the young woman without her clothes. As he describes his "inverted sympathy" with Shylock, imagining how the Jewess would be perceiving the play, he feels "as though I had myself been a Jew."[19] Even before knowing her, Harrington undergoes a superficial conversion to Judaism because of the theatrical intensities at work, but he still does not "pity" Shylock.[20] From the third act he changes seats so that he can see Berenice without being seen, focused wholly on how he imagines her reactions to each part of the drama, reading her "soul" and "countenance." When she nearly faints, he comes to her rescue, his attention leaving the drama on stage for another kind of drama on another kind of stage. Like Recha and Jessica, Berenice has sexual power, which enchants Harrington and forces him to overcome his psychological demons. Saying little, looking beautiful and vulnerable, Berenice performs her Jewess role well enough to win Harrington. As a Sephardic Jewess she has a little more status than an Ashkenazi would have; similarly, the vulgar nouveaux riches family the Coateses seem to have the sole function of illustrating how comparatively aristocratic and polished the Monteneros are. Although Harrington has an emotional conversion to Jewishness while watching Berenice's reaction to Macklin's Shylock, he never seriously entertains requiring either her or himself to change religious identities, so that when her father discloses her secret Protestantism, a potentially thorny difficulty is conveniently evaded.

Berenice is a revisionary Jessica in the area of art and education because she does not have Jessica's aesthetic disability. Her father provided her with a rich aesthetic education in painting, literature, and music. Unlike the wealthy Jew in the chapbook vignette, Montenero is knowledgeable about "boetry" and does not view it as hostile to his money-making enterprises and his religion. In her passivity and dependence on her father, Berenice is more like Recha than the assertive and willful Jessica. Even in her passive dependence Berenice is the mediator between the Jewish and Christian worlds because her sexual attractiveness inspires Christian men to overcome their antisemitic prejudice. In her very person—similar to Recha—Berenice contains the two religions, the experience of being both an insider and an outsider. As with Recha, Berenice and her hybrid identity promote social harmony and reconciliation rather than the tragic in-betweenness of Shakespeare's Jessica. Edgeworth's novel avoids making Berenice a kind of tragic mulatto. It is worth noting that in the Romantic apologies for and revisionary commentaries on Shylock Jessica's difficult situation is largely ignored.

The prominent theme of theatricality provides scenes for actors and audience, performance and reaction. Even before uttering a single word to Harrington, Berenice has been performing as a Jewess. The novel's villain Mowbray has an erotic adventure with the actress who plays the role of Jessica, which parallels ironically Harrington's own erotic investment in his own Jessica. The reason Berenice's father conceals his daughter's true religious identity is to test the liberal tolerance of the suitors, just as Portia's father devised a test for his own daughter's suitors. Despite the baptism, Berenice still has a Jewish father, a Jewish name, and skin darker than most English women; even as a Protestant, she is in some ways a Jewess. From the reaction of some readers at the time, for example Walter Scott, who exclaimed he could "breathe more freely" when he discovered that "Miss Montenero was not an actual Jewess," it is apparent that the baptismal water still counted for something.[21]

The final character I want to consider is Rachel, the false Jewess in one of the most popular operas in the nineteenth century, *La Juive* (1835). Translated into English the same year it was staged in Paris,[22] *La Juive* circulates a compelling version of the Jewess. The music composed by Fromental Halévy (1799–1862), a French Jew, and the libretto by Eugène Scribe (1791–1861), a popular playwright who had worked with Meyerbeer, the opera borrows from Shakespeare's *Merchant of Venice*, Lessing's *Nathan the Wise*, and Scott's *Ivanhoe*. Set in fifteenth-century Constance (much of Godwin's *St. Leon* was set in sixteenth-century Constance; see ch. 4), the plot hinges on two critical acts of deception: the Christian Prince Léopold disguises himself as a Jewish painter, Samuel, to romance the beautiful Rachel, and Rachel's father Eléazar conceals from his daughter Rachel that not he but the Cardinal of Brogni is really her father. Rachel, unaware that her suitor is a Christian who is already married to Eudoxie, innocently accepts Samuel's attentions until she discovers the truth, which she makes public. As Jews and Christians are prohibited upon penalty of death to have sexual relations, the Cardinal Brogni has the magistrate jail Rachel, Prince Léopold, and for good measure Rachel's father Eléazar, the Cardinal's old nemesis, to await death for the sexual crimes. Eudoxie, Prince Léopold's wife, persuades Rachel to perjure herself in order to clear her husband of any wrongdoing. After the Prince is released from prison upon the new testimony of Rachel, the Cardinal oversees the execution of the two Jews, but Eléazar taunts his long-time enemy that he knows where Brogni's living daughter can be found, information he does not disclose until the Cardinal sees Rachel—his daughter—go to her death. Eléazar's death follows and the opera concludes.[23]

Unlike Lessing's Recha who discovers at age eighteen about her non-Jewish parents, Scribe's Rachel goes to her death believing she is Jewish by birth, not just by upbringing. The infant Rachel was saved from a deadly fire by Eléazar, who raised her as a Jew; this part of the plot reworks several aspects of Lessing's drama, Nathan adopting Recha as an infant and the Templar much later saving her from the deadly flames. Lessing's Templar did not have to disguise himself as a Jew to court his *belle juive*, only because of Nathan's extraordinarily liberal views on religious toleration. Given harsh medieval Christian laws, the Prince has to perform his best version of Jew to get what he wants. Michael Ragussis's recent study of ethnic performance obtains here because Scribe's plot assumes that ethnic and religious identities are performative not essential. Like Jessica, Recha, and Berenice, Rachel falls in love with a Christian rather than a Jew, reinforcing a pattern of ethnic sexual politics that feminizes the Jewish male, who is never a serious candidate for the most desirable Jewess. The Jewish male, who is usually too old for the sexual competition anyway, claims masculinity by threatening Christian men—threats the Christians usually deflect. Rachel's physical and moral sacrifice of herself for the sake of the Christian Prince establishes her ethical superiority and unassailable spirituality, accented however as Christian rather than Jewish. The conjunction of her own sacrifice with her father's refusal to convert to Christianity to save his daughter's life—a deal offered by the Cardinal—restages the Shakespearean contrasts of Jewish revenge and Christian mercy. By forgiving and sacrificing, Rachel performs Christian spirituality, even though she does not change religions outwardly. By hating and exacting revenge on his enemy, Eléazar performs the role of Shylock, the Christian-loathing Jew. Her father refuses to convert to Christianity but in effect Rachel herself has already become a Christian not just by birth but by her actions. In this respect my reading differs somewhat from that of Nadia Valman's forceful interpretation of *La Juive* and Rachel, whom Valman sees not as an overdetermined Christian but as someone with an uncertain identity who has been victimized by two religiously inflexible men.[24] If Scribe had wanted to attribute a Jewish spirituality to Rachel, he would have constructed a sacrifice beneficial to the Jewish community. Eléazar's refusing to convert and dying for his Judaism are represented as selfish, narrow, hateful, and vengeful, completely outside of religious virtue. The aspect of Shylock that returns with Eléazar is not Shylock's love of his ducats but the moneylender's hatred of Antonio—of Christians. During the century of Jewish emancipation, this opera is liberal only in an equivocal way, but it is clear that Rachel the Jewess is the mediator whose spirituality and self-denial point the way for versions of social integration and tolerance.

As I direct my attention now to the literature of conversion and counterconversion, it has been apparent that the texts of the false Jewesses are readable too in terms of conversion, a central event in Shakespeare's *Merchant of Venice* and its later revisions. Julia Reinhard Lupton has offered an unusual perspective on Shylock's forced conversion, which has been seen traditionally as an episode of scapegoating from one angle, and of religious coercion from another. Lupton reads the conversion in terms of a "limited universalism" and citizen naturalization in the context of early modern Venice, which had numerous New Christian and *converso* merchants. Shylock exemplifies not the tragic victim of antisemitic hatred but of the modern citizen, with mixed feelings and multiple memberships, as the play tries to imagine what Jewish emancipation would be like in terms of its foundation and costs. Lupton also points to what others like Susan Handelman call a Jewish textuality in the play, in Lupton's own vocabulary a Pauline hermeneutics in which scriptural categories lose their ethnic and national anchoring, as the Jewish Shylock aligns with Laban and Esau rather than the reliably "Jewish" Jacob.[25]

Lessing's Nathan is surely within the spirit of this limited universalism, as are Edgeworth's Montenero and Scribe's Rachel. That being said, forced conversion was without question a historical catastrophe for Jews.

CONVERSION AND RESISTANCE

When Walter Scott writes his own tale of religious toleration in *Ivanhoe,* he sets the action in England at the same time as the action in Jerusalem is set in Lessing's *Nathan the Wise*; he also makes a Templar one of his central characters. Scott's Rebecca is one of the most influential literary Jewesses in the nineteenth century, a revisionary Jessica who becomes a model for both Christian and Jewish writers. Emphatically Jewish in some ways and emphatically Christian in others, she is a hybrid creation that mixes different qualities inherited from her ancestor Jessica. It goes without saying she is a *belle juive,* one who is not shy about putting her beauty on public display at the Ashby tournament:

> Her form was exquisitely symmetrical, and was shown to advantage by a sort of Eastern dress, which she wore according to the fashion of the females of her nation. Her turban of yellow silk suited well with the darkness of her complexion. The brilliancy of her eyes, the superb arch of her eyebrows, her well-formed aquiline nose, her teeth as white as pearl, and the profusion of her sable tresses, which, each arranged in its own little spiral of twisted curls, fell down upon as much of a lovely neck and bosom as a simmare of the richest Persian silk, exhibiting flowers in their natural colours embossed upon a purple ground, permitted to be visible.

Moreover, the narrator adds, "the three uppermost" clasps on her vest "were left unfastened on account of the heat, which something enlarged the prospect," making her diamond necklace "more conspicuous."[26] Rebecca's Orientalized beauty, the description of which echoes the Song of Songs,[27] is part of her character and its power. A "noble savage," Rebecca is more moral than the Christians and more "sexually arousing" than Christian women.[28] In appearance she could not "pass" as a Christian, as the insistently "white" Jessica apparently could. Other emphatically Jewish qualities include her medical knowledge and her loyalty to Judaism. Rebecca, however, also demonstrates qualities over the course of the novel that are coded as Christian rather than Jewish, especially her generosity, love of Christians, and sexual self-denial.

Scott's narrator, commenting on Rebecca's ability to heal the sick and injured, remarks that medieval women were usually the community's healers and that Jews were especially advanced in the science of medicine, which was shrouded in kabbalistic mystery, inviting Christian distrust and envy. According to the novel, Jews, "with the exclusive spirit arising out of their condition," carefully concealed their medical secrets from the Christians,[29] a spiteful exclusiveness exhibited by Isaac who chides his daughter for helping an injured Ivanhoe; he believes it violates Jewish law to help Gentiles. Rebecca argues with her father by claiming that "in wounds and in misery, the Gentile becometh the Jew's brother."[30] Even in an area as markedly Jewish as medicine, Rebecca pushes it in a Christian-friendly direction contrary to her father. Isaac, as many have noted, is a lesser Shylock, a miser who cares much for his ducats but even more about his daughter; the paternal love softens his image. Serving as a contrast to Rebecca, Isaac is stingy where Rebecca is charitable; he is hateful to Christians where she is loving; he cares more about money than people, she more about people than money, and so on. To her kidnapper and possibly future rapist, if not murderer, Rebecca says: "But I do forgive thee, Bois-Guilbert, though the author of my early death."[31] Within the cultural norm Scott is assuming, that Christians and the New Testament are more merciful, forgiving, and loving than Jews and the Old Testament, Rebecca displays signs of "Christian" spirituality.

One of the characteristic traits of Jewesses in conversionist narratives is their yearning for a spirituality that Judaism stifles. Rebecca is the model for the later Jewesses who move toward conversion. According to Nadia Valman, Rebecca exerted a huge influence with the pattern of exotic beauty, excessive passion, and the need to convert not to Christianity but to Christian moral norms of "forgiveness and self-sacrifice."[32] Like Jessica, Rebecca falls in love with a Christian but unlike her precursor, she becomes in effect a Jewish nun because she cannot have the choice of her heart, Ivanhoe. The denial of her sexual desire, which is directed exclusively toward a Christian man, in effect makes her spiritual in a Christian sense, even though she does not convert to Christianity. Like Scribe's Rachel, for whom Scott's Rebecca is a prototype, the daughter of Isaac the moneylender does not have to convert to perform a Christian role.

For all the apparently Christian things that Rebecca does, her most heroic action is refusing to convert and remaining loyal to the Jewish community. In contrast with Shakespeare's Jessica, Rebecca's steadfastness as a Jewess strongly resists the established pattern, thus making *Ivanhoe* what Michael Ragussis calls a "critique of conversion."[33] Seen from another angle, Rebecca's spirituality illustrates that virtues, which are universal rather than religiously specific, cross ethnic, national, and theological boundaries. One of the most appealing characters in the novel and in the many plays and operas constructed from the novel, Rebecca is the mediating figure binding together the Jewish and Christian worlds, but she has no interest in making a Jewish family. Her mixed and hybrid character, with Jewish and Christian qualities, makes her an evocative model for the cultural ambivalence.

In this section of the chapter I describe literary Jewesses from conversionist narratives that derive from the spiritual side of Rebecca as well as more nationalistic heroines who derive from Rebecca's ethnic and religious pride, and her strength to resist conversion. The conversionist narratives harshly critical of Judaism include those by Amelia Bristow, Bulwer Lytton, and Madame Brendlau. Another set of narratives by Mary Leman Grimstone and Julius Ursinus Niemcewicz is more ambivalent about Judaism. Finally, Maria Polack's novel strongly supports Judaism, while Thomas Wade subverts most of the established paradigms of Jewish representation.

Amelia Bristow's *Sophia de Lissau: A Portraiture of the Jews* (1826) is a mixed-genre text similar in some ways to *The History of Mary Prince* (1831). The latter memoir, although subtitled as *Related by Herself,* is actually an oral history taken down in writing by Susanna Strickland and edited by or coedited with Thomas Pringle. It is impossible to tell how reliable the memoir is in terms of representing accurately what Mary Prince actually told Susanna Strickland.[34] Similarly, if the stories of Sophia and Emma de Lissau are not invented out of whole cloth but have at their core the oral histories of two Jewesses whose narrative Amelia Bristow is trying to render, at the very least what the reader confronts is a heavily mediated and edited account of so-called real life. It is not simply the editor's numerous notes that try to explain Jewish customs and practices that indicate the presence of an intrusive editor but the very structure of the memoir is novelistic, for the text is divided into chapters with various twists in the plot, reversals and recognition scenes, withheld information later disclosed to regulate the reader's sense of involvement, and so on. The Preface to *Emma de Lissau* concedes that "dates and names are changed, and anachronisms purposely committed"; moreover, the ostensible author claims that "many events are wholly omitted."[35] Even if the actual experiences of real people who once existed are reflected in Sophia de Lissau and Emma de Lissau, it is difficult to separate the authentic from the fabricated. That being the case, the best approach is to treat as a novel what appears to be a novel.

The novels tell the stories of two sisters, Emma the eldest who is initially raised by the maternal grandparents, and Sophia, the mother's favorite. The back story is that their parents, Polish Jews now living in London, Solomon and Anna, were betrothed when Anna's father tried to marry her off to a rich, old, sick man. Anna resisted and appealed to the chief rabbi who ruled against the father and in favor of the daughter. Anna married Solomon as she wished, but her father extracted a deal stipulating that he and his wife—the maternal grandparents—would get Solomon and Anna's first daughter to raise as they wished. That eldest daughter turns out to be Emma, who for reasons not clearly explained turns to Christianity. In her account, she acquires a conviction of depravity and sin from reading an English translation of the Old Testament, and her desire for salvation can be satisfied only by the ideas and practices of Christianity; she never explains how she learned about the religion. With a Christian teacher and several Christian friends she acts like a secret Christian, a parody of the Spanish crypto-Jews, hiding her sacred texts like contraband, reading her gospels secretively. Her liberal merchant father allows her to attend church, but her mother and the rabbi give Emma much abuse. After her mother dies she gets closer to her father who encourages her to write the family history, honing her skills as a writer. The whole time she lives openly as a Christian and even develops friendships with observant Jews, friends of her father, who know she is Christian but accept her anyway. In the last chapter after both parents have died, she finally marries a Christian and all is well for her. The other sister, Sophia, the mother's favorite, is courted by James Sydney, a ward of Sophia's father. He wants to convert to Judaism to marry the love of his life, but he is discouraged from doing so by his guardian, and he finally leaves the family, after which Sophia declines in health. Sophia finally marries Leoni, a Jew who seems acceptable but turns out to be abusive. While Sophia's father is trying to arrange a divorce, Leoni robs her and not long afterward an emotionally devastated Sophia dies.

Although the narrator of the novels seems to think that the "real" story is the Providential emergence of Protestant Evangelical Christianity as the salvation for Emma de Lissau, a less religiously focused attention suggests other things. Although Anna the mother is portrayed as a vicious abuser of her daughter Emma, Anna is also a bold actor in the Jewish world, standing up to her father, persuading the rabbi to rule in her favor, and marrying ultimately for love.

Although Protestant English culture is supposed to be freer than Judaism, with the Talmudic rigidities, especially as they oppress women, Anna's story suggests otherwise. Another narrative that does not fit well within the programmatic Protestantism of the two texts is the sad tale of Sophia and James Sydney. Regardless of the theological issues, the young people seem in love and might have been happy. Things could not have turned out worse for Sophia when she marries Leoni. Although Sophia dies before a divorce can be obtained, the Jewish culture at least permits divorce, something not possible in Britain except for the wealthiest. Both Sophia and Emma seem to love their father, the liberal merchant who is open to the novelties of the English culture, whereas the mother is depicted as loathing English and Christian ways. The mother's conflict with her father was harsh and debilitating, as it became expressed through the battle over the eldest Emma. No wonder Emma came to loathe Judaism.

Emma, the converting Jewess, scarred from small pox, is not the *belle juive*; her father is not an authoritarian brute but her mother seems to hate her. She witnesses a number of unhappily married women, her aunt and her sister among them. In most regards Emma does not resemble Shakespeare's Jessica. Rather, she seems more like a gothic heroine, who gets kidnapped from the home of her grandparents by her mother and the family rabbi, who grotesquely and gratuitously kills her pet bird. The mother and the sadistic rabbi also act as jailers and censors for Emma, regulating what she can read and whom she can meet. Emma demonstrates Jessica-like strength and willfulness in becoming a Christian in a family hostile to the conversion, but it should be noted that the father, no Shylock, seems to have accepted his daughter's conversion. She remains in the family home the whole time her father is alive. Although she complains about being oppressed by Jews for her religious convictions, it is certainly not her father who is giving her difficulties.

Because the Amelia Bristow conversionist texts are not polished literature but are zealously sectarian, they are not strongly controlled by stereotypes and conventional plots. The awkward story-telling is a virtue in some sense, for what appears to be authentic gets expressed: destructive feuds between a daughter and a father that harms both of them, making the daughter mentally ill; a loving, mutually supportive relationship between a Jewish father and a Christian convert daughter, who does not fully understand or appreciate her good fortune; a young woman who turns away from a Christian man who is willing to convert and who loves her to marry a Jewish man who abuses her so severely that the resulting illness kills her. These interesting plot lines are not as fully or as effectively developed as one might wish, but they suggest some genuine elements in what is packaged as religious propaganda.

The next text I am looking at is by a professional writer who knows his literary business, Edward Bulwer Lytton (1803–73). Despite the jokes about his bad writing—"It was a dark and stormy night"—he actually is knowledgeable about constructing plots and characters. *Leila* (1838), set in Spain in the pivotal year of 1491 just before the defeat of the Moors and the expulsion of the Jews, yields some rewards, for there are compelling characters, including a Jewess who falls in love with a Muslim warrior, perhaps the most admirable male character in the novel; she converts to Christianity under female tutelage, and a few moments before she takes her vows as a nun—with the Inquisition's Torquemada looking on—her father intervenes and kills her. Her father, Almamen, is a fascinating character, a crypto-Jew and magician who works for both the Moors and the Christians. While his politically neutral fellow Jews are content to make money selling to both sides, Almamen displays courageous initiative to guide the forces of history. While Michael Ragussis is correct that Lytton is depicting the Catholic Torquemada and the Jewish Almamen as fanatics to make British Protestants appear reasonable and humane,[36] the novel does more than promote the British Empire. The novel records the Christianization of Spain, but it does not celebrate it. The conversion of Leila, who is never taught the doctrines and history of Judaism by her father, is not a triumph for the Christian reader because Leila loves a Moor and feels deeply for her Jewish father. Almamen and Muza (the Muslim warrior) are powerful characters, not idealized allegorical abstractions, so that the reader becomes emotionally invested in what happens with them. Almamen is ambivalently portrayed, acting for the Jewish community, contemptuous of the Jewish merchants, exciting as a magician and double—even triple—agent. Boabdil the Moorish king, in contrast, is not heroic. Leila the Jew's daughter who converts to Christianity does not fall in love with a Christian but with a Moor, who is about to be defeated; the Jessica pattern obtains but only to a point, and her inclination toward the monastic life suggests Marlowe's Abigail.[37] Almamen's killing of her conforms to the Christian stereotypical slander that Jews would rather kill their children than see them convert. The Jew with the knife killing the young convert in church evokes medieval images of ritual murder, even sacrificial murder with Abraham and his son Isaac. The other Jews in the novel are represented as predatory merchants, odious war profiteers and cowards sitting on the sidelines while the manly Christians and

Moors fight one another. When popular violence breaks out against the Jews, the reader is given no reason not to applaud.[38]

Lytton, whom the Moss sisters treat as though he were one of the most unblemished and heroic philosemites in their dedication of *The Romance of Jewish History* (1840), a text I will be discussing later, has actually written a novel that does the Jews very few favors. (Lytton was friendly too with Grace Aguilar.) Leila's conversion to Christianity does not resonate completely with the conversions of other Jewesses like Jessica and Emma de Lissau because she knew nothing about Judaism and because she was emotionally neglected, easily turned to the religion by an attentive and loving older woman. The literary ancestors of Almamen the Jewish magician and triple agent are the medieval Satan and early modern Jewish alchemists and kabbalistic sorcerers, but the peculiar mixture of his qualities suggests the Rothschild banking family as they were popularly represented in the nineteenth century: financial wizards working both sides, moving unpredictably but always landing on top. Almamen hates the actual Jewish merchants but at the mythic level that only suggests the tycoon's contempt for the mere businessman. Leila ironically is not a mediating force for harmonizing the three contending forces; rather, her connections with all three worlds make her a catalyst for masculine competition and violence. Also, even as she is about to take the nun's vow of chastity, Leila has never stopped loving the Muslim warrior Muza, making her an incoherent symbol for Christian triumph and feminine spirituality. I trust the Mosses were just opportunistically taking advantage of the attention Lytton paid them in order to help advance the cause of Jewish emancipation; they could not have read *Leila* as anything but a conflicted text.

With Madame Brendlau's *Tales of a Jewess* (1838), one is again with awkwardly constructed narratives like the de Lissau novels; also like them, Brendlau's has some rewards for the patient, generous reader. These subliterary works have their own conventions, as Nadia Valman points out: insisting that the stories are factual not fictional, and trying to bolster the realism with notes and addenda explaining Jewish customs to promise the reader insider information being passed to the Jewishly ignorant readers.[39] The author of *Tales of a Jewess* claims to be Jewish from a foreign-born family that moved to London. Her "rich and beautiful" mother married a German physician who was educated at the French court and who converted to Judaism to marry. Throughout the work the author inserts her father's stories, many of which feature Napoleon, whom he served as a physician. Although the author and her brothers all married Christians, she wants to have the moral capital of being a victim, emphasizing the family disgrace within the Jewish community of marrying outside the faith and making the claim that if it were not for Christianity, she would have been stoned to death for following her heart in marriage.[40] The novel's main plot is simple and Richardsonian: Judith, with dark hair and blue eyes—physically marked as both Jewish and Christian[41]—resists an arranged marriage with her slave-dealing American cousin Mr. Davis because she loves William Hartford, a Christian. (The detail I especially like is that Judith met her beloved Christian at the theatre.) Her family uncompromisingly forces Judith to choose between her Christian boyfriend and her own family, whom she ambivalently loves, especially her father, whose stories she enjoys retelling and whose German-accented English she reproduces in mocking italics. Although there are several chapters recording Judith's spiritual enlightenment in Christianity, the novel suggests, despite what Judith herself says to the contrary, that her attraction to the Protestant world is for the social resources and higher status. Her already wealthy family has as much status as it is going to get, so the children look elsewhere for opportunities to move higher; indeed, Judith concedes that her brothers married Christians "only" for money, whereas she had more spiritual motives.[42] In some respects this is an immigrant tale of a daughter ambivalent about her foreign-tongued parents whose old-country ways are holding her back from fitting in completely in the new society. Because of what Michael Ragussis calls the "culture of conversion" that prevailed in the nineteenth century, Brendlau splices her Richardsonian immigrant tale onto the conversionist narrative.[43]

That her conversion seems mostly social (with sexual and racial undercurrents) rather than religious becomes apparent in the key chapter 9, entitled "The Book," to signify her receiving William Hartford's gift of the New Testament. Judith's guilty handling and reading of the Christian book are risibly sexual: afraid to read it, she hides it in a drawer, but her "excited curiosity" makes her return to it again and again like "Eve with the forbidden fruit," and she "promiscuously" opens it. Her reading causes "sensations" and "feelings that can never be forgotten." At family gatherings she yearns to be alone with "*that forbidden book*," and then one day she is so absorbed in the transcendent pleasures of the Testament she does not notice her mother entering the room to discover Judith's secret practices.[44] A racial discourse structures the chapter in several ways. The New Testament enters her room by way of the family's black servant Joseph, who is a Christian and who supports Judith discreetly in her Christian aspirations. Although Joseph's Christianity makes him someone like Judith, the novel never ceases to remind the reader that Joseph is black. His speech is rendered in italicized dialect, in much the same way that Judith's father's speech is represented as emphatically foreign and un-English. Here is a sample of Joseph's speech: "*Disse, missee; disse, missee; dat your mamma and your papa have been told dat dare was a box in de floar, and so day say day* will open and see; and day *callee me,* and say, '*Go open, dake, and bring de rascal's letters here!*' "[45] Blackness itself is represented throughout the novel as a sign of inferiority and ugliness, of the very antithesis of Englishness. In the first chapter Judith's father darkens the skin of his sister-in-law in Amsterdam to make her too unattractive—ugly like a "negro"— for the invading French soldiers to rape.[46] Judith's Jewish suitor Mr. Davis is also represented as black, in the words of Joseph the servant, "*terrible blackafied.*" Judith thinks that "even black Joseph would be preferable to this Jew."[47] Judith's father, although born a German Christian, becomes black by means of his foreign speech, which also functions to align Jewishness with blackness. Here is a sample of the father's speech: "*I vos shetting in de parler, ven Josef informed me dat a gentlehomme vonted to shee me. 'Let him come in,' said I. So in volks a tall strait man, mit his hat on. 'Vot is de matter mit you sar?*' "[48] There is no difference between this dialect and the Jew dialect current on the London stage, from which Brendlau obviously borrowed it. By marrying William Hartford the novel's heroine escapes the taint of foreignness, blackness, and Jewishness, following the example of her literary ancestor Jessica.

In Mary Leman Grimstone's *Character* (1833), the dominant influence is not Shakespeare's *Merchant of Venice* but Mary Wollstonecraft and the tradition of the 1790s novel of purpose, or "Jacobin" novel. Although the climax of the novel suggests a racist stereotype of a "carnal" Jewess (Esther) who kills her husband (Marmion) and then herself in a frenzy of jealousy,[49] the novel in fact works against stereotypes at several levels, including the plot and characterization. Tracing the ill effects of bad education, especially on women, Grimstone shows a contrasting pair of women, one a poorly educated beautiful woman (Amelia) whose bad decisions ultimately bring ruin to herself and her family, conforming to the social diagnosis in Mary Wollstonecraft's *Vindication of the Rights of Woman* (1792), and another (Agnes) who is a highly educated, broadly experienced widow, who has a happy second marriage and a morally exemplary son Arthur. A Jewish subplot intersects with the main plot eventually, but the novel belongs mostly to the Christian characters. The most destructive characters in the novel are Christian men: Peter Coverley who is a hurtful miser,

Smith who seduced a Jewess and sold their baby, and Malfort who is a murderous embezzler. Although the novel does not critique property and class relations, as *Caleb Williams* (1794) does, it forcefully provides a critique of gender relations. The Christian Amelia, who has an affair with the villain Malfort, is shown to be as carnal as any of the Jewesses. The conversion the novel promotes is a cosmopolitan, universalist one of mutual forgiveness and religious tolerance: "to make us more liberal, more considerate towards each other."[50] The novel does more than enforce a sentimental solution to deeply rooted social problems because it also systematically argues for a new regime of egalitarian education for women.

Another novel, *Fiction Without Romance* (1830), assigns Jews a subplot as well, but in Maria Polack's fiction the Jewish role is very different from the one in Grimstone's *Character*. Although the main action of the novel concerns Christian characters, most notably Eliza Desbro, who discovers as a young woman her status as a bastard, the subsidiary Zachariahs function in two ways: to illustrate sympathetically and accurately how modern English Jews live in terms of Shabbat and the various festivals and fasts, and to provide a melodramatic parallel to the Eliza Desbro story with their own tale of their daughter Sarah, a lively and independent *belle juive* who elopes with a Christian man, has a child that dies, and perishes herself but within the bosom of her own forgiving Jewish family. Jewish herself, Polack constructs a novel that highlights forgiveness of sins under the benevolent authority of Protestant Englishness; a subplot about Evelina St. Clair is a harshly anti-Catholic morality tale, which makes both Protestantism and Judaism look much better. The novel's two moral authorities are a strict, almost puritanical Anglican clergyman, and the Jewish Zachariahs, whose Sarah, when she plays the Jessica role, destroys herself. The Christians visit the Zachariahs and applaud their piety and intelligence, but the two worlds, though morally equal, are quite separate. The Christian heroine Eliza Desbro is indeed a catalyst for moral reform and social harmony, precipitating a spiritual conversion to what the novel deems humane values. Her origins as someone born out of wedlock allegorize the parallel disability for Jews, who look for emancipation after the Catholics have secured theirs. It is no accident that the subscription list for Polack's novel includes most of the Anglo-Jewish notables. The novel aspires for another kind of conversion, for the English political nation to accept Jews as equals.[51]

The anonymous translator and editor of *Levi and Sarah* (1830) unequivocally looks forward to the conversion of the Jews,[52] but the text of the novel favors *Bildung* and reform as articulated by

Moses Mendelssohn and the *maskilim* for Polish Jews. The plot of the epistolary novel is that Sarah, an emancipated Jewess, seeks to marry another enlightened Jew, Levi, against the wishes of her father, Moses, a caricatured Shylock who delights in cheating Gentiles, and who has already arranged a mercenary marriage for his daughter. Moses suspects his daughter has been corrupted by too much education ("boetry") for she is attracted to the liberal Levi, who socializes with Christians, cuts his beard, and does not pray with *tefillin*. Like Richardson's Clarissa, Sarah runs away from her family, and corresponds with her best friend the liberal enlightener, Rachel (Sarah's "Miss Howe"). After much storm and stress, Count Tenczyn, friend of liberal Jews, forces Moses to reconcile with Levi and to reform his corrupt commercial practices. The benevolent, despotic Count requires that Jews learn to use the Polish language. The conversion that most interests the novelist Niemcewicz is to modernity, not so much a regime of mutual tolerance as one of assimilation to the already existing Polish culture. The theological niceties matter far less than appearances, as Jews are expected to look and talk like Poles. The template of the *Merchant of Venice* is strongly evident here but with unique revisions, for all the actors are Jewish except the Count, who plays the Portia role of imposing Belmont values on an unruly Jewish Venice. Moses, the Shylock character, endures a forced conversion to liberal modernity, which he accepts cheerfully if implausibly. The Jessica and Lorenzo roles are played by Polish Reform Jews, reflecting far more Niemcewicz's wishful thinking than historical reality.

Another text of 1830, Thomas Wade's play *The Jew of Arragon*, undermines the established patterns of Jewish representations from the *Merchant of Venice* to *Ivanhoe*. While Shakespeare's drama was seen and read by countless thousands, who also read Scott's novel and the dozens of theatrical versions, Wade's tragedy had one single showing in Covent Garden where an audience vehemently rejected it because the tragedy uncompromisingly justifies Xavier, an early thirteenth-century court Jew in Arragon, who makes two important decisions: (1) he refuses to comply with the king's decree that the Jews pay an exorbitant special tax for the royal wedding and celebration of the victory over the Moors; (2) after he fails to persuade the king to withdraw the edict, he encourages his daughter Rachel to seduce and hopefully marry the king to influence policies affecting Jews. Xavier's objection to the decree is not that he cannot afford to lose that much money, but that in the past Xavier's financial dealings with the king were privately arranged, not publicly negotiated. As official and public policy, the edict sets a precedent for arbitrary dispossession of the Jewish community, which would be placed in a position of impossible weakness and vulnerability. It was in thirteenth-century England that a succession of kings repeatedly taxed and fined the Jews to such an extreme extent that they were practically dispossessed even before they were finally expelled from the country in 1290. The well-known account of the medieval oppression of the Jews in Henry Hart Milman's *The History of the Jews* (1829) relates how English kings, when they lacked money, took what they needed.[53] Although Milman does not dramatize the expulsion of 1290, he never justifies it or other acts of violence and theft against Jews. Wade's play reminds his audience of the guilty past about which they do not want to be reminded, and he forces the audience to experience the dispossession and expulsion from the point of view of the victims.

The character of Rachel is even more subversive of complacent English opinion. After the king declines to withdraw the edict, Xavier mulls over the situation, at first insulted by the king's suggestion of giving his daughter to the king for his sexual pleasure, but then thinking "She might aspire to crowns—a Christian crown!" and with power she could "quash" the edict and "turn the streams / Of power and greatness towards her countrymen— / And Saragossa make Jerusalem!"[54] As a powerful *belle juive* who deliberately sets out to seduce the king in order to influence him politically, she ought to be, by ordinary norms, harshly judged. The parallel of the biblical Esther and Ahasuerus applies to daughter Rachel and King Alphonso, to be sure, but most appropriately as a narrative that resonates with a Jewish community that has fought for survival more than a few times and that observes Purim annually to commemorate that kind of experience. The play illustrates how under emergency conditions of imminent extinction something that is ordinarily immoral—using sex to influence political decisions—is justified. The play also depicts as tragic the ultimate failure of Rachel and her father; their downfall is not poetic justice for malefactors. Rather, the play is designed to provoke cathartic fear and pity in the audience, which must identify with the terrible choices forced on the Jewish characters. Fanny Kemble, who played the role of Rachel in the Covent Garden production, remarked that she knew the play would fail because it exalted "the Jews dramatically at the expense of the Christians."[55] If the audience could have suspended their identity as English Christians, they could have entered the spirit of the play, but Wade was making demands the audience could not endure.

Rachel is no Jessica because when she seduces the Christian king, she has no intention of converting. Her excessive sexual beauty is something she controls for her own purposes. The Christian men, however, can hardly control themselves around her, as she is much more alluring than her Christian rival, Isabella. She is not at odds with her father Xavier, who has no moral disabilities because of his position as the rich court Jew. The play tantalizingly creates what look like opportunities for English Christians to feel morally superior to the carnal and materialistic Jews, but Wade frustrates each and every attempt to accumulate moral capital at the Jews' expense. The tragedy of the play is that the Jews do not survive; they are exterminated; the efforts of Xavier and Rachel do not work as they were intended to do, but even in defeat Xavier expresses hope in Israel's eventual rebirth.

As a play to promote the case for Jewish emancipation, *The Jew of Arragon* is a huge miscalculation, for it attacks the English investments in Jewish representations at a too radical level. Nathan and Sheva are deferential, eager to promote social harmony and tolerance, allowing the Jewish community and its desires a subsidiary position, if acknowledged at all. Scott's Rebecca, as alluring perhaps as Wade's Rachel, is in passionate love with the Christian Ivanhoe and deferentially denies herself a sexual life. The Jewess in conversionist narratives is supposed to effect social harmony and mutual understanding, whereas Wade's Rachel provokes bloody war. Some details reinforce a Judeocentric perspective: the Christian ladies at court take a sexual interest in Xavier, who turns Isabella down in a brutal retort: "They've Christians plenty, dame, to serve the turn / You drive at. Lucky! Strange beasts couple not."[56] When Xavier gazes at Isabella in a sexually evaluative manner, the Christian Manrique protests: "Thy presence does inflict a circumcision."[57] The encounters with Isabella and Manrique establish the dominant masculinity of Xavier, despite his age. When the partisans of Isabella rise up against Rachel and the Jewish community, Wade does not portray their victory as a triumph of justice; rather, the Christians cannot bear to see Jews in a position of power. Similarly, when the king favors Rachel, he does so because he is in thrall to her sexual power; he loses whatever political judgment he might have had. His desire for Rachel humiliatingly makes him helpless, as he futilely protests Rachel's supernatural power over him.[58] The Christians, none of whom rise to the occasion to assume heroic roles, are turned into a murderous mob by the events initiated by the Jews. The Christians have the power of numbers but in nothing else does their superiority consist in Wade's play.

THE KING SISTERS: "LOVELY LITTLE JESSICA"

The paternal grandfather of Sophia and Charlotte King, Moses Rey, dressed up like a Turk, was called "Sultan" and supplied coffee-house patrons "from Cornhill to Charing-cross" with "cane-strings, c-d-ms, sealing wax, and bawdy books." As a boy John King doubled the profits of his North African-born father by selling candy made by his mother.[59] I begin the account of the King sisters with this vignette to establish the commercial theatricality of poor Jews who sold goods on the street and surely of the King family as well, including father John and his two daughters. The grandfather's role-playing to please an audience eager for sweets and sex is not remote from the literary granddaughters, who fashioned anti-Jacobin and gothic fiction as well as lyrical poetry for readers eager for sensational eroticism and violence.

Although Charlotte King's novel *Zofloya* (1806) has been reprinted many times in the twentieth century and is still in print in paperback, and although her two pseudonyms, Rosa Matilda and Charlotte Dacre, were demystifed long ago in Lord Byron's *English Bards and Scotch Reviewers* (2nd edition, October, 1809), more than a few contemporary specialists in the gothic novel still refer to *Zofloya*'s author as Charlotte Dacre as though that were her real name. The King sisters produced innovative poetical and fictional work that represents, according to Jerome McGann, an alternative Romantic tradition to the more canonical Romanticism of Wordsworth and Scott. For McGann the key features of this Romanticism are sensibility, sensation, and experiential temporality, the triumph of uncensored embodied imagination over idealized, sublimated, and Bowdlerized creativity.[60] Charlotte published three books of poetry, numerous poems in newspapers and periodicals, and four novels, while Sophia published five novels and two books of poetry. They both married wealthy Christians, Charlotte marrying Nicholas Byrne (1760/1–1833), editor of the *Morning Post*, and Sophia marrying Charles Fortnum (1770–1860), related to but not directly part of the Fortnum-Mason empire. Both sisters also died young, Sophia in her twenties (1781/82–1805?) and Charlotte in her early forties (1779/80–1825).[61] Although both also took after their father in their ambition, their leaving the Jewish community, and their literary accomplishments, their written work also suggests a painful ambivalence toward their father who left them as infants when he divorced their mother and married (or perhaps not) Lady Lanesborough and who as a political radical and moneylender known as "Jew" King did not enhance their chances to enter respectable Christian society. The cultural myths reflected and embodied in Shakespeare's *Merchant of Venice* and conversionist narratives made it easier for Jewish women than men to become part of Christian society as Jessica was a trope for both the convert and for the exotically beautiful object of Christian male desire. One way to see how the King sisters worked out some identity themes is to examine how they presented themselves in their publications and how they were themselves represented.

I will start with a note appended to the second edition Lord Byron's *English Bards and Scotch Reviewers* where part of the satire of contemporary writers is directed against "Rosa Matilda," who receives fourteen lines (ll. 756–64, 926–30). Byron's note on Rosa Matilda reads as follows:

> This lovely little Jessica, the daughter of the noted Jew K[ing], seems to be a follower of the Della Cruscan School, and has published two volumes of very respectable absurdities in rhyme, as times go; besides sundry novels in the style of the first edition of the Monk.[62]

Byron (and Shelley) borrowed money from John King, a fact that might explain Byron's desire to get back at King through exposing his daughter. Jerome McGann suggests another motive. Discovering that "The Mountain Violet," thought to be one of Byron's poems, is actually in Charlotte Dacre's *Hours of Solitude* (1805), McGann argues that Byron's *Hours of Idleness* (1807) was strongly influenced by Dacre. To distance himself from and repudiate a style of poetry he earlier practiced and for which he was criticized in reviews, Byron scapegoats Rosa Matilda in what McGann aptly calls "a typically Romantic act of displacement."[63] I also want to note the power of Shakespeare's play to establish the lens through which Charlotte King is viewed by examining the ways she fashions her authorial identity by strategic framing. King's first work was a book of poetry, *Trifles of Helicon*, published in 1798, jointly authored with her sister Sophia. The volume was dedicated to their father in the following way:

> To John King, Esq. Instead of the mature fruits of the Muses, accept the blossoms; they are to show you that the education you have afforded us has not been totally lost:—when we grow older, we hope to offer you others with less imperfections.
>
> Your Affectionate Daughters,
> Charlotte King
> Sophia King
> January 14, 1798

By early 1798 John King had many of the external signs of respectability: an elegant house in a fashionable neighborhood, an aristocratic wife, and party guests from the most prominent strata in politics and the arts. However, he was also invariably called "Jew" King, known everywhere as a moneylender whose activities in the political and criminal underground were widely suspected. For the daughters to align themselves with their father in 1798 was perhaps a matter of affection or material self-interest but as a public action it was an embrace of a controversial and ambiguously Jewish and ambiguously respectable father. The year 1798 was in fact an especially bad one for John King who became bankrupt, fought against charges that he had assaulted two prostitutes, and saw the publication of *Authentic Memoirs*, an exposé of King's private life and criminal activities. At this time King also moved closer to Judaism as his legal troubles intensified.

The *Trifles of Helicon* dedication was the last publicly affirmative allusion to their father. Sophia's first two novels, *Waldorf* (1798) and *Cordelia* (1799), reject the New Philosophy of Godwin, alert readers to the sexual dangers of immoral cosmopolitans, and in the form of a roman à clef represents her father's abandonment of his young family and his living with Lady Lanesborough and her two children. After the *Trifles of Helicon* volume Charlotte seems to dissociate herself from her father but she also seems to resemble his ambiguous performance of respectability. Using the *nom de plume* Rosa Matilda, she publishes poetry in the *Morning Post* and the *Morning Herald* that attracts popular attention. The name Rosa Matilda evokes two strong literary associations, Della Cruscan poetry, and Matthew Lewis's notorious gothic novel, *The Monk* (1796), in which a major villain, Matilda, seduces Ambrosio the monk by exploiting the ruse of appearing to be Rosario, the shy young novice. Her first novel in fact was dedicated to Matthew Lewis. The provocative Rosa Matilda, which also evokes Hannah Cowley's Della Cruscan *nom de plume* Anna Matilda, is a deft marketing strategy to draw attention to the poetry but veil her identity. Della Cruscan poetry and Lewis's *Monk* provide a safely transgressive allure that was enhanced in 1805 when she adopted yet another *nom de plume*, Charlotte Dacre, for her volume of poetry, *Hours of Solitude*. The title page of the 1805 volume suggests that Charlotte Dacre is the real name of Rosa Matilda. Moreover, the frontispiece displays an image of the author that reinforces the reality-effect of the Dacre name. Underneath the image of Rosa Matilda that appears in the *Hours of Solitude* is Rosa Matilda's handwritten name, as though the *nom de plume* were the most authentic aspect of the author's identity. Not unlike her father who changed his own name, Jacob Rey, when he was young man, Charlotte assumes two new names. Living women writers rarely included images of themselves in their books, and certainly not sexy images. Indeed, in an 1809 pamphlet about Mary Anne Clarke, "The Royal Concubine," there is an image of the notorious prostitute and it is the exact same image that appears in Charlotte King's book as Rosa Matilda. The Rosa Matilda image lent itself to be appropriated for erotic representations. If Charlotte King wanted respectability, it made sense to cloak her name in pseudonyms but her writerly personae had scandalous associations that were only enhanced by the writing itself that disapproving reviewers found sexually improper. As Lisa Wilson characterizes the poetry, although King's poetry denounces seduction, the poems also "imply the pleasures of committing the errors they so vehemently condemn."[64]

The poet after whom Charlotte is modeling herself is clearly Mary Robinson, the most famous Della Cruscan poet who generated countless images of herself in prints and in the frontispieces of her poetry books, and who as a Della Cruscan poet in the 1790s used numerous *noms de plume* to theatricalize her identity. As poetry editor of the *Morning Post* Robinson perhaps accepted some of Charlotte's poems and Robinson, after her death, occasions a poem of tribute in the *Hours of Solitude*. Did Charlotte find the connection between Robinson and her father inspiring because the two had once perhaps been lovers or because they had become enemies or both? That Robinson ideologically was more on the left than the anti-Jacobin right with which she and her sister aligned complicates the modeling but also is symptomatic of the King sisters' ideological ambivalence: their novels and poetry can be read both as cautionary tales against excessive passion and individualism, as well as individualistic narratives of passion that violate various codes of authority.

Another part of the framing of Charlotte's poetry is the dedication of the volume to an extremely wealthy John Penn (1760–1834), poet and Burkean writer well known for the architecture and landscaping of his estates. As a member of parliament, a sheriff of Buckinghamshire, a Lt. Colonel in the Army, and governor of Portland, Penn is as firmly established in English society as John King's position is tenuous. Further anchoring the effusive identity of Rosa Matilda in the conservative, stable identity of Charlotte Dacre, Charlotte King performs a maneuver not unlike those financial schemes of her father, manipulating representations to simulate legitimacy and respectability. Charlotte Dacre, patronized by John

Penn, cannot be the emotionally and sexually transgressive author that Rosa Matilda appears to be; rather, Charlotte Dacre creates an ironic distance between herself and her literary creations, and generates a false identity behind which Charlotte King, the mistress of a married Nicholas Byrne, can be the mother of three children before Byrne and King eventually marry. When they marry in 1815 with their three children baptized in 1811, Charlotte achieves a brittle respectability, for she will still be able to read in a poetical satire that she is the daughter of "the notorious Jew King."[65] Perhaps she did not mind being associated with her father, whom she honored when Charlotte's mother Sara sent to the Bevis Marks Synagogue 50 pounds in the name of her daughter—Rachel Charlotte Rey—after John King died in 1823. This donation along with another 50 pounds in Sara's own name was earmarked for "communal institutions," and "treated as legacies paid in advance."[66]

To explore the literary work of the King sisters I first discuss Sophia's anti-Jacobin fiction, then her sister's gothic novels, and finally their poetry.

As described in the previous chapter, Sophia met several times with the most famous of the "Jacobin" novelists, William Godwin, friend of her father. It seems to have gone unnoticed that this novel by a sixteen-year-old probably influenced both *St. Leon*, published a year after *Waldorf*, and daughter Mary's *Frankenstein* (1818). Recently reprinted by Pickering and Chatto, and edited and introduced by Adriana Craciun, this anti-Jacobin fiction is receiving the attention it deserves in literary history. Craciun shrewdly observes that *Waldorf* as a Voltairean philosophical tale can avoid the standard anti-Jacobin "conflation of loyal subject and good Christian."[67] If the novel had a contemporary English setting, religious identities would be unavoidably specific, but Sophia as a Jew makes national and religious identity somewhat vague by having her eponymous hero Ferville Waldorf raised by Chalcot and Maria Louvain in Speyer, Bavaria. Waldorf discovers later (vol. 1, ch. 18) that his biological father is really the Duke of N----, whom he already knew under the name of Frederic Zenna, the alchemist and magician he had previously addressed respectfully as "father." Somewhat French and somewhat German, the novel's hero is born and dies just outside Speyer, a city with one of Europe's earliest Jewish communities and a long history of religious conflict and violence, Jewish expulsions and sectarian warfare between Protestants and Catholics. With much of the novel taking place in Vienna and Spain, the abstracted distance from modern England and its system of social identities is deliberate.

Like *Candide*, *Waldorf* sets its hero on a series of adventures to illustrate various moral truths, and like a *Bildungsroman*, the novel makes the hero face and reflect upon the consequences of his choices. Waldorf leaves his loving home at age fifteen for Vienna only after his elderly guardians have died and the blood relations have expelled him. The trauma of the Kings' divorce and the experience of Sophia and Charlotte being replaced by their father's new family gets represented in the fiction of both sisters on numerous occasions. Lady Lanesborough and her two children, Augustus Butler-Danvers and his sister, the Marchioness of Mariscotti, become John King's family after he divorces his wife Sara in 1784. Expulsion, displacement, and neglect appear in various forms in the sisters' fiction, which allegorizes paternal abandonment as symptomatic of larger social failures. The same age as the author, the hero in his naïve innocence gets robbed on the road to Vienna and then taken in by a misanthropic solitary and recluse, with whom he lives for several years before he leaves the simple life for the sophisticated life in a European capital. The Recluse tries to impart his wisdom to the impatient, ambitious youth: "The heart of man is radically corrupt—barbarians, that prey on each other—cannibals, devils, that glut themselves with the blood of their own species."[68]

The pattern established in Vienna where he tries his hand as a literary adventurer repeats itself for the rest of the novel: after adopting the radical opinions of Hardi Lok—glossed by Cracium as a fusion of Thomas Hardy, treason trial defendant of 1794 and leader of the London Corresponding Society, and John Locke, empiricist philosopher of the Enlightenment[69]—Waldorf wins the affection of his host's daughter Millroh, who eventually becomes an atheist and dies from her loss of traditional beliefs and her disappointment in Waldorf's neglect of her. The philosophy of Lok is primarily anti-religious and libertine, with the political dimensions of the New Philosophy only hinted at. By the sixth chapter of volume one Waldorf is a complete convert to Lok's ideas on marriage, faith, and personal responsibility. The defense of tradition is taken up by the fatherly Zenna, who as a magician and alchemist makes a curious Burkean because alchemy was associated with Jews and the disruptive energies of modernity, most famously at the time by the notorious figure Cagliostro. Guiseppe Balsamo (his birth name), peripatetic healer, reformer, alchemist, magician, and con man, blazed his way through the Europe of the 1770s and 1780s, incurring the wrath of religious and political authorities; he was at the center of the French queen's necklace scandal, friend and associate of Lord George Gordon (whom the next chapter discusses), and he was finally vanquished by the Inquisition, which tortured him in prison, where he died in 1795.[70] In 1798 the only famous magician and alchemist is the recently deceased Cagliostro, whom Waldorf's actual father calls to the reader's mind. (That John King and William Godwin would have met Cagliostro at some point is a possibility.) Godwin's *St. Leon*, published after Sophia's novel, features a Cagliostro-like alchemist as well, one who travels through central Europe and Spain where he, like Waldorf and Zenna, encounters the Inquisition. Zenna counters Lok's radicalism in two ways, arguing against it for abjuring God, trampling on human and divine laws, inverting the order of nature, and crushing links of society (vol. 1, ch. 7), and administering a psychotropic "liquor" that sends Waldorf into a hallucinatory state where eyeless sockets and bloody cheeks are supposed to frighten him away from the New Philosophy (vol. 1, ch. 9). Neither technique is effective in dissolving the tight bond between Waldorf and Lok. The shocking revelation that Zenna is Waldorf's real father also discloses why two peasants were parenting Waldorf: Zenna discovered his wife's adultery and assumed her child was not his (vol. 1, ch. 18). In terms of allegorizing the King family drama, here is an inversion of the King father's sexual betrayal but a similar repetition of paternal abandonment. Waldorf does not turn against the New Philosophy until his guilt becomes insupportable for all the damage he has caused to those close to him by the "poison" of the radical doctrines. The trope of "poison" is strongly developed in the novel where young women characters absorb the toxic skepticism about tradition and morality. As Don Herzog illustrates, the metaphor of a democratized print-culture "poisoning the minds" of innocent people is a pervasive one in the eighteenth century.[71] Waldorf ruins with his destructive ideas the three young women who actually care for him, an allegory for King leaving his wife and two daughters. Millroh and Sophia die from the disillusionment with religious, social, and sexual norms, while Helena out-libertines the male radicals but dies as embittered and as disappointed as the other two women. The climax of the plot is when a brother who is avenging a sister for whose death Waldorf is responsible kills in front of Waldorf the infant son of Helena and Waldorf (vol. 2, ch. 11). The novel's hero returns to Speyer ("Spire" in the text) where Helena sickens and dies, to be followed by Waldorf's predictable suicide (vol. 2, ch. 30–31). The final chapter has the traditionalist Zenna and the radical Lok disputing over the tragedy, but Lok loses his enthusiasm and so sinks into depression and death.

The parallel with *Frankenstein* is the trail of destruction left by the hero's good intentions and determination to realize bold new initiatives in philosophy. All of those closest to Waldorf are destroyed by his own words and actions. Of course *Frankenstein* is a much more complex novel with other units of meaning at play, but the crude anti-Jacobin cautionary tale is visible in Shelley's work. The Jewish themes get developed obliquely and subtextually. Waldorf witnesses an execution of heretics by the Spanish Inquisition, exclaiming: "*This* then is *religion!*"[72] Such a scene, which is also in *St. Leon*, shows that anti-Jacobin novels also express Jacobin meanings along the way toward proving the ultimate emptiness of philosophical radicalism. The Inquisition killing heretics is a *topos* in the antireligious discourse for which the novel has no Burkean confutation. There was no mystery about the identity of most of the Inquisition's victims, something about which a Sephardic Jew would have been especially aware. Lok, the villain of the novel, nevertheless gets many good speeches for which there is no rebuttal. Attacking religious violence, for example, Lok concludes that "*Real* devotion consists in acts of humanity, not in offering *human* sacrifices at the shrine of the Deity" (vol. 1, ch. 25).

If John King operates in the text as both the good and bad father, he becomes an idealized magician arguing against sexual libertinism—extremely wishful thinking—and the Moorish robber chief denouncing morality: "Interest is the pursuit of mortals—friendship is an empty name, a coward virtue....Self-preservation, self-interest, is the law of nature....Honour is the dream of madmen—the vision of folly—a casualty that depends on the opinions of others....Follow your passions; they were given for your happiness"[73] Following your passions regardless of the moral consequences is a major theme of gothic fictions like Charlotte King's *Zofloya* (1805); the genres of the anti-Jacobin and the gothic overlap in many respects. The philosophical robber chief suggests Godwin's similar character Raymond in *Caleb Williams* (1794), while Moorishness is an oblique way to figure Jewishness, especially in a Spanish setting with the Inquisition nearby. Moreover, King's daughters had to know of their father's criminal associations.

At another level, the Jewish tradition is as susceptible as Christianity to the corrosive skepticism and negative dialectic of the New Philosophy. That the three female converts to the New Philosophy come to a bad end reinforces the ideological disciplining of the reader. As Craciun points out, *Waldorf* like most anti-Jacobin novels rejects debate on principle as something anti-social and unpatriotic.[74]

Accordingly, it is not in the playing out of point/counterpoint in an extended argument that the narrative consists, but in student/mentor and child/father relationships that whole worldviews are accepted or rejected. The operating figures are not enlightenment and discovery but seduction and betrayal, trust and loss of faith.

Sophia's second novel, published by the spectacularly successful Minerva Press, is another anti-Jacobin fiction that carries forward the tropes of seduction and betrayal by merging an English domestic novel (first eighteen chapters and the concluding three) with a gothic Italian section (twenty-three chapters), both of which are accented as a roman à clef commenting on the King family drama. The English half of the novel polemically attacks the New Philosophy while simultaneously describing an attempt by a young woman to achieve an independent life first as a writer and then in the theatre as an actress. The heroine Cordelia is frustrated by incompetent literary mentors (Miss Milner, who seems to represent Mary Robinson), and disappointed in the Bath theatrical opportunities, most of which seem to be for prostitution. Cordelia seeks Wollstonecraftian independence but harshly condemns the "innovating doctrines" with their "pernicious effects."[75] The apparent contradiction is easily accounted for: she blames the cultural radicalism for her father's abandonment of the family for a more beautiful woman, Lady Lindern (Lady Lanesborough), and her two children (Augustus Butler-Danvers and the Marchioness of Mariscotti). If the old morality of loyalty to "Heaven" and "King" had prevailed, Mr. Arden (John King) would not have left his family of Rosina (Charlotte), Cordelia (Sophia), Collville (Charles), and their mother (Sara).[76]

The Italian gothic section revolves around three other characters who are symptomatic of the typical splitting of the gothic: Cordelia's lover in his good aspect is Mandani, and in his bad aspect Leoni; Cordelia herself has a wicked double, Lucinda, a libertine without a conscience. After many twists and turns in the plot Cordelia, who agreed to accompany Mandani to Italy only after Bath seemed too immoral, finally succumbs to Mandani's desire, even though she is aware of his problematic character. That Italy was where John King and his wife Sara got their divorce perhaps accounts for the setting of the sexual drama. Shortly after the sexual consummation Leoni kills Mandani and then imprisons Cordelia. Her imprisonment occasions some harsh anti-aristocratic rhetoric against legally sanctioned despotism and the *lettres de cachet*, which is ironic in an ostensibly anti-Jacobin text. Leoni finally allows her to leave prison with 5,000 pounds, money rightfully hers because it was Mandani's. Apparently

Cordelia's anxiety over prostitution has diminished because she accepts the compensation without a murmur, using it in London to reform her wayward brother. The novel concludes with a cozy family harmoniously resigned to their situation. The novel condemns "sophisticated education,"[77] as Rosina has made a vow of celibacy, and Cordelia herself seems content to stay home.

The hostility toward Mary Robinson, whom sister Charlotte idolized, is perhaps an expression of sibling rivalry. The mixture of blindness and insight throughout the novel is something that is typical in the work of both sisters and characteristic of the gothic and anti-Jacobin genres. Mr. Arden is not identified as Jewish, nor are any other characters, which suggests that Jewishness has been erased at least superficially from the novel. Sophia King, however, whose name is on the title page, is undeniably Jewish. She does not change her name until she marries Charles Fortnum. That she does not use a pseudonym for a popular novel published by Minerva Press is remarkable not because it suggests she was so courageous but that apparently the publisher did not think it would hurt sales; maybe the "Jew" King notoriety and the roman à clef elements interested readers back then as they do now.

Turning next to the four gothic novels of sister Charlotte, one has to pause at Sophia's *The Fatal Secret* (1801) for its confrontational preface, the gothic plot that her sister will use in her own fiction, and finally the numerous inserted poems authored by "Rosa Matilda," thus making this text a joint production. Complaining that anyone who shows intellect is marked like Cain as an outsider and homeless wanderer, Sophia chastises the reviewers who have unfairly treated her writing. Identifying herself as nineteen years old, she mocks two male literary authorities, first "sage Godwin" and then "Legislator Lewis," for using gothic conventions invented by women writers like Radcliffe but for escaping the opprobrium and contempt heaped on women writers for using those same conventions. Announcing she too will be partaking of the supernatural resources of that genre, she scorns any critical abuse on those grounds alone.[78] Not unlike *Northanger Abbey* (1818), where Jane Austen pays tribute to the insufficiently esteemed women novelists,[79] *The Fatal Secret* frames the gothic as possessing literary value that cannot be misogynistically dismissed. Sophia's novel, in a stylized medieval setting, shows Lady Altona on her twentieth birthday about to marry Orand, someone arranged for her, but she falls in love with a mysterious stranger, Morven, who turns out to be after several gruesome murders and supernatural fireworks, the Prince of Darkness himself, the suitable mate for a rebellious daughter discontented with what her family plans for her. Published around the same time as Coleridge was working on *Christabel*, a similar narrative in the style of the medieval ballad, Sophia's novel includes numerous of her sister's poems, some of which are later placed in her *Hours of Solitude* (1805). The basic plot structure of *Zofloya* (1806) Charlotte took from her sister Sophia, as the heroine Victoria also finds herself in love with a handsome man who is unfortunately Satan.

Most but not all the literary criticism on Charlotte's fiction has been on *Zofloya*, deemed either a racist and xenophobic work (Hoeveler) or a Sadeian subversion of gender and sexuality norms (Craciun).[80] Arguably the novel is both, for the plot punishes both virtue and vice almost equally, shunning the distributive rewards of poetic justice.[81] Although the novel's actions are sensationalistic, readers keep returning to the text because of the heroine Victoria, who demonstrates courage and inventiveness without any male assistance in escaping her prison at Il Bosco (ch. 7–8), and who resists the condescending mentorship of Berenza who tries to "new model" her (ch. 9). Indifferent to her virginity, she manipulates her supposed seducer into having sex (ch. 10). The second half of the novel concerns her attempt to free herself from the husband she no longer loves and capture the affections of Henriquez, her husband's brother. Minutely describing her desire and frustration, as well as the steps she and Zofloya, the Moorish servant, take to further her plans, the narrative provides the reader with an intricately drawn sexual consciousness unusual in women's fiction, except perhaps some of the Restoration/early eighteenth-century writing by women like Aphra Behn (1640–89) and Eliza Haywood (1693–1756). Haywood's *Fantomina* (1725), whose heroine displays inventive sexual initiative in her pursuit of the man she wants, is surely a precursor of *Zofloya* and Charlotte's other novels.

Also the novel intriguingly does not correspond to what Anne Mellor calls a female Romanticism accenting women's self-control and rational restraint to assume leadership in guiding the nation toward nonviolent reform.[82] Although *Zofloya* and her other novels follow in some respects what Mellor calls a masculine Romanticism of unrestrained individualistic rebellion linked with an emancipation of the imagination, Charlotte's fiction also never entertains affirmatively radical alternatives to established social practices and beliefs; indeed, some novels are deliberately anti-Jacobin, and all of them in some sense take the loyalist position against revolution and radical reform. As one critic points out, Charlotte's writing assumes the stance of neither the "proper lady" nor "didactic maternalism," two major options women writers take in the Romantic era.[83]

Because Victoria becomes a spectacular murderer near the end of the novel, stabbing her blonde rival Lilla dozens of times in a jealous and erotic frenzy (ch. 29), one might forget that for the first half of the narrative she behaves in a comparatively restrained manner. First, Victoria is hardly "depraved" before Satan/Zofloya arrives. Cleverly and boldly escaping the repressive confinement in her cousin's house, she has premarital sex with Berenza whom she then marries, and to whom she is faithful for five years. She resists Berenza's ambitious *Emile*-like plans to reshape her character; she repels these authoritarian schemes instinctively rather than philosophically like Wollstonecraft in *Vindication of the Rights of Woman*. She pretends to obey outwardly, but inwardly she has growing contempt for her witless husband. Earlier in the novel she had circumvented the coercive discipline established for her by her mother and Ardolph. In these respects, Victoria is a Romantic rebel, individualistically claiming an identity for herself not determined by parents and husband. The reader is made to share her subjective world and there is very little to object to until Henriquez and Zofloya come on the scene. The turning point is when she develops an immediate attraction to Henriquez and a disgust with Berenza (ch. 16). That in itself is not extraordinary, for one can sympathize with her unequal situation *vis à vis* her husband, who had many years of sexual freedom before settling down and she has had sex with one man, him. If the gothic premise is that Zofloya/Satan entered her world by way of dreams, then the reader leaves the world of ordinary moral judgments for the unconscious world of dreams, wishes, and nightmares. In this fictional space to experience those desires is to carry them out as well; to have those transgressive desires is the same as acting on them. "I wish my husband were dead" becomes, after a few vials of poison, a real deed of murder, just as "I wish my rival Lilla were dead" becomes a dagger to her breast.

If *Zofloya* is a critique of marriage, it is not a Wollstonecraftian one because it never develops or opposes doctrines. The novel invents a young woman who experiences authoritarian social practices designed to regulate her sexuality and the reader witnesses her subjectivity at work, including her "unconscious," a rather unlovely thing at times but perfectly ordinary and human. The cautionary tale that frames the narrative—wayward wives will go to hell for eternal punishment—is a convenient device but the novel is not earnestly moral in a religious way; there is no mistaking this novel for the writing of Hannah More and genuine Christian moralists. Her hideous deeds are more dreamlike than actual because the gothic permits exploring dreams and the unconscious. Insofar as social institutions figure in the novel, their power and legitimacy are not questioned. The absurd blaming of Victoria's mother Laurina, who is not nearly as bad as the satanic and sadistic Ardolph, a kind of Zofloya figure but German style, indicates the feeble degree of real social analysis.

The oblique Jewish references are considerable. The fifteenth century is when Jews were expelled from Spain and Portugal, from where her own ancestors probably came. The slippage between Moor and Jew in this context is fairly obvious, as both are "defeated" people hunted down by Catholic Spanish. Zofloya's expertise, passed down from ancestors, in herbs, drugs, chemistry and medicine sounds more Jewish than Muslim (ch. 18). Blackness being aligned with Jewishness is ancient and continues into the nineteenth century. Much of the novel's action is in Venice, scene of the most famous Jewish representation in English literature. Charlotte herself is a "Jessica." Victoria's rage at Berenza for thinking she was not good enough to marry because of her adulterous mother (ch. 16) is homologous with anger at antisemitic snobbery. The dichotomy of dark Victoria and light Lilla represents an ethnic competition on the level of sexual beauty; similarly, the eroticizing of Zofloya, the dark male body, expands and relativizes the ideal of male attractiveness.

Charlotte's first novel, *Confessions of the Nun of St. Omer* (1805), is not as spectacular and sensationalistic as *Zofloya*, perhaps a reason for its neglect, but it has strengths not evident in her sister's fiction, especially the ability to explore the emotional complexities of sexual relationships, something Charlotte does also in her last two novels. The title alludes to Rousseau's notorious *Confessions* (1782), considered an immoral book in the England of the early nineteenth century because of the frank revelations about sexuality. Rousseau's emotional excesses and lack of restraint were read onto the violent excesses of the French Revolution, of which he was considered the father. Although Rousseau's example authorizes the novel's bold expression of sexual experiences, the anti-Jacobin construction of Rousseau necessitates that emotional intemperance be treated harshly, as it is in Charlotte's *Confessions*, where the heroine Cazire does penance in a convent for the rest of her life for her sexual sins. Percy Bysshe Shelley's first book of poetry, entitled *Original Poetry by Victor and Cazire* (1810), is one of many tributes the most famous Romantic poets made to Charlotte "Dacre," whose *Hours of Solitude* (1805) helped shape Byron's own first volume of poetry, *Hours of Idleness* (1807). Later in their careers the male poets are anxious to erase their debt to Charlotte, thus repeating a pattern of taking what is needed from women writers and then concealing how it was taken—something like a debtor who does not pay back his loan.[84]

Structured as a letter to her son as an apology and explanatory justification, the novel identifies two kinds of influence that can lead to immoral actions: bad parenting and bad reading. The first is a Rousseauvian truism, and the second became a staple in the anti-Jacobin and loyalist campaign against revolutionary and liberal ideas. Cazire points to Countess Rosendorf, a freethinker and feminist, as the source of all her troubles because she lured her father away from Cazire's mother (ch. 1). The biographical subtext is obvious: Countess Rosendorf is Lady Lanesborough, and her two children whom Cazire loathes are Lanesborough's son and daughter. Another biographical subtext, not as obvious, is her relationship with the editor of the *Morning Post*, Nicholas Byrne, who was married and with whom she had their first child in 1806, shortly after the novel was published. Speaking the rhetoric of the New Philosophy, the Countess sets a treacherous example for the impressionable Cazire. Unhappy with her family situation, she takes refuge in reading, "my chief delight." The novel depicts reading as dangerously seductive: "whatever was calculated to inflame the senses, and enervate the heart to *rational* pleasures, was drawn with dangerous fascination."[85] Unsupervised and promiscuous reading poorly trains her for the temptations and difficulties of courtship. A charming proponent of the Godwinian philosophy, Fribourg, wins her heart, but she tries to resist his attractions because he is married. Another suitor, Lindorf, pretends to be unmarried, impregnates and abandons her. She is rescued by a childhood friend, St. Elmer, a man of benevolence who marries her and accepts her child. Disaster follows when Fribourg, now a widower, comes to live with the St. Elmer family and the inevitable infidelity leads to further catastrophe, as Fribourg kills first St. Elmer and then himself. Unable to sustain the guilt and remorse, she gives her child to her mother to raise and enters a convent to do penance for her sins.

An anti-Jacobin novel with debates on religion and politics between the loyalist Cazire and the Godwinian Fribourg (vol. 1, ch. 14), it excels not in ideological combat but in the ebb and flow of emotional turmoil. Cazire resists falling in love, reflects on her desires and moral choices, is compelled by sensations, experiences guilt and self-loathing, and so on. With St. Elmer, the benevolent friend from childhood, she feels so morally inferior that she does not desire him sexually, for which she feels guilty. The infidelity with Fribourg is developed step by step, with various moments of guilt, resolution to resist, and sensations of desire. At one point she expresses her feelings in a letter, then reflects on those feelings, turning them over this way and that, adding yet another layer of affective discourse. She wants Fribourg to return to his family, but she does not know if she tells the truth that she loves him, her telling will make it easier or harder for him to do the right thing. If she lies, she will lose whatever influence she has. But is she not just creating a trap for herself by conversing with and writing to him? And so it goes, as the reader witnesses a passionate, intelligent, morally sensitive young woman reacting and thinking during a difficult love affair (vol. 2, ch. 2). The novel records only one episode of intentional adultery, for which Cazire experiences crushing guilt and remorse; the sex with Lindorf, which was under false pretenses, is outside the moral calculus. The novel attends to the consciousness of Cazire, her daily trials of temptation and moral action; the reader hears her thinking about her desires, recording her physical feelings, and reflecting on her experience. Charlotte as a writer lyricizes the novel by representing the subjective world of her heroines so minutely, and as I will show later, she novelizes her lyrical poetry. Charlotte literally makes her novel lyrical by inserting poetry under the guise of Cazire expressing herself in that form.

Charlotte's other two novels, *The Libertine* (1807) and *The Passions* (1811), similarly develop with depth and complexity the subjectivity of the heroines. Gabrielle, daughter of a Rousseauvian who distrusts society, loves a libertine Angelo, who before killing himself in the last chapter has two children with the heroine. To illustrate redundantly the novel's lessons that bad parenting—in this case caused by the father's sexual promiscuity—produces wretched offspring, both of their children have miserable lives, with daughter Agnes headed to the convent and son Felix a thief on the way to the hangman. The novel's section taking place in Naples where Gabrielle, disguised as a swarthy male servant, stays close to her beloved libertine Angelo, has some of the best writing Charlotte produced. Like the cross-dressing heroines of Shakespeare's comedies (including Portia), Gabrielle exercises the freedom permitted only to males and finds herself in awkward sexual situations, such as being the object of women's erotic attention (her rival Oriana, Angelo's mistress). Her disguise and masculine freedom also permit her a wider scope for acquiring useful information about people's actions and motives. Using her knowledge to advance her interests in ways she cannot as a woman, the cross-dressed Gabrielle allegorizes the woman writer who can move freely in fiction where she is barred

in real life. The disguised Gabrielle also suggests *Fantomina*'s heroine who finds a new identity in the freedom produced by theatrical
disguise and performance. In a delightful episode illustrating the
ironies of theatricality, Gabrielle's libertine Angelo becomes infatuated with Paulina, the daughter of a poor fisherman. He falls in love
with her performance of youthful, naïve innocence and helplessness,
when in fact she is deliberately seducing him, whom she leaves for a
wealthier man. In her final letter to Angelo she anticipates his anger
at her deception; her reply resonates beyond the specific situation:
"You loved the deception, which, till now, I suffered you to fancy
real: and, in the midst of your invectives against me, remember, that
for once at least I have dealt with you sincerely."[86]

The final novel, *The Passions*, has Charlotte's most memorable villain, the beautiful Countess Appollonia Zulmer, and her most fully
realized heroine, the virtuous Julia who is destroyed by the conflict
between her morality and her passions. The whole novel, modeled
after Rousseau's *Julie*, includes a Count Wiemar after Rousseau's
Wolmar. As the Countess tries to get the innocent Julia to read
Rousseau's novel, she confides to her fellow libertine:

> There is not in my estimation a more dangerous work extant, or one
> better calculated for the purposes of seduction: for I defy the female,
> however pure in her heart, however chaste in her ideas she may be,
> before reading this book, to remain wholly unaffected, and unim-
> pressed by its perusal. I aver that it is utterly impossible so many
> highly-coloured and voluptuous images as are there depicted, can be
> permitted to take their passage through the mind, and leave no stain
> behind.[87]

In Charlotte's fiction the imagination consoles, provides pleasure and
allows entry of unwanted, dangerous images that overcome a stable
moral identity. Both sisters assume a Lockean metaphysics of radical
empiricism as it applies to reading and other forms of discourse.

In another letter to her libertine confidante and former governess,
Countess Zulmer exults over the success of her interventions:

> How much, my dearest gouvernante, are we indebted to Voltaire,
> Rousseau, Helvetius, Diderot! those writers have been of no small
> service to me. They have not, in the profundity of their good will
> towards mankind, benefited less the cause of morality than of philoso-
> phy. Books have been no small engines of my skill, in relaxing by their
> seducing doctrines the fibres of my fair one's mind. When I found
> my arguments fail, or that I was at a stand for new ones, a volume of

philosophy was the force I rallied, and it always proved an host [helpful agent] in my favour.[88]

Philosophy can weaken traditional restraints because human nature is strongly irrational and seeks some excuse to pursue pleasure. Rozendorf, the novel's voice of reason and responsibility, cautions his friend Darlowitz who is experiencing an adulterous obsession:

> The *Passions* may be called the wild horses of the soul; virtue alone can tame or keep them in subjection; but if once they overpower and hurl her from her height, fiercely they announce their dreadful victory, and drag the prostrate soul even to perdition.[89]

Alluding to Plato's famous metaphor in *Phaedrus* of the horses and chariot to figure how the mind works, Rozendorf warns his friend that the passions are so powerful that granting them much freedom will result in moral catastrophe.

The scheming Countess Zulmer, imitating the Marquise de Merteuil from *Les Liaisons Dangereuses* (1782), cleverly destroys her rival Amelia with subtle manipulations and skilful interventions because the characters are already oriented to do the immoral things the Marquise wants them to do. It takes only a little pushing to get things headed in the wrong direction to destroy two marriages. Although *The Passions*, an anti-Jacobin text to its core, thoroughly repudiates Rousseau and the New Philosophy, the novel shows that family stability rests on a weak foundation because of ordinary human frailties. The wicked Countess Zulmer likens herself to Satan,[90] but she does not use any supernatural tricks to effect her designs. Ordinary human nature is quite enough; there is no need for a Zofloya. The powerful and unpredictable inclinations fit into established institutions only with great care and difficulty. Although the evil Countess comes to a bad end, she has a fairly easy time disrupting the harmony of two families.

Charlotte's fiction, consistently anti-Jacobin, connects her father's new wife Lady Lanesborough with the modernizing trends of the New Philosophy that destroys customary family relationships, religious faith, and moral certainties. The corrosive skepticism and individualism, by weakening restraints on the selfish pursuit of pleasure, victimize women who are seduced, betrayed, impregnated, and abandoned. Both Sophia and Charlotte target their father's friend Godwin opportunistically, as the loyalist writers scapegoated him routinely, but also to avoid criticizing their father, whom they shield from harsh criticism by deflecting it elsewhere. If Judaism is a religious faith with moral truths constituting its traditional teachings, then the New Philosophy is anti-Jewish, but neither sister in poem or novel makes a direct reference, positive or negative, to Judaism. When Christianity is discussed, it is never expressed in the Evangelical terms of Christ becoming a personal savior. Indeed, in all the sisters' vignettes of young women suffering from betrayal and abandonment, there is not a single instance of turning to the consolations of Christian faith. The convent in Charlotte's novels is a figure for the complete extirpation of sexual desire and removal from social and sexual interaction, the female version of the misanthropic retreat. The absence of Christian resolutions in the King novels expresses a presence of Judaism. A staple of loyalist and anti-Jacobin writing is an aggressive and explicit Christianity, which in the King fiction is always muted.

As Charlotte's fiction displays a lyricization of the novel, so her poetry shows a novelization of the lyric. The sisters' poetry volume, *Trifles of Helicon* (1798), shares with their novels the same moral-psychological preoccupations. One of Charlotte's poems, "Sonnet. To Prudence," rejects one of the standard virtues, especially for young women, because it creates suspicion and checks spontaneous generosity.

> Hence, Prudence! bane of ev'ry virtuous deed,
>   Child of cold Prejudice and selfish Fear,
>   Insensible to Sorrow's bitter tear,
> Wrung from the heart thou bid'st unpitied bleed![91]

The lyrical subject created by Charlotte's poetry demands a subjective responsiveness that honestly attends to feelings and impressions. Prudence may be sensible advice delivered by Rozendorf to the infatuated Darlowitz in *The Passions*, but such a virtue if adopted by the lyrical voice would be death. The dilemma for Charlotte is that what most sustains lyrical expression is most fatal to the social morality she tries to uphold. She never finds a solution to this contradiction, which is at the core of her writing's energy.

Charlotte's poetic Muse and role model do not fit well within a loyalist and anti-Jacobin framework because Mary Robinson (1757–1800)—actress and mistress of the Prince Regent and several prominent aristocrats, feminist friend of Wollstonecraft and Mary Hays—was anything but the darling of the cultural conservatives. Intimately connected at one time with Charlotte's father, "Perdita"

Robinson embodied theatricality in different venues. Displaying herself elegantly dressed in public at the theatre and elsewhere in London, she used her public image and notoriety in her own writing.[92] As a Della Cruscan poet, Laura Maria was her first role, as she later assumed other identities like Tabitha Bramble and Oberon in her lyrical poetry of the 1790s.[93] The Rosa Matilda and Charlotte Dacre role-playing that Charlotte adopted served her throughout her whole literary career because as a writer with a mask and disguise she was freer to invent and express than she would have been *in propria persona*. Matilda is the notorious character in Matthew Lewis's *The Monk* (1796), the woman disguised as a male monk in order to seduce Ambrosio to further Satan's plans. Just in case readers did not realize the full intentions of her pseudonym, Charlotte dedicated her first novel to Matthew Lewis.

The *Hours of Solitude* has a poem of tribute, "To the Shade of Mary Robinson," which laments that the poet did not know her while she was alive but celebrates her strength in defying her critics. Thus far a conventional elegy, but then the poem turns to call up Robinson's presence to provide comfort and support for the poet.

> Oh! say, from thy cold, narrow bed, lovely Mary,
>   Say, couldst thou not wander, to smile upon me?
> Oh! why not, sometimes, in thy form light and airy,
>   Deign in the deep wild my companion to be?
>
> Oh! why not, sometimes, when I wander in sadness,
>   Glide distant before me—seen dim thro' the trees?
> Or how would my heart bound with mystical gladness
>   If thy *voice* were heard, sounding sweet in the breeze!
>
> Or why not, o'ershadow'd by yon drooping willow,
>   At eve let me mark thee reclining beneath?
> Or by moonlight upborne, on the edge of the billow,
>   Fantastic, and light as of zephyr the breath?

The poem generates images of vivid interaction between lyrical subject and the ghost of Mary in the form of a prayer and incantation. What in gothic fiction would be a frightening and uncanny spirit is here the wished-for presence of a maternal Muse. The poem concludes:

> Then grant, O great God! since to Mary 'twas given
>   *Most* perfect among erring mortals to be,
> That chief of thy slaves she may serve thee in heaven,
>   And bear, when I die, my frail spirit to thee.[94]

In the poetic world created here, "Matilda" the lyrical subject finds religious consolation in imagining Mary one of God's favorites whose errors are forgiven. The presence of Robinson as Muse and precursor strengthens the poet's literary resolve and solidifies her poetic identity. The antithetical companion poem that closes volume one of *Hours of Solitude* clarifies the poet's position by rejecting the model of "The Female Philosopher," the poem's addressee, who inspires but does not feel erotic attachments and romantic affections. Stoicism is too high a price to purchase the kind of Wollstonecraftian independence associated with the female philosopher.

> Life is a darksome and a dreary day,
>   The solitary wretch no pleasure knows;
> Love is the star that lights him on his way,
>   And guides him on to pleasure and repose.[95]

The choice for the lyrical subject is between a philosophical stoicism and a wild romanticism of spectacular Robinsonian theatricality. There is no option for the pious Christian, the Proper Lady, and the moral teacher.

The persona of the *Hours of Solitude* is a novelistic character who undergoes various intense experiences usually in sexual relationships. The volume attends to the ages at which various poems were written, to give a historical account of the lyrical subject's development over time. Blurring the lines between invented female characters, performative lyrical voice, poet as inventor and the real individual Charlotte King, the *Hours of Solitude* becomes a novel of sensibility as well as a *Kuenstlerroman*. Imitating the Robinson example of using private experience for public consumption, Charlotte represents her persona as losing her sexual innocence and undergoing a series of romantic adventures. The very first poem, "The Triumph of Pleasure," written at age sixteen, receives special attention because it is the first and because she has a lengthy appendix of juvenilia composed when she was thirteen through fifteen. The volume is presenting as a fully adult expression the work of a sixteen year old, who in this allegory as "Beauty" is tempted by Pleasure and Love, after being warned by Age to take a rational path. Instead she chooses Pleasure and Love, introducing the dominant theme of the whole volume: a woman's sexual "fall," "ruin," and "redemption," usually within passion itself. The second poem, "The Exile," also composed at sixteen, represents in the third person a suicidal young woman in despair, ruined by a man who betrayed her. "In secret let my anguish'd bosom swell, / In secret all my faults and sorrows dwell!"[96] Expressing remorse, guilt, and the loneliness of solitude, the frustrated female speaker wants "vengeance" and "justice" but is certain she will not find either. Another poem, "Passion Uninspired by Sentiment," is one of many dialogic poems in the Della Cruscan tradition of responding to another voice, in this case *Addressed to him who denied their existing together.*" The sixteen-line poem is short enough to reproduce in its entirety.

> Oh! Passion, seducer of heart and of soul!
>   Thou transport tyrannic! half pleasure, half pain!
> Why consum'st thou the breast with such madd'ning controul?
>   Fly quickly—yet, ah! come as quickly again.
> Without thee, what's life but a wilderness drear,
>   Or a chill, gloomy vale, where stern apathy reigns?
> Like Phoebus, thy vivid refulgence can cheer,
>   And brighten, in rapture, e'en Memory's pains.
> When pleasure seduces the wild throbbing heart
>   In moments ecstatic of tender excess,
> When Fancy refines, and when Passion takes part,
>   The lover existence too fondly may bless.
> Yet Passion alone, to the delicate mind,
>   Aspires not a simple *sensation* above;
> Unless sentiment yield it an ardour refin'd,
>   It degrades, not ennobles the essence of love.[97]

In a poem that makes the words "seduction," "pain," and "excess" have affirmative connotations, the reader knows the lyrical subject is not valorizing self-control and restraint, the common moral instruction in loyalist and anti-Jacobin writing by women, clearly not the model for King's verse. Rather, the poem's four rhymed quatrains of abab indicate Charlotte's strong affiliation with another Charlotte, Charlotte Smith whose *Elegiac Sonnets* (1783) established the Shakespearean sonnet of sensibility as one of the most popular genres of the Romantic era. Smith's attention to personal feeling, the immediacy of the moment, interaction with the landscape, and melancholy reflection on the past influenced many others not just Charlotte King.

Finally, Charlotte's "The Sovereignty of Love," another explicitly dialogic poem addressed to an imagined interlocutor, vindicates the lyrical subject's embrace of intensity over security and caution. "O! I have lov'd to such a mad excess," she proudly declares. "How oft the solitary shade I've sought, / To brood with pleasure o'er my own fond thought! / Reason has stagger'd on her trembling throne, / And wild imagination reign'd alone."[98] This lyrical voice, situated in one of her four novels, would find deadly disappointment before too long, victimized by a libertine or betrayed by a weak lover and thwarted by a hostile, misogynistic society. In the poetry, however, even death and betrayal provoke lyrical triumphs and elegiac melancholy, the bittersweet beauty of defeat.

Conclusion

As Shakespeare's Jessica occupies two worlds in a hybridized state of ambivalence, so too the King sisters and many of the literary descendants of Shylock's daughter. The King daughters like their father enter the Christian world as literary adventurers, marry Gentiles, and assimilate to the English culture, but like their father they also register marks of difference, notably the absence of explicitly Christian themes in any of their loyalist and anti-Jacobin writing. The fundamental contradiction of Charlotte's work between a literary commitment to full imaginative expression and psychological description and a political commitment to the traditional values undermined by the Enlightenment and the democratic revolutions in America and France reflects the circumstances of her parents' divorce and her ideological interpretation of what caused it. The contradiction begins with Jessica herself, who demonstrates extraordinary courage and willfulness in leaving her home and community, but who must fit into a Christian world where women's passivity and obedience to masculine authority are primary virtues. The suspicion is that the willfulness of the convert does not cease after joining the new community, a suspicion one sees expressed in the conversionist fiction as well. One can point to Lytton's Leila, who still loves her handsome Muslim warrior even as she is about to take the nun's veil, as the symbol for the culture's ambivalence about Jessica.

CHAPTER 6

EXILES AND PROPHETS

The story is simple in its bare outlines. A political nation and civilization with a thriving literature occupied the land of Israel for about a thousand years, interrupted by the loss of the northern kingdom to Assyria in the eighth century BCE and by the Babylonian Exile of the sixth century BCE. The Roman Empire delivered the catastrophic defeat in 70 CE when Jews were dispersed to other parts of the Near East, North Africa, the Iberian Peninsula and Europe. Although Jews continued in parts of Israel—Hebron, Jerusalem, Safed, and Tiberias—more or less continuously with fluctuating population numbers all during the time of the Diaspora, they lived without political sovereignty. Rabbinic Judaism adjusted to the new conditions but envisioned a messianic gathering of the exiles, return to Zion and rebuilding the Temple.[1] Although there were a few moments of enthusiasm like the movement sparked by the false messiah Shabbatai Zevi (1626–76), modern Zionism dates from the latter half of the nineteenth century.[2]

The Christian myth of the Wandering Jew is an ideological rendering of Jewish history from a partisan Christian perspective to account for the Diaspora and to justify Christian oppression of Jews and contempt for Judaism. The core story, of which there is a written account from the sixth century CE, is that a Jew, rather than assisting Jesus on his way to Calvary, taunts him with cruel words—"Walk faster!" Jesus replies, "You will walk until I come again."[3] Both a mythological character and an allegory for all Israel, the Wandering Jew is a thoroughly antisemitic construction until the eighteenth century when versions of the story start to express sympathy for the deathless sufferer who begins to represent humanity. The myth has a spectacular textual history from the early Middle Ages up through the nineteenth century when it becomes enlisted in the conflict over Jewish emancipation. The Wandering Jew, whose primary cultural function has been to express Christian European religious anxieties, was available for revisionary appropriation by Romantic writers like Godwin, Byron, Coleridge, Wordsworth and Percy Shelley who make the figure a symbol of social and metaphysical alienation.

A related literary topos, the Fall of Jerusalem, attracted Romantic writers influenced by the Higher Criticism of the Bible, according to E.S. Shaffer, who reads *Kubla Khan* as Coleridge's fragmentary epic that substituted for the unwritten epic he could never manage to create on the master theme of his age. The Fall of Jerusalem was a historic moment when East met West, Judaism mixed with Christianity, Hellenism with Roman imperialism; the Fall addressed Romantic modernity as no other historical event could.[4] It is not, however, just philosophically sophisticated writers like Coleridge who are drawn to the Fall of Jerusalem, for as Eitan Bar-Yosef has shown recently, mainstream English Protestant culture was fascinated with the Holy Land as it was mediated through biblical narratives and historical reconstructions. Quite independent of imperial designs on the land, popular English Orientalism cathected with the biblical terrain at a literal level in terms of physical visits (which often disillusioned the visitors), archaeological studies, and representations of the destroyed Temple. Coleridge and his fellow intellectuals who no longer read the Bible literally required a vigorous symbolic translation of divine revelation to salvage scripture from complete secularization, but the middle-class consumers of Holy Land books and paraphernalia assumed they were in touch with something transcendently real.[5]

The Fall of Jerusalem and the notion of a New Jerusalem resonated with Romantic-era public opinion at large and the other Romantic writers as well. For Christians the theological-historical drama involves the return of the Messiah, not his initial appearance. For English Protestants the apocalyptic and millenarian performance is the interplay between prophetic biblical texts—Revelation, Isaiah, Daniel—and the unfolding events of history guided by God. The astonishing episodes of the French Revolution, each radical change more startling than the next, convinced sober Unitarians like Joseph Priestley (1733–1804) that the prophecies of the Book of Daniel were coming to be realized in the living moment.[6] More politically radical religious enthusiasts like Richard Brothers (1757–1824), who challenged royal authority, were imprisoned, and more plebeian prophets of the divine word like Joanna Southcott (1750–1814) attracted thousands of followers. Attracted by the ideas of a Mosaic Commonwealth and egalitarian concepts of justice, some writers, under the pressure of the French Revolution that illustrated it was possible to "new-model" the social world, like Thomas Spence, Coleridge, and Lord George Gordon synthesized a radical politics out of elements from Jewish scripture.

In the Romantic era different conceptions of biblical prophecy seek legitimacy. The rival positions of two eighteenth-century theological writers define what is at stake: for Thomas Sherlock (1677–1761) prophecy is poetic and approximate because God is not obligated to be precise; for William Whiston (1667–1752), prophecy has only one meaning, and if the predicted outcome is not realized in the actual historical world, the fault rests with corruptions of the text.[7] From the Sherlock notion of indeterminate prophecy come formulations like William Blake's well-known passage in his marginalia to Bishop Watson's *An Apology for the Bible*:

> Prophets in the modern sense of the word have never existed Jonah was no prophet in the modern sense for his prophecy of Nineveh failed Every honest man is a Prophet he utters his opinion both of private & public matters / Thus / If you go on So / the result is So / He never says such a thing shall happen let you do what you will.[8]

The Whiston approach to prophecy, however, had many adherents who teased out historical predictions from Isaiah, the Book of Daniel, and especially Revelation. Some eighteenth-century interpreters, notoriously the Hutchinsonians, were not reluctant either to "correct" the biblical text when it seemed to be corrupted. The philological dispute was both a genuine scholarly search, using scientific methods to achieve the most reliable biblical text, and a fiercely sectarian battle over determining God's word.[9]

Jews such as David Levi (1742–1801) and Solomon Bennett (1761–1838) challenged the Christian reading of biblical prophecy at several levels, the Hebrew meaning of the biblical text itself and the supercessionist assumptions of Jewish inferiority that pervade most Protestant interpretations. Jewish women also claimed within certain gendered limitations a prophetic authority to criticize prevailing social and religious practices. The Jewish position on exile diverged from that of Byron and Shelley, who fashioned it as an empowering stance from which to satirize and judge a society that had scorned them. While not ruling out a messianic moment when a return to Zion could be made, Jews sought to consolidate their status as English citizens not yet granted their full civil liberties, while they insisted that their exercise of Judaism did not constitute a repudiation of English identity. This chapter has two sections, the Hebrew Commonwealth (Spence and Gordon), and the Daughters of Miriam and Huldah (Lyon, Moss sisters, and Aguilar).

HEBREW COMMONWEALTH

If we except the Spartan, the Jewish has been the only Republic that can consistently boast of Liberty and Equality.

S.T. Coleridge, "Lecture 2,"
Lectures on Revealed Religion *(1795)*[10]

One source of Coleridge's political radicalism in the 1790s was the tradition of the Mosaic republic, a divinely instituted polity with ideal and historical qualities. He gave concentrated attention to the Hebrew Commonwealth in a lecture of May, 1795, in Bristol, where he mixes harsh judgments against actual Jews—"a people of a stupid and earthy imagination and blindly addicted to idolatrous Rites"—with supercessionist ideas on Judaism as a "preparatory" religion. Making clear he is not giving comfort to Jews or Judaism, he teases out of Leviticus and other biblical texts radical political ideas about property, equality, and representative democracy. His radical Christian politics has a huge debt to Jewish scripture, as he fully acknowledges.[11] Nicholas Roe has described vividly how exactly Coleridge, with his friend Wordsworth, fashioned a radical politics during the revolutionary decade, and I will not repeat what he says in that splendid study.[12] I wish to point out that Coleridge, even when he comes closest to Jewish ideas, feels compelled to separate himself roughly from what he finds appealing, performing the characteristic ambivalence of the British culture toward Jewishness.

Thomas Spence (1750–1814) and Lord George Gordon (1751–93) also found in Jewish scripture an inspiring set of social ideals applicable to the social world in which they lived. Spence, almost as well acquainted with Enlightenment and republican literature as Coleridge, paid tribute to James Harrington especially for the outlines of his land reform proposal (see ch. 2). For Spence, however, the center of his political program was Leviticus 25 and the biblical treatment of property as belonging to God rather than individual humans. Lord George Gordon came to his close identification with Judaism's social ideals of justice through his passionate Protestantism and fanatical anti-Catholicism. One of the most famous converts to

Judaism, Gordon was arrested and jailed for his libels against the Queen of France during the Diamond Necklace scandal with which he was involved along with his friend Cagliostro, who was imprisoned and tortured by the Inquisition. From Gordon's own jail cell he spoke out boldly for prison reform and Jewish civil rights across Europe.

Thomas Spence[13]

The eponymous leader of a land reform movement, Spence experienced success popularizing his ideas and suffered considerable repression. The worst repression Spence endured in Newcastle-upon-Tyne was his expulsion from the Philosophical Society for publishing a cheap edition of his land plan lecture, but otherwise he conducted his work as an English teacher and participated in the city's political culture. London was not so tolerant. He was arrested on seven separate occasions, being released fairly promptly or acquitted five times (December 6, 1792; December 10, 1792; January 1793 arrested then acquitted in February 1793; December 1793, arrested and acquitted; in 1798 he was arrested for his suspected role in the United Englishmen group, but he was released shortly afterward without being charged with any crime). In two instances he spent considerable time in jail. On May 20, 1794 he was arrested as part of the repression of radicals leading to the treason trials; he spent seven months in jail before being released. Shortly after the government allowed the suspension of habeas corpus to lapse, he was arrested yet again, this time for publishing one of his most accomplished works, *Restorer of Society to Its Natural State*. Upon being convicted he spent a year in Shrewsbury Gaol where his health suffered, and he was fined 20 pounds and charged 500 pounds security for good behavior for five years.

He was born to a large laboring-class family—one of nineteen children—in 1750 in the northeastern part of England, Newcastle-on-Tyne. Spence's father, who came to Newcastle from Aberdeen, Scotland in 1739, taught his children to read and interpret the Bible while they all worked. "My father used to make my brothers and me read the Bible to him while working in his business and at the end of every chapter encouraged us to give our opinions on what we had just read. By these means I acquired an early habit of reflecting on every occurrence which passed before me as well as on what I read."[14] One informing context for Spence's writing is biblical, especially the ways radical Dissent interpreted the Bible, highlighting messages of social justice from the Pentateuch, prophets, and apostles. According to

H.T. Dickinson, "Although he later denounced religion as a delusion, Thomas Spence's writings were always replete with Biblical references and shaped by a millennial vision."[15] Spence as a young man became an associate of an "extreme Presbyterian," the Reverend James Murray (1732–82) from 1765 until Murray's death. "Murray taught Thomas Spence to see the stark contrast between biblical promise and harsh social reality."[16] Spence's texts like William Blake's are saturated with biblical references, allusions, influences, and even cadences. To illustrate how Spence uses the Bible I will discuss some prose works and then some of his songs.

In the 1796 "Coffee-House Dialogue" in *The Reign of Felicity*, Spence stages a discussion among a farmer, clergyman, courtier, and esquire. They debate how best to "civilize" the native Americans without conquering them. Although the dialogue concludes inevitably that the Spencean land reform system is the only way to insure the natives of their independence while enjoying the benefits of civilized culture, each of the four participants in the dialogue makes cogent points along the way. In searching for ethical models by which to formulate ideas about the natives, the dialogue turns to the Bible, rejecting pointedly the lesson of the Gibeonites who purchased their lives only at the price of remaining in perpetuity "hewers of wood and drawers of water." Unlike the Deists who use the biblical account of the conquest of Canaan to illustrate Jewish evil, Spence sees in the Book of Joshua some moral tension to reflect upon conquest in general. Invasions and conquests are the norm: the "Israelites, the Romans, the Goths, the Vandals, the Saxons, the Danes, the Normans, the Spaniards, the English" all were conquerors who dominated the original inhabitants. Spence refuses, however, to equate conquest with "progress." With Swiftian sarcasm, Spence writes that conquest as a "way of instructing mankind appears indeed very harsh, but their conquerors always endeavoured to soothe their sorrows with the consolations of religion, which they introduced at the same time."[17]

Just as Blake insisted that the Bible was the source of the true sublime, the most exemplary literary text far superior to classical literary models, so does Spence promote biblical reading for cultural political reasons. One of his most remarkable works, written in London, is the *Pronouncing and Foreigners' Bible*, whose full title I reproduce:

> containing the Old and New Testament being, not only the properest book for establishing a uniform and permanent manner of speaking, the most sonorous, harmonious and agreeable English and also infinitely perferable to any introductory book hitherto contrived for

teaching children or grown persons upon whose mother-tongue it is, *but* is likewise peculiarly calculated to render English universal, for by this book foreigners of any country may be taught to read English much easier than their own respective languages; recommended as the most proper book for Sunday Schools, by T. Spence, Teacher of English, London.[18]

This passage condenses a number of Spencean preoccupations: his phonetic spelling system by which he hopes to increase plebeian literacy, Bible-reading as cultural empowerment, and the Bible itself as a literary model that blurs the writing/speech distinction. Radical linguistic theory, according to Olivia Smith, stresses the continuity between speech and writing, with speech dominant, thus providing an alternative to the Johnsonian view of language as principally rooted in classical writing.[19] There is here the parallel with Blake's own poetics that, as in the Preface to *Milton,* condemned the "artifice" of classicism to the "Sublime of the Bible."[20]

Because songs were performed at political meetings held at demonstrations and in taverns, they effectively passed on the Spencean ideas to larger numbers of people. An effective and prolific songwriter, Spence used songs as one of the principal means of spreading his political ideas. According to Marcus Wood, Spence had "a gift for compact and striking language" and his verse displayed an "impressive variety of metric forms."[21] Whether through the *Song Book* or individual songs on a single sheet sold or distributed in the street or circulated in a tavern as drinking songs, Spence exploited the form with considerable sophistication. The government recognized the political song as a dangerous vehicle for subversive expression. The 1801 government report on Spence and the Spenceans makes frequent mention of the "treasonable and seditious" sentiments conveyed in the "toasts and songs."[22] His songs acquaint his audience with the unfamiliar details of the Spencean critique and plan, persuade them of its correctness, and urge them to act accordingly. Spence's songs, accommodating the audience's presuppositions as much as possible, employ a popular language to draw upon the authority of the Bible for overturning the aristocratic system of land ownership. He also makes reference to natural law, popular culture, and the Saxon myth of liberty, but the Bible has a stronger persuasiveness than anything else. I want to discuss in depth the "Jubilee Hymn" (1793), which appeals mostly to biblical precedent.

P.M. Ashraf points to a religious influence on Spence's songwriting by way of the Glassites' innovative hymn-singing. "The Glassites introduced a variety of popular verse forms and the more lively metres of secular songs and set them to traditional tunes rather than ecclesiastical music." Consistent with their theology, the hymns of the Glassites were "an affirmation of equality."[23] Spence's brother Jeremiah was a leading figure in the Newcastle congregation, and James Murray, Spence's mentor, was sympathetic to Glassite doctrines.[24] The Newcastle Glassites under the leadership of Spence's brother practice the "most complete republican equality." The congregants "administer the Lord's Supper weekly, dine together every Sabbath day, use the kiss of charity, wash each other's feet, abstain from blood and things strangled, and hold the community of goods, so for that every one is to consider all that he has in his possession liable to the calls of the poor of the church. Their ministers are mostly tradesmen."[25] Abstaining from blood and strangled things reflects the influence of Jewish scripture and kashrut norms, perhaps the Noahide laws of Genesis.

Spence's religious idiom derives from a line of influence from seventeenth-century radical Dissent by way of Murray and the Glassites. Godwin too was also influenced by the Glassites (through the Sandemanians), but the former Calvinist minister tried strenuously to extirpate religion for the sake of his new secular rationalism.[26] Spence in contrast integrated different intellectual traditions, adding new sources of language to the old rather than violently suppressing the old. The degree to which Spence's religious idiom is saturated with Old Testament references is a sign of his radical Dissent intellectual ancestry. So Hebraic is Spence's style that even when he quotes the "Golden Rule" he does so not using the positive formulations of the New Testament (Matthew 7:12 and Luke 6:31) but the negative constructions of Akiva, Hillel and Tobit 4:15: "Do not [do] to another what you would not wish done to yourself."[27]

Spence's "Jubilee Hymn" (1794), his most well-known work, negotiates the rhetorical difficulties of advocating radical land reform by means of a religious idiom.[28] Associating the biblical Jubilee with social ownership of land is not unique with Spence (there are precedents in Moses Lowman and James Harrington), but Spence was the one to popularize the association for the reform movement.[29]

[Jubilee Hymn] From Spence's Rights of Man. A Song, to be sung at the Commencement of the Millennium, when there shall be neither Lords nor Landlords; but God and Man will be all in all. First printed in the year 1782.

Tune—"God Save the King."

1

Hark! how the trumpet's sound*
Proclaims the land around
   The Jubilee!
Tells all the poor oppress'd,
No more they shall be cess'd,
Nor landlords more molest
   Their property.

2

Rents t' ourselves now we pay,
Dreading no quarter day,
   Fraught with distress.
Welcome that day draws near,
For then our rents we share⁺,
Earth's rightful lords we are
Ordain'd for this.

---

*See Leviticus, Chap. 25.
⁺Though the inhabitants in every district or parish in the world have an undoubted right to divide the WHOLE of the rents equally among them, and suffer the state and all public affairs to be supported by taxes as usual; yet from the numerous evils and restraints attending revenue laws, and number of collectors, informers, &c. appendant on the same, it is supposed, they would prefer, that after the whole amount of the rents collected in a parish from every person, according to the full value of the premises which they occupy, so much per pound, according to act of parliament, should be set apart for support of the state instead of all taxes; that another sum should next be deducted for support of the parish establishment, instead of tolls, tythes, rates, cesses, &c. and that after these important matters were provided for, the remainder of the money should be equally divided among all the settled inhabitants, whether poor or rich.

3.

How hath the oppressor ceas'd,⁺⁺
And all the world releas'd
   From misery!
The fir-trees all rejoice,
And cedars lift their voice,
Ceas'd now the Feller's noise,
   Long rais'd by thee.

4.

The sceptre now is broke,
Which with continual stroke
   The nations smote!
Hell from beneath doth rise,
To meet thy lofty eyes,

From the most pompous size,
  How brought to nought!

5.

Since this Jubilee
Sets all at Liberty
Let us be glad.
Behold each man return
To his possession
No more like doves to mourn
By landlords sad!

⁺⁺ Isaiah, Ch. 14.

In the first stanza the poet refers to the "poor oppress'd" in the third person, but from the second stanza to the poem's end Spence uses the first person plural. All of Spence's songs try to abolish the distance between the poet and the poor whom he tries to persuade and urge to action. Lending his plan authority and making it seem less unfamiliar, the song cites, echoes, and assumes a set of biblical references. Moreover, Spence wrests religious concepts from an aristo-cratic monarchy by redefining the poor as "lords" who are "Ordain'd" (st. 2). The millennialist imagery throughout the song portrays pro-phetic fulfillment of biblical truth. Moreover, the social reorganiza-tion of property is portrayed as a "return" (st. 5), a restorative process healing a breach in the natural order, not a violent innovation.

By seeing how Spence engages specific biblical passages one can discern his overall logic. The concept of the Jubilee, the imagery of the old society's destruction, the imagery of celebration, and the con-cluding symbol of prophetic fulfillment are all biblical.

Spence starts with Leviticus 25 and the Jubilee idea, whereby every fifty years each family recovers whatever land and property it had lost, as the entire society has a yearlong sabbath or sabbatical: "The land shall not be sold forever: for the land *is* mine, for ye *are* strang-ers and sojourners with me" (*KJV*, v. 23). The land is owned only by God and is subject to religious law and morality, so that private property must give way to a higher authority. The Levitical Jubilee lasts for a year only, but Spence makes it permanent, so that the Jubilee trumpet at the song's beginning—citing verse 9—is reminis-cent also of an apocalyptic trumpet, the kind that announces the end of time, the Last Judgment, and the New Jerusalem in Revelation. Spence partakes of the rhetoric and assumptions of radical Dissent, the same stream of cultural meanings that sustain William Blake as well as Christian millenarians like Richard Brothers and Joanna Southcott.[30]

From Isaiah 14, prophesying Israel's emancipation from the Babylonian Captivity, Spence gets the imagery of celebration. The allusions to verses 4–5 and 8–9 are pointedly anti-monarchical. Verse 8 reads: "Yea, the fir trees rejoice at thee, *and* the cedars of Lebanon, *saying*, Since thou art laid down, no feller is come up against us." The rejoicing fir and cedar trees are delighted because there are no more tyrants who need palaces constructed with fir and cedar, the most valuable kinds of wood at that time. The innocent trees are no longer cut, but cut down now is the "sceptre" of power (v. 5). The lines on hell in the fourth stanza are obscure unless one is familiar with Isaiah 14:9: "Hell from beneath is moved for thee to meet *thee* at thy coming: it stirreth up the dead for thee, *even* all the chief ones of the earth; it hath raised up from their thrones all the kings of the nations." In Isaiah Israel's power is so great that even the dead kings from hell come to pay homage. In Spence's fourth stanza, the tyrants are "brought to nought" from their previous "pompous" grandeur; now the liberated people are "lofty." In the Old Testament (as opposed to the Hebrew Bible, where Sheol signifies rather neutrally the place for the dead), the "hell" of Isaiah 14:9 suggests inevitably the place where damned souls are punished for their sins, prominent among which are the sins of disobedience. So here is yet another way in which Spence reverses traditional meanings: those who "disobeyed" established authority are now in a position more powerful than even the tyrants of the past and the very system itself of "divine" punishment.

The doves in stanza five are biblical (Genesis 8), suggesting Noah's dove as one of the symbols of the peace and mercy following the violent flood of judgment. As a sign of finality, the doves that "mourn" by the landlords are yet another reversal, as the former victims of landlords no longer need the imagined comfort from the doves whose mourning no longer echoes the sadness of the oppressed people. Now the oppressors need some comforting, as they have been dispossessed.

The title's prose framing of and commentary on the song, as well as the long footnote are ways for Spence to compete with other reformist writers by claiming priority for putting forward original ideas, so that the date "1782" declares that Spence's ideas preceded even the French Revolution. The title also dramatically contrasts illegitimate power with legitimate by announcing the end of "Lords" and "Landlords" and the new rule of "God" and "Man." One of the names for God, "Lord" is embedded in the language of established power, so that

Spence seeks to reinforce the new connection between God and ordinary people in a number of ways, including, as already mentioned, the "ordaining" of the people as "rightful lords" in stanza two. Using the tune of "God Save the King" was not unique with Spence, as there were other ironic uses of the nearly sacred song by the reform movement, but this is an especially effective use of the irony, as the song celebrates the downfall of not just kings but every other kind of monarchical vestige. The long footnote explaining how the new parochial system works is clever propaganda, as the song's lyrical and prosaic components reinforce one another. Spence's hostility to the Church of England did not stop him from naming the basic unit of his new society a "parish." The word may be the same as the word used by the church, but what it signifies in Spence's system is very different.

In the second stanza Spence refers to an aspect of ordinary life that indicates his position with this audience. "Dreading no quarter day, / Fraught with distress." Quarter days were the four times of the year when taxes and/or rents were due: Lady Day (March 25), Midsummer Day (June 24), Michaelmas Day (September 29), and Christmas Day (December 25), corresponding more or less to the four seasons. Laborers were also hired—or not rehired—on a quarter day. Evoking the intimate details of ordinary lives is typically Spencean. Thee oppression of the poor is not an abstraction but a felt experience, something he has in common with his audience, not something he has to prove.

The song, although brief, refers to a number of different levels of reality. There is the contemporary England with its dreadful quarter days, and the apocalyptic future when such things will not exist. The biblical level of reference originates in a legendary past but exists as a mode of contemporaneous interpretation. Spatially, the primary reference is to England but "nations" and "Hell" provide a broader focus. Remarkable is the interpenetration of different realms, so that in the last stanza the English landlords of the historical present are imagined in an apocalyptic future where the doves from Genesis mourn. Within the temporal horizon of the song itself Spence cleverly orchestrates the various referential worlds.

Lord George Gordon

The scholars Iain McCalman and Marsha Keith Schuchard have demonstrated convincingly that Gordon was not politically idiosyncratic, "Mad Lord George," as some have called him, but "with all his eccentricity and recklessness," Lord George Gordon "represented an authentic tradition of Scottish philo-Semitism and British millenarianism that had deep religious roots."[31] On Gordon's conversion to Judaism, which made him at least as famous as the London riots of 1780 named after him, historian Christopher Hibbert succinctly points to the continuity in his intellectual development: "For the Jewish view of humanity, the Jewish sense of justice and the Jewish hope for the world were all very much his own."[32] McCalman sets the context for Gordon's style of radicalism, which he calls a radical restorationism—that is, restoring Jews to Zion—and Dissenting philosemitism, a political orientation shared by not just Gordon but the Unitarian Joseph Priestley (1733–1804), the self-proclaimed prophet Richard Brothers (1757–1824), and William Blake, whose greatest poem was titled *Jerusalem* (1820). Whether restoration was imagined as occurring literally (Brothers, Priestley) or figuratively (Blake), it provided a discursive and ideological focus for popular radicalism for about forty years.[33]

Converting to Judaism in 1787 attracted huge public attention in the form of a stream of antisemitic discourse, prints, caricatures, and satires that stigmatized him with madness—a charge that has held to this day. McCalman and other scholars have shown that the conversion was not mad but within the logical premises of a religious-political tradition of prophetic millenarianism and philosemitism, extending back to the Dissenters Richard Price (1723–91) and Priestley who articulated a vision of the New Jerusalem. "But government officials, press, and prints alike agreed," according to McCalman, "that his prophetic excess had to be halted when he began in 1787 to preach and distribute handbills amongst male and female convicts in Newgate denouncing capital punishment and transportation as contrary to the laws of Jehovah."[34]

The text that occasioned his imprisonment until he died is probably his best literary effort, taking the form of a petition by prisoners headed to Botany Bay who are protesting the capital punishment levied against them for acts of theft. Gordon ventriloquizes the prisoners who are made to address their complaints and reform proposals to Lord George Gordon, public representative, Scottish aristocrat. In the late eighteenth century convictions for property crimes were capital offences, receiving punishment that could be hanging or transportation to Australia for seven years (or life), as we saw in chapter 3. If Gordon had merely published the petition in a journal or newspaper, he would not have attracted the court's attention, but he published a pamphlet that he then distributed at

Newgate Prison to the jail officials and, according to witnesses, to prisoners. As someone who had been charged with treason for inciting the London riots of 1780 when there was widespread property damage and hundreds of casualties, Gordon did not get the benefit of the doubt from the government, as deferential as it usually was to aristocrats.

The pamphlet, *Prisoners Petition to the Right Hon. Lord George Gordon, to preserve their Lives and Liberties, and prevent their banishment to Botany-Bay*, makes a simple argument: property theft should not be a capital offense because such punishment is too harsh, offending the moral sensibility, and more decisively it violates divine law. Offending moral sensibility is not an unusual appeal but the religious argument is uncompromising, based on biblical maxims, and the style of the petition is oratorically biblical, as though it came from the lips of an impassioned preacher delivering a sermon. Using the idiom of the King James Bible Gordon creates something that approaches a Blakean prose poem in its fierce condemnation of the "Heathen" legislation that violates religious law. The persona of the petition has many roles that he plays, humble victim who entreats Gordon for help, guilt-ridden and repentant sinner and criminal confessing his wrongdoing, reverent petitioner who utters prayers and blessings, prophet declaiming against injustice and calling down divine judgment against the oppressors, and Enlightenment moral philosopher synthesizing points of evidence and damning immoral legal authorities. One oratorical flourish uses anaphora to generate a breathless tension from the self-abasing rhetoric reminiscent of the Yom Kippur liturgy that is broken only by an unexpected prayer phrased like a Jewish blessing:

We are not so shameless of face, or hardened, as to say that we are righteous, and have done no sin; for verily we have sinned, we have been guilty, we have deceived, we have spoken falsely, we have waylaid the unwary in his footpath, we have arrested the traveler on the highway, we have robbed, we have committed iniquity and wickedness, we have infested the streets of the city, we have done violence, we have caused the terror by night, we have occasioned distress by day, we have erred and set bad examples, we have led a rising generation astray, we have been suffered to grow up as a plague to the people, for their sins, as a pest in their play-houses, in their churches, in their courts of justice, and at their executions; our young ones also swarm and nestle in their avenues; even the king's companies are dishonoured by thieves and plunderers: we have departed from the commandments of God, and refused to keep his laws.—Blessed art thou, O Lord our God, King of the Universe, that thou bestowest graciousness, confession, and repentance to sinners![35]

The catalogue of sins and errors echoes the Yom Kippur liturgy in King James English with balanced pairings, parallelisms, antitheses, and imagery. Gordon is ventriloquizing a Christian persona who speaks in the accents of Judaism but those same sonorities and rhythms also characterize Protestant "Old Testament" rhetoric as well. In yet another section the pamphlet has a translation of the opening lines of another Jewish prayer, the Ve'ahavta ("May they love the Lord our God with all their hearts, with all their souls, and with all their might, and diligently teach his statutes and judgments unto their children, and remember all the commandments of the Lord, and do them").[36] A Jewish reader picks up readily where the rhetoric of the pamphlet comes from, but a reader from a Christian background would just register the effect of emotionally intense religiosity presumably Christian, although the petition has no Christian references whatsoever. In an especially pointed sequence Gordon withholds a Christian reference where one would expect one: "when the people forgot God their Saviour, which had done great things in Egypt."[37] In Christian rhetoric the Savior is Jesus, not the God of the exodus. A Christian could still read this within a Christian framework but a Jewish reader would detect the many departures from Christian *topoi*.

Identifying the legal code as bloody and heathen is similar to what Blake does in *Jerusalem* by often connecting modern injustices, including the executions at "Tyburn's fatal tree," to Druidic sacrifices: "the fires blaz'd on Druid Altars / And the Sun set in Tyburns Brook where Victims howl & cry" (3: plate 62).[38] The petition, as is common in Dissenting rhetoric, also develops the analogies between contemporary oppression and the Israelites enslaved in Egypt, as the persona characterizes the prisoners as "bitter with hard bondage" facing "perpetual exile," while likening the appeal for mercy to the court to Moses asking the Pharoah to let the people go.[39] The pamphlet does not argue against capital punishment as such because it cites biblical precedent for exacting a life for a life. It even goes so far as to cite Phineas as the biblical hero and role model in this context without fully describing what he did: in Numbers 25 he spears to death an Israelite and his Midianite lover to dispel the plague. Phineas seems to be likened favorably to the executioners of Charles the First. If the court unjustly and against God's law murders thieves, then the court deserves the biblical punishment meted out to those who kill unjustly. "Let him be known among the heathen in our sight by the revenging of the blood of his servants which is shed."[40] If one theme is harshly punitive, another appeals to "mutual forgiveness and reconciliation as brethren."[41] The petition's strongly biblical cadences, syntax, and allusions make the pamphlet's arguments rest on the absolutes of divinely sanctioned law. Similarly, Spence rests his land reform on biblical texts, assumed to be God's word, unanswerable in its authority. It is not for Spence and Gordon to celebrate the ambiguity of the biblical text and its numerous possible meanings. Rather, the Lord speaks with no uncertainty.

Never lacking moral conviction, Gordon intervened in national and international affairs, urging an alliance between the Ottoman Empire and Protestant Europe against Russia and the Catholics, chastising Emperor Joseph for his treatment of the Jews, protesting the ill treatment of Jews in Poland (where one of his cousins was the king), urging Jewish financiers to withhold funds from warmongering European states, chastising liberal politicians for being soft on Catholicism (his inflexible hatred of Catholicism is a blind spot on which he never gets any critical distance), Gordon was, until his death in 1793, "the unofficial leader of the distinguished band of radical state prisoners incarcerated in Britain's Bastille for political sedition and treason." According to McCalman, he "always adhered to the most strenuous libertarian principles of the rational Enlightenment."[42] I will add: as long as he could articulate those principles in the idiom of biblical rhetoric.

DAUGHTERS OF MIRIAM AND HULDAH

The difficult road for Jewish prophetesses is evident from scripture and rabbinic commentary. For apparently the same offense against God and Moses (Num. 12:1), Miriam gets punished with a hideous skin disease (Num. 12:10) and then dies shortly afterward (Num. 20:1), while brother Aaron receives no disfiguring affliction and dies much later (20:28). Huldah, who teaches at an academy in Jerusalem, is the authoritative prophet for determining the significance of the newly found scroll (Book of Deuteronomy) in the Temple (2 Kings 22:14–20), but because her address to King Josiah does not acknowledge sufficiently his royal status when she speaks to him, the rabbinic sages immortalize her as "haughty" and "Weasel."[43] If the premodern prophetic women are only grudgingly accepted by the religious culture, it is not surprising that later women would take a cautious approach, as indeed the four women writers we are turning to now do indeed take. Emma Lyon (1788–1870) probably would not have published at all if it had not been for the family emergency when father Solomon became blind and unable to work. Her *Miscellaneous Poems* (1812) published by subscription was framed as an exercise of charity relief. The Moss sisters, Celia (1819–73) and Marion (1821–1907), test the limits of what the male-dominated community can tolerate, especially with Marion's Jewish women's journal that enjoys a brief run before Abraham Benisch (1814–78), editor of the *Jewish Chronicle*, condemns and thereby kills it. Michael Galchinsky's account of Marion's *Jewish Sabbath Journal* (1855) leaves no doubt that it failed only because powerful men opposed it.[44] Grace Aguilar (1816–47) had a difficult relationship with Isaac Leeser (1806–68) who encouraged her writing but also tried to control and censor it, according to Galchinsky. Leeser published her *Spirit of Judaism* (1842) but included a running critique and correction of its ideas within the text.[45] The three women find ways to circumvent obstacles and disguise what most threatens anxious male authorities.

"Pretty Little Poems" and the Biblical Sublime

Generic identity and critical reception are ways women's writing, even when it is published, is contained within safe reading methods governed by gender hierarchies. The *Monthly Review* found nothing objectionable in Lyon's "pretty little poems."[46] It is not known whether the reviewer got as far into the 152-page book to read the Psalm paraphrases and the poem addressed to the Society of Friends of Foreigners in Distress, two kinds of poems that are neither pretty nor little, so one assumes the *Monthly* critic was characterizing the numerous short lyrics of rhymed tetrameter or pentameter quatrains on traditional poetic subjects, such as tributes to the poet's friends and family and to various abstract personifications like melancholy, beauty, the seasons, and so on. If not read attentively, these lyrics seem harmless effusions by a rabbi's daughter performing with the pen rather than on the piano at her own charity benefit. All the subscriptions taken by the royals and academics from Cambridge, Oxford, and Eton provide a cultural imprimatur to the book, which might only have been skimmed by the reviewers, who would have missed the darker themes of the lyrics, not to mention the bold Psalm paraphrases and the politically assertive poems that conclude the volume. It is doubtful that the respectable people who subscribed to Lyon's book knew that her mother a decade earlier cooked kosher food for Lord George Gordon and brought it to his prison cell at Newgate.[47]

Celia and Marion Moss begin their literary career with a book of poetry whose full title is somewhat apologetic: *Early Efforts: A Volume of Poems, By the Misses Moss, of the Hebrew Nation, Aged 18 and 16.* Following this is a rhymed quatrain inscription to set the tone:

> For O! the soul of song hath power
> To charm the feeling heart,
> To soothe the mourner's sternest hour,
> And bid his griefs depart.
> Korner.[48]

No cultural incursions into traditional masculine territory seem threatened here, as the poems are "efforts" by Jewish teenagers who cite the melancholy "feeling heart" as their touchstone. As usual, all is not as it appears. The "Korner" quotation, for example, is the second stanza of a poem by Karl Theodor Körner (1791–1813) translated by G.F. Richardson. The poem, "Three Stars," celebrates song, love, and wine in the conventionally anacreontic style, hardly what readers would associate with unmarried misses not yet twenty years old.[49] The quatrain seems to be what a "poetess" would admire but the larger context tells another story of literary sophistication. Just as with Emma Lyon's book, if one actually reads the poems within the feminizing frame one finds various affronts to gendered norms, such as political poems about recent massacres of Greeks by Turks, "The Destruction of Setia," cosmopolitan protests like a "Lament for Poland," several poems on the fall of Jerusalem, and most notably a long poem about the York massacre of 1190. The Mosses have managed to sneak into their book Zionist poems that affiliate the Jewish nation with the Romantic nationalism of the nineteenth century and poems that bring back one of England's most shameful acts of racist violence against Jews. I will first look at Lyon's poetry then that of the Moss sisters. One prominent theme in Lyon's poetry is her relationship to her muse and to her vocation for poetry, sometimes even a prophetic calling. Although the Preface points to the circumstances of her poverty and father's blindness that make publication a necessity rather than a choice, she clearly writes poetry whether it ever gets published or not. Her enthusiasm about poetry begins as a child when her imagination inspired her and "the Muse smiled when I endeavoured to harmonize the scenes she drew." Lyon adopts the inspirational model of composition, with its affinity with prophecy. One of her recurrent words that registers desire is "lure" or "allure"; she employs this word to describe poetic inspiration: "Allured by her [the Muse's] fairy charms, and impelled to seek solace from the gloom of surrounding embarrassments, I soothed my anxieties in her mazy bower, twining garlands to deck the dark brow of fate."[50] The logic of her metaphor suggests that "fate" can be decorated with the products of imagination but cannot be transcended.

The poems that explicitly explore "inspiration" as it affects and is affected by cultural authority are ambivalent about entering the public world of conflict, competitive envy, and masculine power, but the nine Psalms that conclude the volume resolve the ambivalence by incorporating the earlier figures of inspiration into a model of prophecy and by transforming poetic ambition into eagerness to spread the wisdom of God.

Not counting the dedicatory poem to Princess Charlotte that is located in the prefatory section, the book's first poem positions Lyon in relation to the dominant culture in "Address to the University of Oxford."[51] Her "weak" feminine muse hesitantly and tremblingly appears among "contemplation's studious sons." While ostensibly describing her situation as a unlearned young woman, these lines seem to record a note of protest: "Had it been mine in learning's path to tread, / The Muse, perchance, had smil'd as fancy led: / But fortune's cloud gloom'd o'er my earliest hour, / And cares domestic drove me from her bow'r; / Or I had haply trac'd each mystic page, / And reap'd, like you, the fruits of ev'ry age." It is hardly just gender that keeps her from learning at Oxford; Jews of course cannot enroll at either Cambridge or Oxford where her father teaches Hebrew but not with the full privileges of a professing Christian. Is "fortune's cloud" her Jewishness in an antisemitic Britain? Or is it her gender? Or her poverty? The plain sense indicates that she is emphasizing the prohibitions of gender that entail "cares domestic," but one can also read the other prohibitions. She declares throughout the book a muse that is hobbled by a lack of learning, a lack about which she is not quiet, so that while she appears to be modest, making no excessive claims for her writing, she is also calling attention to an injustice.

The second piece, "Lines to D. F*****, Esq. Barrister," is another poem of positioning, in this case in relation to a Gentile friend, Daniel French, the husband of one of her good friends, to whom she also writes a poem.[52] He provides encouraging advice and a sympathetic reading of her work. Ironically, this same Daniel French, who was one of Emma Lyon's Hebrew students, intervened on her behalf shortly after the publication of the book when she was assaulted verbally and physically by a William Simmons, who lived in the same London building as Emma Lyon.[53]

French is deemed "patron," a sympathetic mediator between herself and the public before which her "blushing Muse still shrinks" (l. 10). French's role is to validate the poet's sincerity, honesty, and modesty—her "moral" status, in short. The poem is not about French or their friendship but about her relationship with her muse, who is called here "Goddess" and addressed in the second person. The classical idiom of the Muses and their shrine that the poem deploys for her relationship to her own poetry pays no heed at all to the traditional Jewish anxieties about the idolatry of art—anxieties of which her Gentile audience in any case would probably not be aware. The forty-seven poems that precede the nine Psalm paraphrases are almost exclusively secular, and consistently exploit and develop the figures of inspiration from classical culture; in these poems there is a proliferation of female deities and female-gendered human qualities that provide the basis for Lyon's poetics. The Psalm paraphrases silence the suspicions about idolatry the previous poems might have generated. Rather, the Psalms reinforce the themes and figures Lyon had developed in the prior poems.

The tribute to French has a five-part structure, beginning with a prologue (ll. 1–14) that is grateful for French's generosity and encouragement while echoing the Preface in renouncing poetic ambition: "No thought of fame, or yet ambitious pride / Bade me all fearful to the world confide" (ll. 7–8). Her Muse blushes and shrinks at competition, but on the speaker's first encounter with the Muse (ll. 15–36) she vows and prays to her goddess, who then speaks to her.

> "Sure some rude thorn
> Impels to seek me in life's early morn;
> They seldom wander near my mystic cell,
> Whom pleasure has not bid a long farewell.
> But if thou com'st a lonely hour to cheer,
> Remember! 'tis not happiness dwells here:
> The pow'r I boast is but to soothe the mind,
> When cares perplex, and fortune low'rs unkind." (ll. 25–32)

The Muse does not offer pleasure but relief from misery; however, the "mystic" power to which only the few, the elect, and the spiritual elite ever have access appeals to the poet. Although only those who are unhappy seek the Muse for solace, the pleasures of poetry seem more than just compensatory and therapeutic. The Muse's words are described thus: "so gently flow'd / Each accent sweet, that still my bosom glow'd; / Still long'd to trace the varying shades of rhyme, /

And catch the glimm'rings of a thought sublime" (ll. 33–36). Like someone who has just fallen in love, her body, her feelings, and her intellect yearn and long for the presence of her Muse.

Precisely at this moment of her greatest pleasure—acquainting herself with her desire and identity as a poet—and her greatest embarrassment when she is aware of her poetic inadequacies in relation to the source of her inspiration, she returns to the figure of French for reassurance and guidance (ll. 37–54). As a Gentile man educated in the most prestigious kinds of secular poetry, he is Lyon's projection of cultural authority, whether he was really knowledgeable or not. By thanking French so profusely, she distracts herself from the more decisive encounter with her Muse who reappears in the next section side by side with French (ll. 55–72). It is as if French's presence makes the Muse, "the fair Queen" (l. 62), and her "Sisters" (l. 58), less subversive. She steels herself against harsh criticism with the following logic: if French approves of the poetry, then so will the critics (ll. 65–66). Reassured and strengthened, she turns again to her Muse, referring to the necessity of *reining* her "erring fancy" with "wisdom" because of all that she lacks: an education in Milton, Homer, and Virgil (ll. 67–71).

When Lyon turns to the Psalm paraphrases she is playing out the Hellenic/Hebraic conflict of modern literature, as she Hellenizes the Hebraic and Hebraizes the Hellenic. Her contained and controlled performance of the Jessica role is to demonstrate her love for the Muse and all that it brings in terms of secular culture. The Psalm paraphrases show that she uses her inspired imagination within the categories and literary canons of her religion. When inspiration gets translated into sacred texts, Lyon surprisingly makes a prophetic turn.

The Psalm first presented is Psalm 19, followed by Psalm 15, 49, 50, 58, 72, 73, 76, and 91. Her paraphrase of Psalm 19, the only one out of order, receives special attention for that fact alone.[54] The last stanza of the paraphrase intriguingly turns the Authorized Version's verse 14, the last verse, "Let the words of my mouth, and the meditation of my heart, be acceptable in thy sight, O Lord, my strength, and my redeemer" into the following:

> O Thou, who erst on David's holiest lyre,
> Didst dart thy sacred vehemence of fire,
>   Come, teach me to reveal thy ways,
>   And scatter round a dazzling blaze;
> Unfolding bright, inspir'd with silent awe,
> The' unclouded prospect of thy heavenly law!

The actual Hebrew of verse 14 is the very familiar *"y'hu l'ratzon imrei fi v'higion libi lifanecha Adonai tsuri v'goali,"* spoken in the daily prayers (after the *Shemoneh Esrei*). Lyon does not challenge the accuracy of the elegant King James translation by playing on the Hebrew roots of the words (Milton's paraphrases are more Hebraic than Lyon's); rather, Lyon transforms a cluster of words on the proper state of mind for praying (*kavana*) into a statement about prophetic inspiration. The grammar shifts from a petitionary "may" to an invocatory command, "come" and "scatter." From God to David to Emma Lyon, the divine authority passes, as the stanza invokes God's power as a prophet. She is deferring to traditional authority but transgressing the gender code, vowing obedience to God's law but claiming for herself a role in transmitting the law that was not permitted at the time by religious institutions. The neoclassical idiom of inspiration in the previous poems is dropped for the biblically prophetic.

The stanzaic form she uses, a sestet comprising a tetrameter couplet sandwiched between two pentameter couplets, moves her paraphrase away from the metrical doggerel of Sternhold and Hopkins and toward instead the more literary versions by Wyatt and Milton.

> The arched heavens ere since the birth of time
> Instruct the earth, in characters sublime,
>   To read aloft with sudden glance,
>   Whose hand stretch'd out the blue expanse;
> Who bade the stars blaze forth from pole to pole,
> And all beneath his high dominion roll.

God's creation as a readable text and nature as a "sublime" language of instruction prepare the metaphysical ground for the final stanza where the poet mediates between the two languages, divine and human, sublime and mundane. Although the first four verses of the King James version also have a linguistic theme, Lyon retains this emphasis in the second stanza with a musical analogy that is not in the original (music as aesthetic expression similar to language), and in the fourth stanza, where God's "name" is written on every beam of sunlight—again in language not present in the original.

Psalm 19 in the first seven verses praises the sun, and in the latter seven praises the wisdom of God's law and commandments.[55] Lyon's structure has ten stanzas, the first six of which praise the creation, the latter four God's law mediated through the prophet. There is a tension between the beauty of the creation—nature's "lovely works" that "allure the gazer's eye!"—and God's holy law (although the Chasidic mystics found God and his law directly in nature). In the ninth stanza when "vanity" opposes "virtue" the "allure" solidifies as a negative judgment against merely superficial beauty purchased at the expense of ethical wisdom. The sensuous descriptions of the creation in the first half of the Psalm become sensuous praise for God's law in the latter half of the Psalm, as even the self-denial of following the law requires the incentive of beauty and sense-gratification: "Thy laws are amiable and sweet indeed, / As virgin honey from the flowery mead!"

If Psalm 19 is one of David's Psalms, then Lyon's eighth stanza seems to claim prophetic power for the lyrical subject: "O give me, Lord! Thy glorious tracks to see." The unforced way to read Lyon's paraphrase is to read the first person in the eighth stanza as referring to Lyon, not David, or better, Lyon performing David, appropriating his role, status, prestige, and authority. It is daring for her to assume the Davidic role, even in a set of ambiguous lines.

The two poems that conclude her book, "Stanzas Sung with great applause at the Anniversary Meeting of the Society of Friends of Foreigners in Distress, Held at the New London Tavern, April 27, 1812," and "Conclusion," have political, social, literary, and prophetic dimensions.[56] She exploits her connection with the Society to emphasize her social acceptance as a poet and as a moral agent by the most powerful members of society. Her own identity as a needy outsider requiring assistance is a point of departure to establish Britain as a multicultural haven for exiles and victims of tyranny. The third stanza, which was censored at the Meeting, is restored in her book:

> When flying from a tyrant's sway
>   In quest of freedom's glorious ray,
> The famish'd exiles wander here,
>   Safe shelter'd from the murd'ring spear;
> They bless the hospitable Isle,
>   And through the clouds of sorrow smile,
> Reposing in the hallow'd rest
>   Of *Friends to Foreigners distrest!*

Because the Russian and Prussian governments supported the Society and would not have appreciated these allusions to tyranny, especially from a Jewish woman, the authorities in charge suppressed the stanza. Lyon's intention is quite apparent: by flattering the generosity of the British, she hopes to mold a myth of national identity quite unlike what was actually normative in 1812. Most of the recipients of aid from the Society were sent back to their country of origin; only the exceptional cases were permitted to receive aid and remain in Britain. Lyon's song does not go as far as Emma Lazarus's famous poem *The New Colossus,* for the fourth stanza refers approvingly of the distressed foreigner returning to his native home, but the principle of assisting everyone who has a need, regardless of religion or national origin, in conjunction with the rhetoric of foreign tyrannies from which people are justifiably fleeing, prepares the way for the myth of a multicultural haven, a myth that had more success in the United States than in Britain. Her poem celebrates the ideal of hospitality that is at the heart of Kant's cosmopolitanism.[57]

The final poem affirms and underlines Lyon's role as an inspired poet with prophetic authority. The self-fashioned image of a modest young woman fearful of public exposure is replaced with expressions of "soaring pride" in her spreading the name of Jehovah "far and wide." She assumes some of the messianic tones of the prophet Isaiah in her hope that all the nations will hearken to the divine message of social justice: "A language that all nations hear / Alike with one harmonious ear: / No clime so dark, no ignorance so blind, / But reads the splendor of th' Almighty mind." As a religious poet she loses her anxiety about public poetry and her gender role. Her path to the Psalms is through the earlier poems with their neoclassical idiom, feminine pantheon of goddesses, and nearly ecstatic celebrations of the inspired pleasures of poetry. That Lyon never published again is tragic because this promising poet never had another opportunity to show readers where her unpredictable and courageous muse would lead her next. In 1815 her father after an operation recovered his sight, Emma married, giving birth to ten children, and she wrote poetry only *"en amatrice."*[58] It is always possible one day a cache of her manuscript poems will be uncovered because such strange things do indeed happen.

The Moss sisters had some literary setbacks, as already mentioned, but they had much encouragement from their father, who read Romantic poetry to them while they performed their domestic chores as girls.[59] Valman describes their literary project as fusing Milman's *History of the Jews* with Romantic poetry and historical romance.[60] From the Byron and Thomas Moore read to them by their father they derive the idiom of a Romantic nationalism within which Zionism has a place.[61] In two ambitious works, *The Romance of Jewish History* (1840) and *Tales of Jewish History* (1843), the Mosses invent stories within the arc of biblical and ancient Jewish history, family conflicts and lovers' problems within events like the Philistine conquest of Judea and the David/Absalom dispute. Following Scott and the model of the historical romance, the Mosses depict Jews as they might have lived in Jerusalem and elsewhere in a biblical context. The purpose here is not midrashic to illustrate moral maxims or give voice to silences and enigmas in scripture. Rather, the stories try to make the biblical world as real as the nineteenth century to the readers in order to "inspire sympathy for the Jewish cause in the present," according to Galchinsky.[62] Another aspect of these historical romances is gaining ground in the gender battles because the Bible is unassailable as a cultural resource and history is one of the masculine intellectual pursuits. Although the stories follow the pattern of domestic fiction, their being spliced onto the Bible and history diminishes the stigma of gender.

Another aspect of these stories is to inspire pride among Jews, clearly also Disraeli's intentions in *Alroy* (1833), a historical romance of the twelfth-century Holy Land, a work that obviously influenced the Mosses deeply. Based on the historical pseudo-Messiah David Alroy, the novel represents a failed attempt to gather the scattered Jews and conquer Zion, but the novel's hero displays so many admirable strengths that he wins by losing. Especially compared with Lytton's *Leila*, another influence on their writing, *Alroy* avoids some of the stereotypes that *Leila* reinforces. First, Disraeli's novel has strong expressions of Zionist yearnings to return to Israel and overcome the humiliations of exile. Displaying physical courage, intellectual ambition and accomplishment by studying kabbalistic and other holy texts, fierce aristocratic arrogance, and sexual charisma, Alroy plays a Davidic role in doing battle against his foes. Esther the prophetess who invokes her precursors Judith and Deborah clashes her cymbals, dances ecstatically, and makes optimistic pronouncements about imminent Jewish victories.[63] Alroy, who ignores Esther's advice to avoid entering Baghdad with his troops, is defeated but he retains his honor. The passionate Alroy is distracted from his messianic mission by the beautiful Muslim Schirene, an Orientalized beauty like Scott's Rebecca; she is strong, willful, self-assertive, rebellious, impulsive, and even violent. After he is captured he refuses to make a deal with the Muslim authorities and rearticulates his Zionist ideals and personal justification of obeying God's inspiration. Unlike the powerful Jew in Lytton's *Leila*, Almamen, the double-dealing trickster who wins the affection of no one, Disraeli's pseudo-Messiah is charmingly reckless and passionate. That Disraeli's heroic, muscular, and courageous fighter is designed to counter stereotypes is evident from the reviews, one of which comments that "there is a deep infusion of the spirit of Judah in it [*Alroy*]—not the fallen and money-changing spirit of these our latter days, but of that martial and devout spirit which kindled in the Hebrew bosoms of old."[64]

The Mosses's heroes and heroines do not match the violent and zealous activities of Alroy or the prophetic theatricality of Esther. Where the Tanakh is understated, plain, direct, and uncluttered, the Moss stories are emotionally hyperbolic with an ornamental prose style and intricate plot complications. The important action in their stories is not military but emotional. In *The Priest's Adopted,* for example, the background is the Babylonian Exile with the action occurring also in Jerusalem.[65] The beautiful daughter of a priest living in a conquered Jerusalem, she falls in love with Ezra, whom her family does not approve. The couple elopes, devastating her family, especially brother Isaac. Asher, an adopted son of the priest's family, deeply in love with Ada, leaves Jerusalem when she chooses the stranger—Ezra—rather than himself. A hunchback, he is a talented musician and prophetic singer, who follows the example of Jeremiah after he reaches Babylon. Ezra turns out to be unreliable and cruel, eventually selling Ada into slavery. Meanwhile Asher is thrown into prison in Babylon because he is blamed for the king's illness. Replaying the Genesis story of Joseph and Potiphar's wife, Luna the wife of the Babylonian prince, is smitten with Asher because of his music, which she describes in erotic terms. Like the biblical Joseph, the Mosses' Asher turns down the sexual invitation of Luna, who is discovered and then killed by her enraged husband. Asher is released from prison but continues as the palace music teacher. One day he is ordered to teach a new student, a Hebrew slave, who is revealed as Ada. The prince's virtuous wife—not Luna—arranges for the marriage between Ada and Asher. Meanwhile, back in Jerusalem, before Isaac's mother dies she urges him to marry. A forlorn and angry Isaac after her death meets at his mother's grave an old man and his grandson. After the old man dies, the priest Isaac takes care of the grandson, who turns out to be a crossdressed and disguised young woman whose betrothed has died. At the story's end, Ada and Asher join Isaac and Edna (the former "grandson") in Jerusalem.

The plot is as intricate as those in the other stories and the themes here are common in the others: the pains of exile, the trauma of being a conquered people, the ever present reminder of lost glory, the intense rewards of family love and the excruciating pains of discord and death. This particular story highlights the Joseph-like artist Asher: the orphan who is adopted and out of his special pain as a hunchback and as someone estranged from the vigorous physical activities of his stepbrother Isaac, he cultivates music in which he becomes expert.

Making art out of pain and loss is a Jewish theme the Mosses express repeatedly. Unlike Disraeli's tough Jew Alroy, Celia's Asher is sensitive and physically limited, but both characters in their respective ways desire to overcome exile. When Asher is alone he would feel that sick longing which only the exile can know, for a return to the haunts of childhood, whose every glade and flower would recall to him his first bright dream.[66] The novel's ending in Jerusalem is a return to the past and almost but not quite a restoration. The tone is melancholy rather than jubilant.

Another aspect of the *Romance of Jewish History* is the function of the inscriptions for the many chapter headings in these three volumes. The favored authors of the inscriptions are Thomas Moore (1779–1852), mostly from *Lalla Rookh* (1817), the Oriental tale, and Lord Byron, who has twenty extracts, more than any other author. Only two of the extracts are from *Hebrew Melodies*, the book one might anticipate as being most relevant to these biblical stories, but in fact the Mosses took from almost every Byron poem: *Sardanapalus, Marino Falerio, Corsair* (four different extracts), *Childe Harold, Mazeppa, Giaour,* the notorious *Don Juan, Siege of Corinth, Two Foscari, Parisina,* "Ode to Napoleon Bonaparte," and the lyric to Mary Chaworth. First, the Mosses knew Byron well, not superficially, at a time when Byron's reputation was sharply declining in respectable middle-class opinion, and rising just as sharply among radicals and working class Chartists.[67] Their biblical Jews are embedded with Byron's verse and especially the Romantic nationalism with which he is associated. The expressions of lonely exile, alienation, and ostracism that Byron expressed resonate with the Mosses in a Jewish way. Another effect of importing so much Moore and Byron into their text is that it removes the book even further from the category of women's fiction. Aguilar has no difficulty importing extracts from women writers into her work—Felicia Hemans being her favorite—but the Mosses have an overwhelmingly masculine set of authors.

The Trials of Grace Aguilar

The centrality of trials and scenes of confrontation between Jews and legal authorities in Grace Aguilar's work probably derives from her background as a descendent of Portuguese *conversos* who escaped the Inquisition and immigrated to England in the eighteenth century. In *History of the Jews in England* (1847) the torture, imprisonment for eight years, and eventual liberation of a crypto-Jew "whom we will call Garcias" from the Inquisition in Lisbon seems like a family story, as the details are so particular, the names are fabricated, and these factual events receive fictional treatment in other texts.[68] A remarkably prolific writer whose work includes a Scottish historical romance, lyrical poetry, theology, biblical Midrashim, and much else beside,[69] Aguilar roots her identity as an author in the *converso* experience of heroism, martyrdom, duplicity, concealment, secrecy, mystery, encryption, and maternal storytelling. During the eight years "Garcias" endures the tortures and privations of the Inquisition cell, he is cheerful, knits socks for his jailer with knitting needles fashioned from chicken bones, refuses to betray his fellow Jews, and finds a way to write—with ink prepared from lamp-black—"several plays and dramas, mostly on Scriptural subjects, which are still in the possession of his family."[70] Here is Aguilar's muse, the inspiring example of a cultivated, gracious, resourceful, and courageous Jew who does not get embittered by his mistreatment and who joyfully creates art in the worst possible circumstances. Although the Garcias story could be true from start to finish, it need not be to function as the narrative of Aguilar's imagined precursor. The detail about the knitting needles and socks integrates a traditionally feminine and domestic activity with the masculine writing.

I will discuss a novella with a *converso* subtext, whose setting is nineteenth-century London, and two fictional treatments of the crypto-Jewish experience in Iberia. Protestant liberal England seems to negate Catholic Iberia fundamentally, but ironic parallels stubbornly appear: Iberian Jews appeared in public like Catholics, just as English Jews were supposed to perform publicly as English. That a performative failure in the one case meant death and in the other scorn and discrimination is consequential but the structure of each model of the public/private division is identical. Aguilar describes the normative situation for English Jews:

> In externals, and in all secular thoughts and actions, the English naturalized Jew is...an Englishman, and his family is reared with the education and accomplishments of the other members of the community. Only in some private and personal characteristics, and in religious belief, does the Jew differ from his neighbours.[71]

As a vulnerable minority, Iberian Jews kept their Jewishness private and secretive, while Aguilar assigns to mothers in the domestic sphere the central role in forming a Jewish identity for their children growing up in a liberal, secularized Christian culture. Trial scenes in Aguilar's fiction are rich with meaning because they are sites where the private experience must defend itself in public in a discourse and on matters wholly alien to Jewishness.

Aguilar has several trial scenes in the novella *The Perez Family* (1843) and the short story "The Escape: A Tale of 1755" (*Records of Israel*, 1843). In both texts the actual trials are only sketchily represented because the real drama is taking place elsewhere.

In *The Perez Family* the character Isaac Levison, a recently reformed thief and the father of the protagonist, Sarah, is convicted and sentenced to transportation to Australia for a robbery he actually did not commit, but after a witness suddenly confirms Levison's alibi, the sheriff detains Levison for a needless second trial, motivated by bureaucratic rigidity or antisemitism. The second trial never happens because Levison, after a tearful reconciliation with his daughter, dies as suddenly as Walter Scott's Bois-Guilbert, the Templar Knight, in his trial by contest with Ivanhoe over Rebecca.[72] The important jury in Aguilar—as it is in Scott—is the reader, the "judicious reader," as Martha Nussbaum would phrase it, who has to determine the aptness of the poetic justice assigned by the text.[73] The important thing for Levison and his daughter is not the legal system and its determinations, but that his innocence has been confirmed publicly if not legally. He is morally if not legally justified, which is enough for his child Sarah, who is the good daughter of a bad father—a permutation of the Shylock archetype—she keeps trying to help and bring back to traditional Jewish values. The divine judgment seems to be that with the father repentant, vindicated, and dead (and therefore not needing Sarah's care), the narrative creates a poetic justice that allows Sarah to marry another repentant Jew, Reuben, thereby effecting a symbolic renewal of the Anglo-Jewish community. With Scott and Aguilar we see the hand of divine justice supplementing the clumsy machinery of social institutions that seem incapable of ever becoming refined enough to dispense authentic justice. Levison's trial, although it failed to effect justice in the judicial sense, was providential, bringing father and daughter to an understanding. The injustice of the second trial, which seems to kill Levison, emotionally devastates his daughter, who finds comfort from the repentant Reuben, her long lost love. Tragedy and suffering bring characters together in Aguilar's fiction.

Sarah has long loved Reuben who married outside the faith, and when his Gentile wife, Jeanie Wilson—a tribute to Scott's Jeanie Deans of *The Heart of Midlothian* (1818)—conveniently dies, Reuben can play out fully the role of *ba'al teshuvah*—someone who returns to the faith as an observant Jew. Reuben's story about overcoming Jewish self-hatred counters the Evangelical conversionist narrative.

Although he loved his Gentile wife and prospered economically, "there was still a void within—I was not happy." He explains his attraction to Jeanie Wilson: "I did but seek her, because I thought a union with a Christian would put a barrier between me and the race I had taught myself to hate—would mark me no more a Jew."[74] Sarah inspires and supervises his return to the Jewish community, whose guardianship in this novella is entirely in the hands of women, Reuben's saintly mother Rachel, and Levison's Angel in the House, Sarah. The wayward men return to the righteous path not by studying Talmud in the yeshiva but by heeding the maternal wisdom, a mixture of traditional lore passed down orally and lessons culled from the Bible. Ann Nichols aptly calls this feminine exercise of influence "empowered domesticity."[75] For Sarah's father and lover the only reliable sphere is the private realm of the home. An ever present threat to the Jewish world is the public world, which has to be handled carefully. Assimilation, crime, and antisemitic discrimination characterize the outside world as Sarah experiences it. A Jewish life is possible only in safe retreat from that world, thus reproducing a milder version of the crypto-Jewish worldview. As Michael Galchinsky comments in this context, "the choice between crypto-Judaism and assimilation [is] one of degree."[76] Miss Leon, the benevolent Christian friend of the family, and Reuben's daughter named Jeanie, who is accepted and loved by Sarah, modifies the nature of the new ideal in a liberal English society. Mixing with the Christian world and maintaining hybridized identities need to be grounded in the Jewish home, a "crypto-Jewish space of maternal power."[77]

Divine justice is illustrated dramatically in Aguilar's "The Escape" as the Rodriquezes, condemned to death by the Inquisition as crypto-Jews, are liberated from their Lisbon prison by an earthquake. The court proceedings have nothing to do with justice, even if the torture had produced a truthful confession. Justice instead is divine and poetic. After the wife Almah, disguised as a Moorish man, is caught by the Inquisition trying to liberate her husband, Alvar, they are both condemned to death, but before the executions can take place, an earthquake devastates the city and liberates the Jewish captives who escape to England not just with their lives but with their wealth intact.

The Lisbon earthquake of 1755, which killed many thousands of people, was a point of reference for skeptical reflections on theodicy and providence, most famously by Voltaire, but Aguilar's story vindicates God by dramatizing a straightforward reversal: fire that would have consumed the bodies of the Rodriquezes in an auto da fé consumes instead the city of Lisbon, thus justly liberating the Jewish captives. Almah's crossdressing as a Moor connects the Jewish victims with the Muslim victims of Spanish Catholicism. Moreover, there is an ironic commentary on *Ivanhoe*, as the Jews in Aguilar's text return to England, which is not Scott's Norman/Saxon ethnic nation but an idealized multicultural haven: "A land whose merciful and liberal government granted to the exile and the wanderer a home of peace and rest, where they might worship the God Israel according to the law he gave."[78] As Jews go from iniquitous Lisbon to merciful and liberal England, Britain becomes the antithesis of the Catholic Iberia.

This story obviously reworks the material about the eight-year imprisonment and torture of Garcias. One difference is that the earthquake of 1755 functions as an apocalyptic liberator of Jews and divine punishment of Catholic oppressors in "The Escape," but in the factual account Garcias remains in his cell during the chaos following the disaster because he knows that trying to escape—proof of his guilt in the eyes of the Inquisition—would lead immediately to his death. Shortly after the quake, the Inquisition in fact released him.[79] His elder daughter urges him to flee from Portugal because her betrothed, Podriques, has already been forced to leave the country a step ahead of the Inquisition, which has imprisoned his father. Not arrested herself, Podriques's mother attends to the father whose ongoing trial occasioned a dream, in which the Inquisition requires the testimony of the prisoner's wife. Just as the torture equipment is being readied to force the truth out of her, she is stopped from testifying. She has a second dream where she survives a catastrophic earthquake, which in fact occurs, as she and her infant are kept from danger by what seems divine intervention. She and her husband, who is eventually released from prison, were not directly liberated by the earthquake, but their escape from Lisbon occurred shortly afterward, whereas the fictional story makes the quake the immediate cause.[80]

Comparing the factual and fictional accounts, one notices the supplement of the Shakespearean crossdressing, gesturing perhaps to Portia and the problematic source of so many Jewish representations, certainly to womanly heroism and initiative. In the factual story Podriques's mother survived the earthquake because of the dream and how she interpreted it—as divine reassurance that she would stay alive. The fictional account dispenses with the mediations and allows God to act directly to administer poetic justice for the crypto-Jews.

The real enigma is not the mechanics of escaping but how Iberian Jews managed to survive as Jews three hundred years after the fifteenth-century expulsions and three centuries of "enhanced interrogation techniques" by the Inquisition. Aguilar knows the reader is curious about how Garcias and Podriques could be public Catholics but private Jews:

> How he [Garcias] contrived, with so many jealous eyes upon him, to adhere to the rigid essentials of the Jewish faith—keeping the festivals and Sabbaths, never touching prohibited meats, and celebrating the solemn fast once a year—must now and for ever remain a mystery. We only know that it was done, and not only by him, but by hundreds of other families.[81]

Putting aside the idealization of her ancestors, many of whom maintained a bare minimum of Jewish observance, for obvious reasons, one notes how she is writing like a crypto-Jew, withholding information, disguising actual names, and obscuring details, as though something like the Inquisition, which finally went out of business in 1834, were an imminent danger. A likely reason for this style is the family inheritance of stories and proverbial maxims from the Old Country, as well as her own experiences as a Jew living among Christians. Galchinsky observes that Aguilar, from her mother and father, absorbed what amounted to an oral history of the Iberian Jews.[82] Moreover, concealment is an overdetermined impulse for Aguilar who is pressured in two directions as a woman who must hide her criticism of the patriarchy and as a Jew who must be guarded about revealing her opinions to the dominant culture.[83]

Aguilar put that oral history to work in her novel about the crypto-Jewish experience, *The Vale of Cedars*, written in the early 1830s, not published until 1850. Because three of the thirty-five chapter inscriptions are from texts published after 1835, it is evident she—or her mother, her literary editor—added to the novel after it was written. As a novel of the early 1830s, it functions, according to Michael Ragussis, "as a sequel and a supplement to" Scott's *Ivanhoe*, subverting several aspects of the earlier novel by having the Rebecca figure, Aguilar's Marie, rescue the handsome knight in distress, Arthur Stanley, the Englishman who plays the Ivanhoe role. It was Ivanhoe who rescued Rebecca at the last minute before the court was going to execute the Jewess (ch. 43). A similar irony operates in the supposed contrast between England and Spain because Arthur Stanley, when he proposes that Marie be his wife in England, neglects to say that she would have to remain a secret Jew there as well. Neither nation state accepts Jews.[84] For Elizabeth Fay, Scott's expelling Rebecca and her father Isaac to Spain at the end of *Ivanhoe* provided a discursive opening for a response.[85] The sheer popularity of *Ivanhoe* and its Rebecca, as noted in the previous chapter, makes it inevitable that Aguilar with her own Jewish heroine will accent differences or similarities with Scott's character. One difference is how their physical appearance functions because Rebecca, drawn as an Oriental beauty strikingly darker than the Saxon Rowena, is Jewish in a visible way, whereas Marie is lighter than the Spanish, darker than the Saxon, but not detectibly Jewish on Iberian soil. Visibility and invisibility is a major trope in this novel about secret Jewishness, as Fay points out.[86] Both heroines are represented as exceptionally beautiful and sexually desirable. The eroticizing of Rebecca was described in the previous chapter, and something similar occurs in Aguilar's novel in her initial physical description (ch. 2) and especially in the scene, meant to evoke Rebecca's spectacular presence at the Ashby tournament, when Marie meets the royal couple in public (ch. 10). The narrator describes how Marie prepared herself for the public event, arranging her hair and body to best advantage, including a "thrown back" collar to disclose her "delicate throat and beautiful fall of the shoulders, more than her usual attire permitted to be visible."[87] The effect of her physical presence on the royal couple and the other dignitaries was as pronounced as Rebecca's at Ashby: "undisguised admiration" and astonishment.[88] Marie, as was Rebecca, becomes the object of unwanted erotic attention from a powerful man who harms her. Don Luis Garcia, Marie's stalker, uses his standing in the Inquisition to imprison and torture her; Rebecca's Templar Knight only manages to imprison her. Marie carries on the Jessica tradition of racialized physical beauty.

In another respect Marie parallels Rebecca and Jessica: she falls in love with a Gentile, which constitutes her youthful error for which she pays a high price. Her father not telling her that she is already betrothed to her cousin and his not anticipating any problems with his daughter, a young woman, mingling socially with young men are the paternal errors that lead to the daughter's crisis. The vain father displays Marie proudly at the Castile court as the prettiest girl. If Marie's mother were still alive, she would have protected her daughter from what inevitably happened because she, unlike her husband, knows that young women are sexual beings (ch. 5). Although Marie tries to end her relationship with Arthur Stanley almost as soon as it became serious, she cannot tell him why they cannot love one another and get married. When Arthur Stanley accidentally runs into Marie after their initial court romance, he forces Marie to disclose the secret obstacle, which she does, anticipating his "aversion" and "scorn":

> Arthur staggered back, relinquishing the hands he had so fondly clasped, casting on her one look in which love and aversion were strangely and fearfully blended, and then burying his face in his hands, his whole frame shook as with some sudden and irrepressible anguish. (ch. 2).[89]

His initial, unrehearsed reaction tells Marie what she already knows, that he shares Christian Europe's hatred of Jews, but he happens to love this particular Jewess. Aguilar revises Ivanhoe, who never declares love for Rebecca, so that her Stanley has a passionate connection with Marie. What is unrequited love in Scott's novel is completely mutual in Aguilar's.[90] If she errs by falling in love with Stanley, she errs even worse by pledging never to love and marry anyone else, a promise she cannot keep after her father discloses her engagement with cousin Morales. Aguilar's novel criticizes Rebecca's vow of celibacy as not just unrealistic but counter to Jewish culture by showing the happy but childless marriage with her cousin Morales, who is cultured, sensitive, and attractive.

Marie's father seems, by ordinary moral standards, to err yet again when he insists that she withhold the information from Morales that she is in love with Arthur Stanley. "Be Ferdinand's bride, and all shall be forgiven, all forgotten" (ch. 6).[91] If she were completely honest, it is possible that neither Morales nor any other Jewish man would have agreed to marry a woman, though still a virgin, who had violated the sexual norms in two separate ways, loving a Christian and loving someone who was not first approved by the parents. Marie's deception of her husband allows her love for Morales to develop over time. Even after the unfortunate revelations about the past that start to come out in chapter ten when Stanley arrives at the royal court, Marie and her husband Morales actually reach an understanding without bitterness shortly before Don Luis Garcia murders Morales and frames Stanley for it (ch. 13). Marie's father was correct, it seems, because the initial deception of Morales was something that was overcome.

Not overcome is Garcia's perverse and murderous obsession with Marie, who cannot tell Stanley why she was able to marry Morales but not him. Stanley demonstrates a failure of imagination on several crucial occasions, after Marie discloses her Jewishness and after he learns of her marriage to Morales, but he learns from the tragedies to which he is witness. Urging her to accompany him to his own country, "my own bright land," he declares that her Jewishness will be invisible and unknown. "What to me is race or blood?" (ch. 2).[92] As mentioned earlier, post-1290 England hates Jews at least as much as 1490s Spain, so that detection in either country will be fatal. Second, if she is indistinguishable from other Spanish, she will not be invisible to the fair-skinned English. Third, he assumes that being Jewish is a matter of blood and birth only. The novel assumes otherwise and shows how Judaism is a civilization, a religion, family connections, and a utopian space identified with the "vale" upon which Stanley stumbles but utterly misunderstands. Stanley, who at that time is not even willing to accept bringing Marie's father to England, expresses the view of a nineteenth-century secular liberal from a Christian background in a Christian-majority society. Why cannot the exotic beauty, *la belle juive,* give up what seems to the cosmopolitan individualist value-less—the culture and religion in which she was raised—for the sake of love? When Stanley learns of Marie's marriage, it is damning of his moral sensibility that he does not imagine Morales must be also a crypto-Jew like Marie. Stung by jealousy and disillusionment, he seeks revenge, which is perfectly human but not heroic. As an exile himself, having lost his family in the War of the Roses, being on the wrong side of the conflict, he does indeed experience some of what Jews had to experience. His assisting Jews near the end of the novel indicates his deepened knowledge of Judaism and exile. After Marie's death Arthur marries a Spanish woman, perhaps as a substitute for his lover, and the narrator refers to him as an "Anglo-Spaniard" (ch. 35).[93] By the novel's end Arthur is far superior to Ivanhoe in his more capacious moral understanding. Ivanhoe at best is intrigued by the alien Rebecca, grateful for her help, but Arthur passionately loves a Jewess from whom he learns what it means to be Jewish in Christian Europe.

Elizabeth Fay attends to Aguilar's reading of the biblical Leah and Rachel for identifying the moral norms governing the novelist's social ideals. God rewards Leah, who is loyal to the patriarchal ideals, with many children despite her not being Jacob's favorite wife, and punishes Rachel with barrenness for her vanity about her beauty.[94] Unlike what Fay calls Scott's eroticized model of the ideal Jewess, Aguilar's is a maternal exemplar after Leah.[95] I want to apply Fay's perceptive observation to Marie's own barrenness, which, following the Leah and Rachel precedent, would be the result of her youthful individualism and vanity, for which she undergoes extraordinary penance. Called to testify in the trial of Arthur Stanley for the death of her husband, Marie cannot answer any of the court's questions because she cannot take the oath of a Christian (ch. 20). The issue of oath-taking was a central political matter for Jews especially but also for Protestant Dissenters and Catholics before their respective emancipation laws in the 1820s. If Marie pretends to be a Christian in the oath-taking ritual, she believes she would make an affront to God. In most cases rabbinic Judaism views that saving a life—*pekuach nefesh*—takes precedence over almost everything. According to the Talmud, martyrdom is permissible only in case of avoiding idolatry, incest and murder (Sanhedrin 74a-b), but Aguilar does not disclose the process of how Marie, no rabbinic scholar, reflected on her decision.

From the point she declines to testify in court on grounds she is Jewish, Marie suffers a long process of martyrdom.[96] The "unconvertibility" of Marie, in Ragussis's phrasing, unsettles the complacency of the represented Christian world.[97] Isabella's patient, extended, and loving attempt to convert Marie is at least as tormenting as the Inquisition's sadistic threats. Nadia Valman suggests that same-sex love and gender solidarity come close to overcoming the respective religious loyalties.[98] Marie's resistance to conversion subverts the Christian conversionist narratives, according to Galchinsky, who also suggests that her martyrdom, which puts the Jewish community at risk, is for the sake of Arthur Stanley, thus proving symbolically that Jews are loyal to England.[99] For Galchinsky, the martyrdom is offered as proof of Jewish sincerity to the English readers ambivalent about Jewish emancipation. For Traci Michele Klass, Marie suffers not for Arthur Stanley but for Judaism and freedom.[100]

All these ways of reading her martyrdom are persuasive. I will make some observations as well. Marie's declaration of her Jewish identity in court does not result in the liberation of Arthur Stanley, who is about to be executed when a crossdressed Marie, who has escaped from confinement, brings the message that the real murderer has been apprehended (ch. 25). Although her public Jewishness shocks Spanish society, which looks for other secret Jews, she gives up no names whatsoever when she is tortured, one of her arms almost amputated (ch. 24, 27). When she argues with the Christian authorities about Judaism, she performs at a high intellectual level and does not appeal to sentiment:

> Marie's intimate acquaintance with the Holy Scriptures in their original tongue—the language of her own people—gave her so decided an advantage over the old monk [with whom she was arguing], that, after nearly three months' trial, he sought his Sovereign, and with the most touching humility, acknowledged his utter incapacity, for the

conversion of Donna Marie, and implored her to dismiss him, and select one more fitted for the task (ch. 31).[101]

In the most hostile circumstances, a young woman with limited but not unusual education in her religion defeats in argument an experienced Christian cleric. Marie, who has strong feelings for Queen Isabella, nevertheless debates her arguments in favor of Christian conversion with skillful use of reason. The queen, whom the motherless Marie hates to disappoint, offers a cruel choice: an exceedingly harsh convent or a forced conversion and marriage with Arthur Stanley (ch. 32). The forced conversion and disregard for intellectual conviction bring one back to Shylock's forced conversion. Marie's baptism and marriage would have some consequence in the queen's managing of public opinion, just as Stalin orchestrated public confessions by political "heretics" to reinforce the impregnability of his rule. When she refuses to deny her faith, the queen accepts Marie's request to die in her place of birth, the Vale of Cedars. An exile from Segovia would be for Marie a return to her one truly safe place.

The dying martyr who returns home has established her heroic status, not the heroism of a military knight like Ivanhoe or Stanley but the heroism of the York martyrs about whom Aguilar wrote in her "History of the Jews of England," an episode also dramatized in Milman's history. Aguilar stages the impossible dilemma in which the York Jews were placed in 1190: the conquest of the besieged castle was inevitable, at which time the Christian mob would have inflicted cruel tortures before slaughtering the men, women and children; another option, articulated by the rabbi, was mass suicide, to die with as much dignity as possible.[102] Marie is terrified of the convent where she expects pitiless handling by Church officials who run St. Ursula's, which for her is the equivalent of being left to the York mob. Dying at home is parallel with the mass suicide, a form of *kiddush ha-Shem*, sanctifying the name of God by an act of sacrifice.

The Vale of Cedars where Marie returns to die is a space rich with meaning: an "edenic valley" that is "entirely secret" and invisible to Christian eyes (Fay); a moveable space essential for Judaism's survival in the Diaspora, including England (Galchinsky); functioning as a pun on "veil," the ironic exercise of hiding and revealing/unveiling Jewish reality (Ragussis).[103] The Vale does not betray its Jewishness because to Christian eyes it is a plain site without significance. Its ordinariness allows it to veil the secret Jewish practices that are permitted there: weddings, funerals, bar mitzvahs, Sabbaths, and the festivals. The novel begins and ends on Sukkot, the harvest festival commemorated by living in impermanent dwellings and studying the biblical book of Kohelet (Ecclesiastes), the theme of which is the ephemeral nature of human efforts. What survive are God and community. Marie dies, as Ragussis observes, but the Jewish community lives on.[104] The novel is not titled "Marie" or "Marie and Arthur"; rather, the Vale names a physical area as well as a symbolic space within which a different temporality prevails, one governed by a religious cycle of Sabbaths, months, holidays, and so on. For crypto-Jews, such a Vale keeps Judaism alive when it cannot be openly practiced. The "cedars" aspect of the Vale is a gesture toward Zion, from which Jews are exiled. A touching episode that illustrates how the Vale functions as a synecdochic allusion to the exile is when Marie's husband Morales discreetly cultivates in Segovia some plants he has transported from the Vale.

> An abrupt curve led to a grassy plot, from which a sparkling fountain sent up its glistening showers, before a luxurious bower, which Morales's tender care had formed of large and healthy slips, cut from the trees of the Vale of Cedars, and flowery shrubs and variegated moss from the same spot; and there he had introduced his Marie, calling it by the fond name of "Home!" (ch. 12).[105]

Like Garcias with his chicken bones used as knitting needles, Morales in his most Jewish actions integrates the feminine virtues of nurturing life. This emotionally satisfying moment will be interrupted immediately afterward by the shocking revelation about Marie's relationship with Arthur Stanley, but that irony does not destroy the necessity and durability of the Vale. One is always losing it, missing it, returning to it, recreating it, and imagining it, for its very structure presupposes the powerfully destructive forces that make it fragile. Exile and prophecy coexist in the Vale because inspired articulation issues from the sacred space, as when Marie convenes Arthur and her grandfather Julien while she is breathing her last words of love and reconciliation (ch. 34). Marie is surely the heroine of the novel, but her grandfather Julien plays a heroic role as well. The original builder of the Vale, he has labored as a crypto-Jew under deep cover within the Church trying to perform deeds helpful for Jews. Displaying energetic courage, he rescues Marie several times and acts as the Jewish community's good angel.

Aguilar imagines her version of Jessica as a martyr who honestly accepts her love of the Christian but who renounces the love for the sake of her religion. If Aguilar mobilizes the always available energies of Protestant anti-Catholicism in making the Inquisition the principal force of evil, she also, as pointed out by Fay, makes all kinds of Catholic tributes in turning Marie into a martyred saint when in England there was a medieval revival championed by writers like Benjamin Disraeli.[106] Moreover, the novel targets not so much the actually existing Inquisition—in the 1830s a nonexistent threat to anyone—but Protestant conversionism, opposition to Jewish emancipation, and European hatred, all of which are symbolized by the old Inquisition. The wildly inaccurate portrait of Queen Isabella betrays a strenuous desire to effect a gender alliance across religions. The figure of Shylock barely exists in Aguilar, somewhat present in the character of Levison in *The Perez Family*, but the Jessica figure looms large and becomes the dominant way of representing the hopeful efforts to take Judaism into a struggle for emancipation at many levels, including the political.

Conclusion

Working through Stereotypes:
After Shylock?

Coleridge's *The Ancient Mariner* (1798–1817) is readable in terms of a harsh antisemitic narrative: the Mariner kills the innocent bird and receives the punishment of eternal wandering, accompanied with guilt and remorse, always feeling alienated from Christian society. He tells his tale to the Wedding Guest outside a church that he never enters. He makes strenuous efforts to convert to Christianity by praying, confessing, and telling his story, but the moral taint of the murder is ineffaceable. His mesmeric "glittering" eye, which compels the Wedding Guest to listen, is a traditional antisemitic image of the Jewish evil eye,[1] and his brown skin suggests the conventional eighteenth-century representation of Jews, especially Sephardim, as black or dark-skinned. The Wandering Jew embedded in Coleridge's poem is hardly critical news; rather, it is too obvious and uninteresting to discuss because there are so many more exciting ways to read the work: as theological drama (Robert Penn Warren and Edward Bostetter); as antiracist slave trade allegory (Debbie Lee); as performative of the Higher Criticism of the Bible and historical hermeneutics (Jerome McGann); and so on.[2] As one of the great Romantic poems, it survives wildly different interpretations that entertain professional critics while also appealing effectively to students. It is unpleasant to notice the Wandering Jew core of the poem, which nevertheless survives the more edifying interpretations that are put on top of it, to cover it over and to make it silent.

The palimpsest one makes out of Coleridge's poem, painting over it repeatedly, is an allegory for how Jewish representation functions with many of the Romantics. If one is looking for constructions of an "inclusive community" achieved by the sympathetic imagination, as Judith Page does in her study, one finds different degrees of failure in all the Romantics. In Page's persuasive account, some like Charles Lamb do not even try very hard—or at all—to overcome their prejudice against Jews, and those who try, like Coleridge and Wordsworth, never achieve sufficient critical distance. As Page and William Galperin show in their separate readings of Wordsworth's philosemitic poem, *A Jewish Family* (1835), the poet fails on several levels to accept the Otherness of Jews as he repeats antisemitic *topoi* in an aesthetic rather than political or religious idiom, even though he thinks he is promoting humanitarian tolerance rather than the medieval hatred of Chaucer's *Prioress's Tale*, the translation of which he published and for which he was criticized and feeling defensive.[3] Although Wordsworth gives no credence to the blood libel about ritual murder that Chaucer's poem immortalizes, he offers the poetic representation of such a libel to readers for their aesthetic delectation, when many people at the time gave it credence. One can argue plausibly on either side of Wordsworth's decision to publish the Chaucer translation, but pervasive Judaeophobia is the broader point that the Chaucer episode illustrates; this fear and hatred permeate European Christian culture from the roots, nurturing powerful stereotypes with adaptable durability. These stereotypes comprise the cultural language by which Christians traditionally have acquired identity.

As numerous critics have already pointed out, Coleridge expresses his ambivalence about Jews by comparing an old-clothes man, for whom he has contempt, and the prophet Isaiah, for whom he has the highest admiration. Exercising a common rhetorical antithesis between dignified Hebrews and scurrilous Jews, Coleridge nevertheless interacted with real Jews, such as his neighbor in Highgate, Hyman Hurwitz (1770–1844), whom he helped get a position as Hebrew professor at the newly formed London University, and even an old-clothes man, with whom he had an argument that remarkably the Jew won.[4] When poets like Blake, Coleridge, Wordsworth, Byron, and Shelley express bigotry, their offences do not compare with what fervent antisemites like William Cobbett were doing in *Paper Against Gold* (1810–15) and *Good Friday; or, The Murder of Jesus Christ by the Jews* (1830). Cobbett fuses the religious argument of deicide and the curse of diasporic wandering with the secular argument of commercial immorality, bringing together Judas, the Wandering Jew, and Shylock. Here is the third paragraph of *Good Friday*, which is using Ezekiel's harsh condemnation of his fellow Israelites in chapter 22 as a point of departure to attack contemporary Jews, Judaism itself, and the Jewish people:

> The life of Jesus Christ had been one of unmixed goodness; of spotless innocence; of bright example. He went about healing the sick, comforting the afflicted, preaching patience, forgiveness of injuries, disinterestedness, charity, peace on earth, and good will amongst men; but, above all things, an abstaining from *extortion*, an abstaining from oppression of the poor, the fatherless, and the widow. But, alas! This was the very thing which gave offence to a people who were living in all the filthiness of "usury and increase;" and who, though themselves the slaves of a Roman despot, who had absolute power over their purses, seem to have had no passion other than that for accumulating money; a passion which has come down, unimpaired, to their descendants, who, while they have been "a mocking to all countries," have been, at the same time, a scourge to every country that has had the weakness and wickedness to encourage any thing approaching towards fellowship with this scattered and wandering and greedy race.[5]

Creating images of pure innocence and vulnerable weakness, he unleashes the full force of his hatred on the Jewish violators of purity. What is specific and occasional in Ezekiel is generalized and essential in Cobbett, as all Jewishness, past and present, has been funneled into this characteristic immorality. By mocking "fellowship" he targets the efforts for Jewish emancipation, which begin in 1830. The Christian virtues of patience and forgiveness do not inspire imitation but provoke the most savage retaliation after those virtues are imagined as being violated by the Jews. The more innocent the victims, the more unforgiving and punitive Cobbett becomes. Defending the Christians, he becomes more like his adversaries the imagined Jews than like the innocents he is supposedly protecting.

Cobbett's antisemitism bolsters his radical populism, whereas William Blake's engagement with Judaism and Jewish texts is entirely from the position as a radical, unorthodox Christian artist. Two dimensions of Blake's writing about Jewishness are relevant. First, he reads the Bible passionately as if his life depends on it. None of the other Romantics are as biblical as he is, for he incorporates the style of the King James Version into his poetry. Sheila Spector has shown that Christian Kabbalah shaped Blake's oeuvre in fundamental and subtle ways.[6] Using Jewish textual resources in the traditions of radical Dissent, he thinks, imagines and perceives biblically, becoming one of the most obvious examples of the hybridized writers in the Romantic canon. As a Christian reading Jewish texts, Blake does not always

express the universalist sentiments of *All Religions are One* and of
"The Divine Image" in the *Songs of Innocence* ("And all must love the
human form, / In heathen, turk or jew").[7] One of many examples of
his decidedly anti-Jewish approach is his making "Law" something
odious, associated with Urizen, a contemptible authoritarian deity,
Nobadaddy, who is identified with the Old Testament Jehovah. Such
writing is not bigotry but the form that his antinomian argument
understandably takes, given his Christian background. That said, just
as with *The Ancient Mariner,* one cannot ignore that what is essen-
tially Blakean, such as his myths of Urizen, the law, and Nobadaddy
are also characteristically and traditionally hostile to Judaism as it has
been constructed by centuries of Christianity. It is unquestionable
that he takes much from Jewish tradition, especially the prophets,
but he takes very little from rabbinic writing except what is mediated through Christian Kabbalah. The second important thing about
Blake and the Jews is that, as Karen Shabetai explains, he does not
give any attention to their social and political difficulties. As for actually existing Jews who are his neighbors in London, these people and
their religion provoke his hostility.[8] Isaiah and Ezekiel the biblical
prophets are his close intellectual intimates; the Isaiahs and Ezekiels
who live in the East End do not interest him, and if he must comment
on them, he expresses the customary bigotry about big noses and
miserliness. One may be disappointed Blake does not transcend the
prejudices, intellectual and social, more than he did, but his oeuvre
is more strongly shaped by an encounter with Jewish textuality than
most of the other Romantics.

Shelley's vehement words against Judaism in *Queen Mab* (1813)
and *A Refutation of Deism* (1814) are harsh and extensive, but
they are routine antireligious polemic in the tradition of Holbach,
Voltaire, and Paine. After these early works he concentrates more on
the more philosophically rigorous Spinoza, whom he translates, and
the Bible itself, which he reads, according to Bryan Shelley's convincing study, to turn "biblically informed language against the biblical
world-view."[9] As a serious reader of both the Jewish and Christian
scriptures, Shelley takes the antireligious argument in sophisticated
directions. Shelley, who does not lack for snide comments in letters
about "Jew bankers," inserts gratuitous anti-Jewish references in
texts like *A Philosophical View of Reform* (1819)—"they [the English
government] would shoot and hew down any multitude [working-
class protesters], without regard to sex or age, as the Jews did the
Canaanites."[10] Instinctively and unrehearsed, Shelley connects cruel
political violence with Jews, just as when Blake imagines the most

authoritarian figure responsible for the worst conceivable evils, the villain has a Jewish appearance; when Coleridge imagines the worst crime to produce the most agonizing guilt, the killing of Jesus comes to his imagination—and it is not the Roman Empire that is the culprit. The Romantics usually work with these cultural myths from tradition and make something far less toxic than the raw material with which they started. They work with the stereotypes. The *Ancient Mariner* becomes something more than a Jewish allegory, Urizen is much more than a trope for the Jewish God, and Shelley investigates cruel political violence from multiple angles and contexts. The bias against Judaism and Jews, however, is the position from which they start because of the many centuries of hostility.

Shelley's bigotry, which does not amount to much, must be put in context with a manuscript transcribed by Tatsuo Tokoo and edited by Nora Crook, "Restoration of the Jews." This remarkable draft essay proposes, within the assumptions of Romantic nationalism, that Jews return to and settle Zion to become one of the great nations. The text is in the form of an address by a cosmopolitan Jew to his community. Although it is roughly similar to the millenarian discourse of Zionist return, it takes a more secular tone and approach, attending to the power politics of the Near East, brushing aside the theological questions about prophecy and the Messiah. Like the late nineteenth-century Zionists, Shelley's imaginary Jew argues in favor of restoration even in the absence of a divine Messiah.[11]

The evolution of Shelley's Ahasuerus, the Wandering Jew, from the early work (*The Wandering Jew* [1810], the gothic fiction *St. Irvyne* [1811], *Queen Mab* [1813]) to *Hellas* (1821) indicates an imaginative investment in the figure that is unusually intense. The *Hellas* figure plays the reluctant prophet role, called in for consultation by the Muslim leader, the Sultan Mahmud. In the context of the "Restoration of the Jews," *Hellas* has another meaning because the new Jewish state would have to extricate itself from the control of the Ottoman Empire. If Greece overcomes the Turks, as Shelley and his friends passionately hope, then a weakened Empire would be more vulnerable to losing another colony. The Jewish character in the play is not simply a gothic curiosity to enliven the drama with exotic color, but a figure who represents the dispersed Jews who actually might be returning in the near future, negating the premise itself of the Wandering Jew. One of the Messengers reports to Mahmud of political revolt in the Near East: "The Christian tribes / Of Lebanon and the Syrian wilderness / Are in revolt—Damascus, Hems, Aleppo / Tremble—the Arab menaces Medina, / The Ethiop has intrenched himself in Senaar, / And keeps the Egyptian rebel well employed" (ll. 578–83).[12] If the Ottoman Empire is collapsing, then "Restoration of the Jews" is not a playful exercise of wit but a thoughtful response to immediate political events; Shelley anticipates the outcome of the conflicts and intervenes with his Zionist essay.

Hellas's Ahasuerus, unlike his previous incarnations in Shelley's work, is emphatically human ("Thou art a man, thou sayest, even as we" [l. 738]) and a cosmopolitan philosopher; he is not the gothic victim-rebel of the earlier work. He stimulates the Sultan to look deep into himself to understand his role in history and how Empire, founded in blood, will end in blood. When Mahmud says to Ahasuerus that "thou disdainest us and ours" (l. 760), he expresses the conventional view that Jews hate Gentiles, but Ahasuerus corrects him: "Disdain thee? Not the worm beneath thy feet!" (l. 762). The stereotype of the Christian-hating Shylock who cares only for money is replaced by the Jewish philosopher who speaks the Promethean language of mystical humility and universal love. Shelley does not always prefer the Hellenic to the Hebraic, for here the Hebraic is the standard of the wisest judgment. Ahasuerus's speech accents a philosophical idealism that is autonomous and unmoored from any place or time. "Thought alone" is the essential dimension of reality, not external reality; only Thought is immortal and free from circumstance (ll. 795–802). If one sees Ahasuerus as representing the Diaspora which is ready to return and which has for many centuries developed its intellectual culture despite its geographical wandering and political misfortunes, then one notices the relevance of the idealism to the Zionist project that becomes possible if the Ottoman Empire truly dissolves. The "Restoration of the Jews" and *Hellas* are not replacing one prejudice against Jews with a prejudice against Arabs and Muslims because the overarching concept is anti-imperialistic Romantic nationalism, not Orientalism.

Lord Byron, who battled against the Ottoman Empire by fighting on the Greek side, plays a positive role in relation to the Jews for several reasons. His strongly expressed Romantic nationalism included Jews after the *Hebrew Melodies* (1815), who were treated as a worthy nation that deserved support. His public collaboration with Isaac Nathan on the *Hebrew Melodies* was courageous because some critics viciously attacked him for blurring the lines between respectable Gentile aristocrats and low-status Jews. The Byronic hero in the Eastern Tales, *Childe Harold*, and other poems is available to sympathetic identification by outsider social groups and individuals. It is not for nothing that the nineteenth-century Hebrew and Yiddish translations of

Romantic poetry are overwhelmingly those of Byron's poetry.[13] In the previous chapter I described how the Moss sisters incorporated twenty Byron extracts into their work of historical fiction.

Nevertheless, Byron expresses casual bigotry about "Jew brokers" and Shylocks with some frequency, mocking Nathan at the same time he works with him. In section fifteen of one of his poems, *The Age of Bronze* (1823), there is an attack on Rothschild and Jewish financiers that is almost Cobbett-like in its ferocity. In an article sixteen years ago I unpacked many of the allusions and recreated the poetic logic to illustrate its antisemitic meanings.[14] I will quote the last eighteen lines of the section:

> Two Jews, a chosen people, can command
> In every realm their scripture-promised land:—
> Two Jews keep down the Romans, and uphold
> The accursed Hun, more brutal than of old:
> Two Jews—but not Samaritans—direct
> The world, with all the spirit of their sect.
> What is the happiness of earth to them?
> A Congress forms their "New Jerusalem,"
> Where baronies and orders both invite—
> Oh, holy Abraham! Dost thou see the sight?
> Thy followers mingling with these royal swine,
> Who spit not "on their Jewish gaberdine,"
> But honour them as portion of the show—
> (Where now, oh, Pope! Is thy forsaken toe?
> Could it not favour Judah with some kicks?
> Or has it ceased to "kick against the pricks?")
> On Shylock's shore behold them stand afresh,
> To cut from nations' hearts their "pound of flesh." (688–705)[15]

The "two Jews" of the poem, the Rothschild brothers, function as the embodiment of Jewish evil, not just two bad Jews. These greedy bankers do not happen to be Jewish; they could *only* have been Jewish, as their greed expresses their essence. The Shakespeare citation about Shylock and the pound of flesh brings up an enormous cultural archive of multifarious appropriations from the play too numerous to identify. All of the hatred evoked by "Shylock" and "pound of flesh" falls onto the Rothschild brothers. The poem justifies the spitting on Shylock, one of Antonio's unrepentantly hateful actions, and laments instead that Gentiles have ceased harming the Jew who instead has become the ruler of the political world. Spitting on the Rothschilds would be perfectly appropriate in the context created by the poem. If Byron wanted to attack just the Rothschilds, as he did in *Don Juan* 12.5, it is not necessary to make them representative of Jewishness. Although Lord George Gordon in the 1780s had proposed to Europe's Jewish financiers to cease funding war, Gordon was making a radical pacifist proposal for bold, principled action. Byron here is taking an entirely different approach: the Rothschilds, who are said to run the world, are the real power, while the political leaders of Europe are their puppets. Such a view is like that of the *Protocols of the Elders of Zion* (1903), propaganda invented by the Russian police, which articulated the worldwide Jewish conspiracy. Byron surely knew that in 1819 the anti-Jewish "Hep! Hep!" rioters in Germany targeted the Rothschilds. Surely he knew the Rothschilds did not control the world, so why would he make the poem say that? I understand why Byron wrote section fifteen no better now than I did sixteen years ago.

That Byron, one of the Jews' better friends among the Romantics, would write as he did suggests the power of the stereotype over merely subjective intention. The overall poem, *The Age of Bronze*, has other aspects that have nothing to do with Jews, and one can say truthfully that section fifteen is only a small part of the whole, that Byron wrote much else. All true.

Returning to the issue of stereotypes again: how to account for their power but the apparent decline of antisemitism in modern Britain? First, the stereotype's power: Frank Felsenstein has pointed to Walter Lippmann's *Public Opinion* (1922) for its surprisingly respectful discussion of the stereotype, which is efficient and saves time ("to see all things freshly and in detail, rather than as types and generalities, is exhausting"), makes "us" feel comfortable and at home in the world, and functions as "the fortresss of our tradition." Moreover, he insists that the ordinary mode of perception is stereotypical:

> For the most part we do not first see, and then define, we define first and then see. In the great bloomy, buzzing confusion of the outer world we pick out what our culture has already defined for us, and we tend to perceive that which we have picked out in the form stereotyped for us by our culture.[16]

An American Jew writing before the Shoah, Lippmann is composing his thoughts also when anti-Jewish sentiment was strengthening not weakening, and lynchings of blacks were ordinary events in the southern United States.[17] Writing as a liberal, he had nothing in common with the Nazis and the Ku Klux Klan, but he is arguing that stereotypes, which the extremists exploit, constitute who we are, all of us, not just the extremists. The evidence from Jewish representations in British literature lends support to Lippmann's view, that from the most well-meaning to the most hateful there is a spectrum of prejudice and stereotypical perceptions, rarely the complete absence of bigotry. The stereotype's role in community maintenance and cohesiveness can be observed in any historical period or geographical region. If one accepts Lippmann's argument, then we have to accept prejudice as common and work from that position, instead of constructing an absolute dichotomy of purity and impurity, innocence and guilt, unbiased and bigoted. Other than wishful thinking, there is not a rebuttal of what Lippmann says about the ordinariness of stereotyping and prejudice. It is not that one is helpless against such ordinariness but that understanding it and working through it is not easy, natural, or inevitable. Left to its own lazy developments, stereotypical discourse will not correct itself.

Why then did British antisemitism, despite the pervasiveness of stereotyping in its literature, seem to decline and result in only a relatively little violence from the Readmission to the present?

A reasonable position is the one taken by Todd Endelman, that the weakening of British antisemitism is due to the overall decline of religion and the flourishing of secularism.[18] The Empire also surely played a role in providing Others against which national identity could be formed. The intensification of European antisemitism from the latter half of the nineteenth century when secularism rises at the expense of religion suggests Britain was exceptional, but perhaps not, for antisemitism in Britain also intensified with the increased immigration from Eastern Europe and Russia, resulting in the 1905 Aliens Act. Because Germany's antisemitism was so much worse than anyone else's, the other countries, including the United States, which resisted accepting Jewish refugees during the Hitler period, appeared more benign than they actually were. European antisemitism weakened greatly after the Shoah because of shame and guilt, not it seems secularization, and now that much time has passed the intensity of the guilt has diminished as well. In demonizing Israel—the now respectable form that antisemitism has taken—the old stereotypes are dusted off and put to use: complaints about the power of the Israel Lobby sound like the diatribes against the Rothschilds and the Goldsmids; Israel's many wars of defense are construed as wars of aggression, with Israel depicted as a ritual murderer and deicide, the assassin of innocence, a nation incomparably more evil than any other.

Because at its very origins Christianity competed with and defined itself against Judaism, and because the Jews who found themselves in Christian-majority societies integrated aspects of the Christian culture to survive, the ordinary social identity is a mixed one. The idea of cultural purity does not survive rigorous scrutiny. When Wordsworth defends his Chaucer translation and invents his "Jewish Family" poem, he is not thinking about the ways his Pedlar and Michael are connected with a figurative Jewishness. When David Levi and Solomon Bennett protest the Christian mistranslations and misinterpretations of scripture, they are not recognizing that any biblical text in the English language will be affected by the King James Version, its phrasing and rhythms, all of which affects interpretation. The mixing of traditions is most forceful with a convert like Lord George Gordon, but mixing is normative, although neither tradition enjoys acknowledging the fact.

The most disputatious point is how to draw the lines of inclusion for community, whether of the state by constitutional criteria, or of religious and ethnic associations by traditions and customs. Despite mixed identities and ambiguous loyalties, one is a citizen or not, one belongs to this congregation and not another, one identifies with and is recognized by this social group and not another. Literature participates directly and indirectly in this line-drawing process as it works out national, religious, and ethnic identities. For reasons already discussed in the earlier chapters, the eighteenth and nineteenth centuries are the era of Jewish emancipation, how it will be achieved, on what terms, and according to what logic. As I hope I have illustrated, the Wandering Jew, the pedlar, the moneylender, *la belle juive*, the Fall of Jerusalem, the *converso*, Shylock, Jessica, Rebecca, and Fagin all play a role in how Jewishness is experienced within Englishness.

I can foresee the moment when the model of ambivalence for reading Jewish representations will no longer serve the interests of accounting most insightfully for the evidence at hand. Accented differently, ambivalence will appear to be intellectual evasion rather than open-mindedness. For the present, however, it seems the best approach, reflecting perhaps my own mixed identity as a convert to Judaism.

Maurycy Gottlieb's great painting, *Shylock and Jessica* (1876), brings one back to art that turns the stereotype into something that challenges preconceptions and conventional beliefs, that tells us things we did not know before. The chapter's title is meant to suggest Freud's concept of *durcharbeiten*, working through, to suggest a cumulative development of intellectual and artistic labor provoked by

Shakespeare's remarkable *Merchant of Venice* and the historical energies it harnessed. "Working through" suggests the admirable goal of
moving toward the other side where the negativity of the stereotype
is not as powerful, but in the process one learns from and interrogates
the distorted truths that make up the stereotype, an all too human
construct.[19]

NOTES

INTRODUCTION

1. Daniel Jonah Goldhagen, *Hitler's Willing Executioners: Ordinary Germans and the Holocaust* (New York: Vintage Books, 1997). Sander L. Gilman disputes Goldhagen's a teleological reading of German antisemitism in *Jewish Frontiers: Essays on Bodies, Histories, and Identities* (New York: Palgrave Macmillan, 2003), 7.
2. Homi K. Bhabha, *The Location of Culture*, new ed. (London and New York: Routledge, 2004), 53–55.
3. Bryan Cheyette, *Constructions of "the Jew" in English Literature and Society: Racial Representations, 1875–1945* (Cambridge: Cambridge University Press, 1993), 1–12.
4. Robert Chazan, *Medieval Stereotypes and Modern Antisemitism* (Berkeley: University of California Press, 1997).
5. Michael Galchinsky, *The Origin of the Modern Woman Jewish Writer: Romance and Reform in Victorian England* (Detroit: Wayne State University Press, 1996), 34.
6. Sander L. Gilman, *Jewish Self-Hatred: Antisemitism and The Hidden Language of the Jews* (Baltimore and London: Johns Hopkins University Press, 1986), 211–14.
7. For insisting that "philosemitism" requires more explanation than I was giving it, I thank my colleague Professor Simone Chess (Wayne State University). A promising alternative to the Semitic terminology is Heidi Kaufman's "Jewish discourse," a neutral phrase. *English Origins, Jewish Discourse, and the Nineteenth-Century British Novel: Reflections on a Nested Nation* (University Park: Pennsylvania State University Press, 2009). Irving Massey finds some forms of philosemitism to be not concealed antagonism, especially the kind that leads to conversion to Judaism and fellowship with Jews. Irving Massey, *Philo-Semitism in Nineteenth-Century German Literature* (Tübingen: Max Niemeyer Verlag, 2000), 30–38.
8. J. Laplanche and J.-B. Pontalis, *The Language of Psycho-Analysis*, trans. Donald Nicholson-Smith (New York: W.W. Norton and Co., 1973), 27.
9. Laplanche and Pontalis, *The Language of Psycho-Analysis*, 27.
10. Laplanche and Pontalis, *The Language of Psycho-Analysis*, 28.
11. Gilman, *Jewish Self-Hatred*, 2.

12. Bhabha, *The Location of Culture*, 95. Bhabha also wrote a foreword, "Joking Aside: The Idea of a Self-Critical Community," to Byran Cheyette and Laura Marcus, ed., *Modernity, Culture and "the Jew"* (Stanford: Stanford University Press, 1998), xv–xx.
13. Bhabha, *The Location of Culture*, 100.
14. Bhabha, *The Location of Culture*, 117.
15. William Shakespeare, *The Merchant of Venice*, ed. M. Lindsay Kaplan (Boston: Bedford/St. Martin's, 2002), 154–59; James Shapiro, *Shakespeare and the Jews* (New York: Columbia University Press, 1996), 122–23.
16. Frank Felsenstein, *Antisemitic Stereotypes: A Paradigm of Otherness in English Popular Culture, 1660–1830* (Baltimore and London: Johns Hopkins University Press, 1995), 243.
17. Anthony Julius, *Trials of the Diaspora: A History of Antisemitism in England* (Oxford and New York: Oxford University Press, 2010), 199–204.
18. J.J. Tobias, *Prince of the Fences: The Life and Crimes of Ikey Solomons*, foreword Ewen Montagu (London: Vallentine, Mitchell, 1974).
19. Jonathan H. Grossman, "The Absent Jew in Dickens: Narrators in *Oliver Twist*, *Our Mutual Friend*, and *A Christmas Carol*," *Dickens Studies Annual: Essays on Victorian Fiction* 24 (1996): 37–57.
20. Edgar Rosenberg, *From Shylock to Svengali: Jewish Stereotypes in English Fiction* (Stanford: Stanford University Press, 1960), 19.
21. Charles Dickens, *Oliver Twist*, ed. Philip Horne (London: Penguin, 2003), Book 3, ch. 3, 337.
22. Grossman, "The Absent Jew in Dickens," 50.
23. For attending to the popular culture of Jewish representations, I am following Frank Felsenstein, *Antisemitic Stereotypes*, and Gilman, *The Jew's Body* (New York and London: Routledge, 1991).
24. Nadia Valman, *The Jewess in Nineteenth-Century British Literary Culture* (Cambridge: Cambridge University Press, 2007).
25. Michael Ragussis, *Figures of Conversion: "The Jewish Question" and English National Identity* (Durham and London: Duke University Press, 1995); Valman, *The Jewess in Nineteenth-Century British Literary Culture*; Cynthia Scheinberg, *Women's Poetry and Religion in Victorian England: Jewish Identity and Christian Culture* (Cambridge: Cambridge University Press, 2002).
26. Richard Popkin and Gordon M. Weiner, eds., *Jewish Christians and Christian Jews: From the Renaissance to the Enlightenment* (London, Dordrecht, and Boston: Kluwer Academic Publishers, 1992).

CHAPTER 1

Parts of this chapter appeared in a different form: "Rethinking Margin and Center in Anglo-Jewish Literature" in *Romanticism/Judaica: A*

Convergence of Cultures, ed. Sheila A. Spector (Farnham and Burlington: Ashgate, 2011), 157–68.).

1. Todd M. Endelman, *The Jews of Britain, 1656 to 2000* (Berkeley, Los Angeles, and London: University of California Press, 2002), 1–13; David Feldman, *Englishmen and Jews: Social Relations and Political Culture, 1840–1914* (New Haven: Yale University Press, 1994), 142; David Katz, *The Jews in the History of England, 1485–1850* (Oxford: Clarendon Press, 1994), 1–14.

2. Endelman, *The Jews of Britain*, 4.

3. James Shapiro, *Shakespeare and the Jews* (New York: Columbia University Press, 1996), 85–86.

4. Sander L. Gilman, *Jewish Self-Hatred : Antisemitism and The Hidden Language of the Jews* (Baltimore: Johns Hopkins University Press, 1986), 391.

5. Anthony Julius, *Trials of the Diaspora: A History of Anti-Semitism in England* (Oxford and New York: Oxford University Press, 2010), 583.

6. Lori Higgins, "Wayne State University Drops Helen Thomas Diversity Award Over Journalist's Controversial Remarks," *Detroit Free Press* (December 4, 2010), on-line.

7. Shapiro, *Shakespeare and the Jews*, 1.

8. Shapiro, *Shakespeare and the Jews*, 199.

9. Shapiro, *Shakespeare and the Jews*, 199–218.

10. Endelman, *The Jews of Georgian England 1714–1830: Tradition and Change in a Liberal Society* (Ann Arbor: University of Michigan Press, 1999), 198–203.

11. Michael Ragussis, *Theatrical Nation: Jews and Other Outlandish Englishmen in Georgian Britain* (Philadelphia: University of Pennsylvania Press, 2010), 29.

12. Ragussis, *Theatrical Nation*, 12–13.

13. Ragussis, *Theatrical Nation*, 27, 138.

14. Ragussis, *Figures of Conversion: "The Jewish Question" and English National Identity* (Durham and London: Duke University Press, 1995), 15–56.

15. Michael Galchinsky, *The Origin of the Modern Jewish Woman Writer: Romance and Reform in Victorian England* (Detroit: Wayne State University Press, 1996), 41–57.

16. Nadia Valman, *The Jewess in Nineteenth-Century British Literary Culture* (Cambridge: Cambridge University Press, 2007), 51–84.

17. Heidi Kaufman, *English Origins, Jewish Discourse and the Nineteenth-Century British Novel: Reflections on a Nested Nation* (University Park: Pennsylvania State University Press, 2009), 1–11.

18. Cynthia Scheinberg, "Introduction: Re-mapping Anglo-Jewish Literary History," *Victorian Literature and Culture* 27.1 (1999): 115–24.

19. Eitan Bar-Yosef, *The Holy Land in English Culture 1799–1917: Palestine and the Question of Orientalism* (Oxford: Clarendon Press, 2005), 1–17, 105–81.
20. David B. Ruderman attends to the Anglo-Jewish writing of the eighteenth and early nineteenth century in *Jewish Enlightenment in an English Key: Anglo-Jewry's Construction of Modern Jewish Thought* (Princeton: Princeton University Press, 2000).
21. Sheila A. Spector, ed., *British Romanticism and the Jews: History, Culture, Literature* (New York: Palgrave/Macmillan, 2002); and *The Jews and British Romanticism: Politics, Religion, Culture* (New York: Palgrave/Macmillan, 2005).
22. Kaufman, *English Origins*, 1–11.
23. Ruth R. Wisse, *The Modern Jewish Canon: A Journey Through Language and Culture* (Chicago: University of Chicago Press, 2002); and Bryan Cheyette, "On Being a Jewish Critic," *Jewish Social Studies* 11.1 (2004): 32–51.
24. David Philipson, *My Life As An American Jew: An Autobiography* (Cincinnati: John G. Kidd & Son, 1941), 18.
25. Valman, "Semitism and Criticism: Victorian Anglo-Jewish Literary History," *Victorian Literature and Culture* 27.1 (1999): 237–38.
26. Philipson, *The Jew in English Fiction*, 4th ed. (New York: Bloch Publishing, 1918), 7–8.
27. Philipson, *The Jew in English Fiction*, 29.
28. Philipson, *The Jew in English Fiction*, 200.
29. Philipson, *The Jew in English Fiction*, 79.
30. Edward N. Calisch, *The Jew in English Literature, As Author and As Subject* (Richmond, VA: Bell Book and Stationery, 1909), 125–27.
31. Ragussis, *Figures of Conversion*, 111–18.
32. Edgar Rosenberg, *From Shylock to Svengali: Jewish Stereotypes in English Fiction* (Stanford: Stanford University Press, 1960), 302.
33. Rosenberg, *From Shylock to Svengali*, 17–19.
34. Montagu Frank Modder, *The Jew in the Literature of England to the End of the Nineteenth Century* (Philadelphia: Jewish Publication Society of America, 1939), 14.
35. Rosenberg, *From Shylock to Svengali*, 38.
36. Adorno, Theodor W. and Max Horkheimer. *Dialectic of Enlightenment* (1944), trans. John Cumming (New York: Continuum, 1972).
37. Harold Fisch, *The Dual Image: The Figure of the Jew in English and American Literature* (New York: Ktav Publishing House, 1971), 51.
38. Rosenberg, *From Shylock to Svengali*, 302–3.
39. Fisch, *The Dual Image*, chapters 5–7.
40. Modder, *The Jew in the Literature of England*, vii–ix.
41. Modder, *The Jew in the Literature of England*, 360.
42. Calisch, *The Jew in English Literature*, 48.
43. Valman, "Semitism and Criticism," 238.

44. M[eyer] J. Landa, *The Jew in Drama* (New York: William Morrow, 1927), 309.

45. H[ijman] Michelson, *The Jew in Early English Literature* (Amsterdam: H. J. Paris, 1926), 1–6.

46. W. D. Rubinstein, *A History of the Jews in the English-Speaking World: Great Britain* (Basingstoke, London and New York: Macmillan and St. Martin's, 1996), 1–35.

47. Rubinstein, *A History of the Jews*, 375–91.

48. Michelson, *The Jew in Early English Literature*, 4–5.

49. See, for example, Claude Lanzmann, "From the Holocaust to The Holocaust," *Telos* 42 (1979–80): 137–43; and Barton Byg, "Holocaust and West German 'Restoration,'" *Telos* 42 (1979–80): 143–49.

50. Philipson, *The Jew in English Fiction*, 161, 189.

51. Philipson, 185; Calisch, *The Jew in English Literature*, 16–17.

52. Gilman, *Jewish Self-Hatred*.

53. Endelman, *The Jews of Britain*, 170.

54. Valman, "Semitism and Criticism," 239.

55. Gilman, *Jewish Self-Hatred*, 241.

56. Calisch, *The Jew in English Literature*, 13–15.

57. Calisch, *The Jew in English Literature*, 16.

58. See Spector, *"Glorious incomprehensible": The Development of Blake's Kabbalistic Language* (Lewisburg, PA: Bucknell University Press, 2001); *"Wonders Divine": The Development of Blake's Kabbalistic Myth* (Lewisburg, PA: Bucknell University Press, 2001); *Byron and the Jews: A Study in Translation* (Detroit: Wayne State University Press, 2010); and Cheyette, *Constructions of "the Jew" in English Literature and Society: Racial Representations, 1875–1945* (Cambridge: Cambridge University Press, 1995), 206–67.

59. Judith W. Page, *Imperfect Sympathies: Jews and Judaism in British Romantic Literature and Culture* (New York: Palgrave/Macmillan, 2004), 53–80.

60. Feldman, *Englishmen and Jews*; Katz, *The Jews in the History of England*.

61. Ragussis, *Figures of Conversion*, 1–13.

62. Modder, *The Jew in the Literature of England*, 187–91, 192–216.

63. Calisch, *The Jew in English Literature*, 162.

64. Philipson, *The Jew in English Fiction*, 107–25.

65. David Sorkin, *The Transformation of German Jewry 1780–1840* (Detroit: Wayne State University Press, 1999), treats this "quid pro quo" phenomenon in great detail.

66. Bill Williams, "The Anti-Semitism of Tolerance: Middle-Class Manchester and the Jews 1870–1900," in *City, Class and Culture: Studies of Social Policy and Cultural Production in Victorian Manchester*, ed. Alan J. Kidd and K. W. Roberts (Manchester: Manchester University Press, 1985), 74–102.

67. Iain McCalman, *Radical Underworld: Prophets, Revolutionaries, and Pornographers in London, 1795–1840* (Oxford: Clarendon Press, 1993), 35–39.

68. Michael Galchinsky, "Africans, Indians, Arabs, and Scots: Jewish and Other Questions in the Age of Empire," *Jewish Culture and History* 6.1 (2003): 46–60.

69. Jonathan and Daniel Boyarin, *Powers of Diaspora: Two Essays on the Relevance of Jewish Culture* (Minneapolis: University of Minnesota Press, 2002); Wisse, *The Modern Jewish Canon.*

70. Michael Ragussis, "The 'Secret' of English Anti-Semitism: Anglo-Jewish Studies and Victorian Studies." *Victorian Studies* 40.2 (1997): 295–307; Rubinstein, *A History of the Jews.*

71. Frank Felsenstein, *Anti-Semitic Stereotypes: A Paradigm of Otherness in English Popular Culture, 1660–1830* (Baltimore and London: Johns Hopkins University Press, 1995), 252.

CHAPTER 2

1. Anthony Julius, *Trials of the Diaspora: A History of Anti-Semitism in England* (Oxford and New York: Oxford University Press, 2010), 250.

2. Cecil Roth, *A History of the Jews in England*, 3rd ed. (Oxford: Oxford University Press, 1964), 163.

3. Robert Chazan, *Medieval Stereotypes and Modern Antisemitism* (Berkeley, Los Angeles, and London: University of California Press, 1997), 74–94.

4. Michael Ragussis, *Figures of Conversion: "The Jewish Question" and English National Identity* (Durham, NC: Duke University Press, 1995), 11.

5. Todd M. Endelman, *The Jews of Georgian England 1714–1830: Tradition and Change in a Liberal Society* (Ann Arbor: University of Michigan Press, 1999), 217; John Gross, *Shylock: Four Hundred Years in the Life of a Legend* (London: Chatto and Windus, 1992), 112.

6. Edgar E. MacDonald, ed., *Education of the Heart: The Correspondence of Rachel Mordecai Lazarus and Maria Edgeworth* (Chapel Hill: University of North Carolina Press, 1977).

7. James Harrington, "*The Commonwealth of Oceana*" *and* "*A System of Politics*," ed. J. G. A. Pocock (Cambridge: Cambridge University Press, 1992), 6.

8. Eliane Glaser, *Judaism Without Jews: Philosemitism and Christian Polemic in Early Modern England* (New York: Palgrave Macmillan, 2007), 113–29.

9. Michael Ragussis, *Theatrical Nation: Jews and Other Outlandish Englishmen in Georgian Britain* (Philadelphia: University of Pennsylvania Press, 2010).

10. Gershom G. Scholem, *Major Trends in Jewish Mysticism,* 3rd ed. (New York: Schocken Books, 1961), 287–324.

11. Mayir Vreté, "The Restoration of the Jews in English Protestant Thought 1790–1840," *Middle Eastern Studies* 8 (1972): 3–50.

12. Todd M. Endelman, *The Jews of Britain, 1656–2000* (Berkeley, Los Angeles, and London: University of California Press, 2002), 20–26; Cecil Roth, *A Life of Menasseh Ben Israel: Rabbi, Printer, and Diplomat* (Philadelphia: Jewish Publication Society of America, 1934), 18–29.

13. Henry Méchoulain and Gérard Nahon, "Introduction," in *Menasseh Ben Israel, The Hope of Israel: The English Translation by Moses Wall, 1652* (New York: Oxford University Press, 1987), 62–63. Cf; Ismar Schorsch, "From Messianism to Realpolitik: Menasseh Ben Israel and the Readmission of the Jews to England," *Proceedings of the American Academy for Jewish Research* 45 (1978): 189, who argues for the priority of the Latin version.

14. Endelman, *The Jews of Britain,* 21.

15. Michel Foucault, "What Is An Author?" in *Critical Theory Since 1965,* ed. Hazard Adams and Leroy Searle (Tallahassee: University Presses of Florida, 1986), 138–48

16. A major theme in Endelman's histories of Anglo-Jewry (1999, 2002) is that many Jews became culturally English, adopting class-appropriate lifestyles, long before official political emancipation in 1858–70s. In the eighteenth and nineteenth centuries, even the most acculturated retained a strong Jewish identity.

17. Menasseh ben Israel, "Humble Addresses" (1650), in *Menasseh Ben Israel's Mission to Oliver Cromwell: Being a reprint of the Pamphlets published by Menasseh Ben Israel to Promote the Re-admission of the Jews to England 1649–56,* ed. Lucien Wolf (London: Jewish Historical Society of England and Macmillan, 1901), 78–80. According to Wolf, the "Humble Addresses" had been composed, translated into English, and ready for publication well before he arrived in London in October, 1655 (xxxviii).

18. Yosef Kaplan, "Political Concepts in the World of the Portuguese Jews of Amsterdam During the Seventeenth Century: The Problem of Exclusion and the Boundaries of Self-Identity," in *Menasseh Ben Israel and His World,* ed. Yosef Kaplan, Henry Méchoulan, and Richard H. Popkin (Leiden, New York, København, Köln: E. J. Brill, 1989), 51–52.

19. Menasseh ben Israel, "Humble Addresses," 81–89.

20. Menasseh ben Israel, "Humble Addresses," 100–03.

21. Menasseh ben Israel, "Humble Addresses," 101.

22. Julius, *Trials of the Diaspora,* 251; Avrom Saltman, *The Jewish Question in 1655: Studies in Prynne's "Demurrer"* (Ramat-Gan and Jerusalem: Bar-Ilan University Press, 1995), 20.

23. H.S.Q. Henriques, *The Return of the Jews to England: Being a Chapter in the History of English Law* (London: Macmillan, 1905), 12–14.

24. Lucien Wolf, "Introduction," in *Menasseh Ben Israel's Mission to Oliver Cromwell*, liv.

25. William Prynne, *A Short Demurrer to the Jewes Long discontinued Remitter into England* (London: Edward Thomas, 1655), 7.

26. Prynne, *Short Demurrer*, 6.

27. Prynne, *Short Demurrer*, 16.

28. Prynne, *The Jew in English Literature*, 10–13.

29. Prynne, *The Jew in English Literature*, 91.

30. Menasseh with six other Jews petitioned Cromwell for resettlement privileges in March 1656 but received no response. Glaser, *Judaism Without Jews*, 12.

31. David Sorkin, *The Transformation of German Jewry 1780–1840* (Detroit: Wayne State University Press, 1999), 68–69.

32. Menasseh ben Israel, "Vindiciae Judaeorum," in *Menasseh Ben Israel's Mission*, 107–21.

33. Menasseh ben Israel, "Vindiciae Judaeorum," 122–45. I accept Jonathan Israel's reading of the text's "Geneva" as a misprint of "Genova" or Genoa. Jonathan I. Israel, "Menasseh ben Israel and the Dutch Sephardic Colonization Movement of the Mid-Seventeenth Century (1645–57)," in *Menasseh Ben Israel and His World*, 153.

34. Roth claims that "Vindiciae Judaeorum" lacks a messianic dimension, which seems inaccurate. *A Life of Menasseh Ben Israel*, 264.

35. According to Rivkah Schatz, 70% of the English clergy at the time were millenarians. "Menasseh ben Israel's Approach to Messianism in the Jewish-Christian Context," in *Menasseh Ben Israel and His World*, 244.

36. Michael Scrivener, *The Cosmopolitan Ideal in the Age of Revolution and Reaction, 1776–1832* (London: Pickering & Chatto, 2007), ch. 1.

37. Menasseh ben Israel, "Humble Addresses," 79–80.

38. David S. Katz, *Philo-Semitism and the Readmission of the Jews to England 1603–55* (Oxford: Clarendon Press, 1982).

39. Richard H. Popkin, "Hartlib, Dury and the Jews," *Samuel Hartlib and Universal Reformation: Studies in Intellectual Communication*, ed. Mark Greengrass, Michael Leslie, and Timothy Raylor (Cambridge: Cambridge University Press, 1994), 129–30. Caraites, viewed as the truest kind of Jews by many philosemites, rejected rabbinic law and followed only the Hebrew Bible. Menasseh, who as a printer would not publish any Caraite text, reflected the strong antipathy to the Caraites by both Sephardic and Ashkenazi Jewry.

40. Endelman, *The Jews of Georgian England*, 19.

41. Glaser, *Judaism Without Jews*, 12.

42. Henry Jessey, *A Narrative of the Late Proceedings at Whitehall, Concerning the Jews* (London: L. Chapman, 1656), rpt. *Harleian Miscellany; or, A Collection of Scarce, Curious, and Entertaining*

Pamphlets and Tracts, As Well in Manuscript As in Print, Found in the Late Earl of Oxford's Library, ed. William Oldys (London: Robert Dutton, 1810), 6: 445.

43. Jessey, *Narrative,* 6: 449.

44. Jessey, *Narrative,* 6: 449–50.

45. Jessey, *Narrative,* 6: 447.

46. David S. Katz, "Menasseh ben Israel's Christian Connection: Henry Jessey and the Jews," in *Menasseh Ben Israel and His World,* 117–38.

47. Popkin, "The Rise and Fall of the Jewish Indian Theory," in *Menasseh Ben Israel and His World,* 67.

48. J. Minton Batten, *John Dury: Advocate of Christian Reunion* (Chicago: University of Chicago Press, 1920), 142. On the Hartlib circle, see Popkin, "Hartlib, Dury and the Jews," 118–36.

49. Mordecai L. Wilensky, "Thomas Barlow's and John Dury's Attitude Towards the Readmission of the Jews to England," *Jewish Quarterly Review* n. s., 50.3 (1960): 256–68.

50. John Dury, *A Case of Conscience, Whether It Be Lawful to Admit Jews into a Christian Commonwealth? Resolved by Mr. John Dury: Written to Samuel Hartlib, esq.* (London: Richard Wodenothe, 1656), rpt. *Harlelian Miscellany,* 6: 438–44.

51. Henry Finch, *The Worlds Great Restavration* (London: William Gouge, 1621). The Hebrew is in the Epistle Dedicatory, which includes the reference to God's winking at the crucifixion; the "nay-ling" of Jesus, 1.

52. Thomas Collier, *A Brief Answer to Some of the Objections and Demurs Made Against the Coming in and Inhabiting of the Jews in this Common-wealth* (London: Thomas Brewster, 1656), 8–9, 14.

53. D. L., *Israels Condition and Cause Pleaded; Or some Arguments for the Jews Admission into England* (London: William Larner and Jonathan Ball, 1656), 15, 25, 47.

54. Popkin, "Hartlib, Dury and the Jews,"in *Samuel Hartlib and Universal Reformation,* 136.

55. D. L., *Israels Condition and Cause Pleaded,* 13.

56. Collier, *A Brief Answer,* 13.

57. Jonathan Karp, *The Politics of Jewish Commerce: Economic Thought and Emancipation in Europe, 1638–1848* (Cambridge: Cambridge University Press, 2008), 54–57.

58. Harrington, *"The Commonwealth of Oceana" and "A System of Politics,"* 6.

59. Pocock, "Introduction," in James Harrington, '*The Commonwealth of Oceana' and 'A System of Politics'*(Cambridge: Cambridge University Press, 1992), xv.

60. According to Jonathan Karp, Harrington's emphasis is humanistic not theological; the Mosaic republic is a human, not divine creation. *The Politics of Commerce,* 56.

61. Harrington, *"The Commonwealth of Oceana" and "A System of Politics,"* 8.

62. Harrington, *"The Commonwealth of Oceana" and "A System of Politics,"* 12–13.

63. Harrington, *"The Commonwealth of Oceana" and "A System of Politics,"* 8–10, 35.

64. Harrington, *"The Commonwealth of Oceana" and "A System of Politics,"* 23, 25, 39.

65. Maria Edgeworth, ed., "Introduction," in *Harrington* (Peterborough: Broadview Press, 2004), 72.

66. Manly, "Introduction," 73.

CHAPTER 3

1. Charles Dibdin, *The Pedlar: A Miscellany, in Prose and Verse, by C. I. Pitt* (London: Harrison & Co., 1796), vi.

2. Betty Naggar, *Jewish Pedlars and Hawkers, 1740–1940* (Camberley, Surrey: Porphyrogenitus, 1992), 66.

3. Todd M. Endelman, *The Jews of Georgian England 1714–1830: Tradition and Change in a Liberal Society* (Ann Arbor: University of Michigan Press, 1999), 181.

4. Endelman, *The Jews of Georgian England,* 166–91; Naggar, *Jewish Pedlars and Hawkers,* 13–40; Frank Felsenstein, *Anti-Semitic Stereotypes: A Paradigm of Otherness in English Popular Culture, 1660–1830* (Baltimore and London: Johns Hopkins University Press, 1995), 58–89.

5. Endelman, *The Jews of Georgian England,* 189.

6. Quentin Bailey, " 'Dangerous and Suspicious Trades': Wordsworth's Pedlar and the Board of Police revenue," *Romanticism* 13.3 (2007): 244–56. Recommendations for the licensing system are in "No. VII. Proceedings on the Tenth and Eleventh Reports of the Select Committee on Finance, appointed in the last Session of Parliament. Hawkers and Pedlars and Hackney Coaches," in William Woodfall, *Parliamentary Register: or, An Impartial Report of the Debates,* vol. 2 (London: T. Chapman, T. Woodfall, T. Bellamy, H.D. Symonds, 1798), Appendix, 58–60.

7. Endelman, *The Jews of Georgian England,* 173–74.

8. Endelman, *The Jews of Georgian England,* 191.

9. Endelman, *The Jews of Georgian England,* 166–67.

10. *Old Bailey Proceedings Online,* www.oldbaileyonline.org (August 24, 2010), February 25, 1789, trial of Esther Elias (t17890225-101).

11. Simon Devereaux, "The City and the Sessions Paper: 'Public Justice' in London, 1770–1800," *Journal of British Studies* 35 (1996): 491–502.

12. *Old Bailey Proceedings Online*, www.oldbaileyonline.org (August 24, 2010), May 17, 1780, trial of Alice Willoughby, Eleanor M'Cabe, Charlotte M'Cave, and Elisabeth Green (t17800510-48).

13. *Old Bailey Proceedings Online*, www.oldbaileyonline.org (August 24, 2010), July 23, 1783, trial of Reuben Wright (t17830723-82).

14. *Old Bailey Proceedings Online*, www.oldbaileyonline.org (August 24, 2010), July 7, 1784, trial of Mary Marshall (t17840707-41).

15. *Old Bailey Proceedings Online*, www.oldbaileyonline.org (August 24, 2010), June 28, 1780, trial of Elisabeth Levi and Judith Isaacs (t17800628-63).

16. *Old Bailey Proceedings Online*, www.oldbaileyonline.org (August 24, 2010), May 10, 1780, trial of Joseph Davis (t17800510-30).

17. *Old Bailey Proceedings Online*, www.oldbaileyonline.org (August 24, 2010), May 10, 1780, trial of Mary Hicks and Mary Hatfield (t17800510-6).

18. *Old Bailey Proceedings Online*, www.oldbaileyonline.org (August 24, 2010), December 5, 1781, trial of Sarah Jackson and Mary Clark (t17811205-12).

19. *Old Bailey Proceedings Online*, www.oldbaileyonline.org (August 24, 2010), January 12, 1785, trial of George Norris, Thomas Freeman, William Johnson, and William Terry Fenley (t17850112-20).

20. *Old Bailey Proceedings Online*, www.oldbaileyonline.org (August 24, 2010), September 12, 1781, trial of Jane Fuller and Elizabeth Hatchett (t17810912-68).

21. *Old Bailey Proceedings Online*, www.oldbaileyonline.org (August 26, 2010), September 12, 1787, trial of Thomas Dean (t17870912-22).

22. *Old Bailey Proceedings Online*, www.oldbaileyonline.org (August 26, 2010), August 30, 1786, trial of Thomas Harwood (t17860830-85).

23. *Old Bailey Proceedings Online*, www.oldbaileyonline.org (August 26, 2010), December 13, 1786, trial of Jacob Abrahams (t17861213-67).

24. *Old Bailey Proceedings Online*, www.oldbaileyonline.org (August 26, 2010), June 3, 1789, trial of John Glover (t17890603-90).

25. *Old Bailey Proceedings Online*, www.oldbaileyonline.org (August 26, 2010), May 11, 1785, trial of Ann Callaghan (t17850511-41).

26. *Old Bailey Proceedings Online*, www.oldbaileyonline.org (August 27, 2010), January 14, 1789, trial of Matthew MacDonald (t17890114-30).

27. *Old Bailey Proceedings Online*, www.oldbaileyonline.org (August 26, 2010), June 29, 1785, trial of Daniel MacKaney (t17850629-110).

28. *Old Bailey Proceedings Online*, www.oldbaileyonline.org (August 26, 2010), May 31, 1786, trial of Henry Asser (t17860531-26).

29. *Old Bailey Proceedings Online*, www.oldbaileyonline.org (August 26, 2010), December 13, 1786, trial of Thomas Neale, Joseph Gabriel, and Sarah Joseph (t17861213-24).

30. *Old Bailey Proceedings Online*, www.oldbaileyonline.org (August 26, 2010), February 22, 1786, trial of Alexander Falconer, James Turner, and Elias Abrahams (t17860222-109).

31. *Old Bailey Proceedings Online*, www.oldbaileyonline.org (August 26, 2010), February 22, 1786, trial of Dorothy Handland (t17860222-131).

32. *Old Bailey Proceedings Online*, www.oldbaileyonline.org (August 26, 2010), February 25, 1789, trial of Esther Elias (t17890225-101).

33. Anthony Bennett, "Sources of Popular Song in Early Nineteenth-Century Britain: Problems and Methods in Research," *Popular Music* 2 (1982): 69–89. A Victorian edition of the three-volume *Universal Songster* sold for 18 shillings.

34. *Laugh When You Can; or The Monstrous Droll Jester* (London: Ann Lemoine, n.d.), 10.

35. All by C.F. Barrett: *Allanrod* (180?), *The Shipwreck* (1803), *Douglas Castle* (1803), *The Black Castle* (1800), and *Tracey Castle* (1800).

36. C. F. Barrett, "The Benevolent Jew," *Laugh When You Can*, 59–60.

37. Bennett, "Sources of Popular Song," 80–81.

38. *Universal Songster*, 3 vols. (London: John Fairburn, Simpkin and Marshall, Sherwood, Gilbert, and Piper, 1825).

39. Iain McCalman, *Radical Underworld: Prophets, Revolutionaries, and Pornographers in London, 1795–1840* (Oxford: Clarendon Press, 1993), 164–65, 171–72, 177, 205–07, 215, 219, 221–22, 224, 227.

40. Eitan Bar-Yosef, *The Holy Land in English Culture 1799–1917: Palestine and the Question of Orientalism* (Oxford: Clarendon Press, 2005), 97.

41. *Universal Songster*, 1: 262–63.

42. *Universal Songster*, 1: 408.

43. *Universal Songster*, 1: 340.

44. Judith W. Page, *Imperfect Sympathies: Jews and Judaism in British Romantic Literature and Culture* (Houndmills and New York: Palgrave/Macmillan, 2004), 1–3, 33, 166–67.

45. Felsenstein, *Anti-Semitic Stereotypes,* 70.

46. *The Works of Charles Dickens*, 34 vols., ed. Andrew Lang (New York: Charles Scribner's Sons, 1900), 26: 87.

47. Maria Edgeworth, *Harrington*, ed. Susan Manly (Peterborough, ON: Broadview Press, 2004), 69. Subsequent references will be parenthetical within the text.

48. Edgar E. MacDonald, ed., *The Education of the Heart: The Correspondence of Rachel Mordecai Lazarus and Maria Edgeworth* (Chapel Hill: University of North Carolina Press, 1977).

49. Anthony Julius, *Trials of the Diaspora: A History of Anti-Semitism in England* (Oxford: Oxford University Press, 2010), 115.

50. William Wordsworth, *Translations of Chaucer and Virgil*, ed. Bruce E. Graver (Ithaca and London: Cornell University Press, 1998), 36.

51. Bruce Graver, "Introduction," *Translations of Chaucer and Virgil*, 18. The reviews were in *British Review* 16 (September 1820), 52, and *Eclectic Review*, n. s. 14 (August 1820), 183.
52. William Hazlitt, "Lectures on the English Poets," in *The Works of William Hazlitt*, 20 vols., ed. P.P. Howe (London and Toronto: J. M. Dent, 1930), 5: 29.
53. See Toby R. Benis, *Romantic Diasporas: French Emigrés, British Convicts, and Jews* (New York: Palgrave Macmillan, 2009), 131–59, for a discussion of hysteria and ventriloquism in *Harrington*.
54. For Edgeworth's earlier representations of Jews, see Michael Scrivener, *The Cosmopolitan Ideal in the Age of Revolution and Reaction, 1776–1832* (London: Pickering & Chatto, 2007), 195–96, and Sheila S. Spector, "The Other's Other: The Function of the Jew in Maria Edgeworth's Fiction," *European Romantic Review* 10.3 (1999): 326–33.
55. For the role of *Bildung* in forming Jewish identity, see Jonathan Freedman, *The Temple of Culture: Assimilation and Anti-Semitism in Literary Anglo-America* (New York: Oxford University Press, 2000), 15–54.
56. Maria Edgeworth, *Maria Edgeworth in France and Switzerland: Selections from the Edgeworth Family letters,* ed. Christian Colvin (Oxford: Clarendon Press, 1979), 16.
57. Marilyn Butler, *Maria Edgeworth: A Literary Biography* (Oxford: Clarendon Press, 1972), 1–2.
58. See my reading of the Widow Levy in *The Cosmopolitan Ideal in the Age of Revolution and Reaction 1776–1832,* (London: Pickering & Chatto Publishers, 2007), 198–99.
59. Bailey, "Dangerous and Suspicious Trades," *Romanticism* 13.3 (2007): 251.
60. James Butler, "Introduction," in *"The Ruined Cottage" and "The Pedlar" by William Wordsworth*, ed. James Butler (Ithaca: Cornell University Press, 1979), 26.
61. "Appendix II," *"The Ruined Cottage,"* 477.
62. "Introduction," *"The Ruined Cottage,"* 24–25.
63. *"The Ruined Cottage,"* 44.
64. Walter Benjamin, "The Storyteller: Reflections on the Works of Nikolai Leskov,"in *Illuminations*, ed. Hannah Arendt, trans. Harry Zohn (New York: Schocken, 1969), 92.
65. Benjamin, "The Storyteller," 109.
66. Benjamin, "The Storyteller," 106.
67. Nikolai Leskóv, "Fish Soup Without Fish," in *Satirical Stories of Nikolai Leskóv*, ed. and trans. William B. Edgerton (New York: Pegasus, 1969), 208, 205–14.
68. S.Y. Abramovitsh (Mendele Moykher Sforim), *Tales of Mendele the Book Peddler. "Fishke the Lame" and "Benjamin the Third,"* ed. Dan

Miron and Ken Frieden, trans. Ted Gorelick and Hillel Halkin (New York: Schocken Books, 1996), 153.

69. For the mediation and remediation of the ballad form of oral culture, see Maureen McLane, *Balladeering, Minstrelsy, and the Making of British Romantic Poetry* (Cambridge: Cambridge University Press, 2008).

CHAPTER 4

1. *An Essay on the Commercial Habits of the Jews* (London: Samuel Tipper and J. Hatchard, 1809), 35.

2. Levy Alexander, *Memoirs of the Life and Commercial Connections, Public and Private, of the Late Benaminj Goldsmid, Esq, of Roehampton; Containing a Cursory View of the Jewish Society and Manners. Interspersed with Interesting Anecdotes of Several Remarkable Characters* (London: Levy Alexander, 1808), 28.

3. *The Torah: A Modern Commentary*, ed. W. Gunther Plaut (New York: Union of American Hebrew Congregations, 1981), 1501.

4. C.G. Montefiore and H. Loewe, ed., *A Rabbinic Anthology* (New York: Schocken Books, 1974), 450.

5. Derek J. Penslar, *Shylock's Children: Economics and Jewish Identity in Modern Europe* (Berkeley, Los Angeles, and London: University of California Press, 2001), 54.

6. Jonathan Karp, *The Politics of Jewish Commerce: Economic Thought and Emancipation in Europe, 1638–1848* (Cambridge: Cambridge University Press, 2008), 17–19.

7. Penslar, *Shylock's Children*, 15.

8. J.G.A. Pocock, *The Machiavellian Moment: Florentine Political Thought and the Atlantic Republican Tradition* (Princeton: Princeton University Press, 1975), and *Virtue, Commerce and History: Essays on Political Thought and History Chiefly in the Eighteenth Century* (Cambridge: Cambridge University Press, 1985) are two major studies that articulate his thesis.

9. Karp, *The Politics of Jewish Commerce*, 1–11.

10. Karp, *The Politics of Jewish Commerce*, 13–15.

11. Karp, *The Politics of Jewish Commerce*, 21–35.

12. Karp, *The Politics of Jewish Commerce*, 12.

13. James Shapiro, *Shakespeare and the Jews* (New York: Columbia University Press, 1996), 122.

14. Janet Adelman, *Blood Relations: Christian and Jew in "The Merchant of Venice"* (Chicago and London: University of Chicago Press, 2008), 110–11.

15. Matthew Biberman, *Masculinity, Anti-Semitism and Early Modern Literature: From the Satanic to the Effeminate Jew* (Aldershot and Burlington: Ashgate, 2004), 3.

16. Biberman, *Masculinity, Anti-Semitism and Early Modern Literature*, 32–37.

17. *An Essay on the Commercial Habits of the Jews*, 3–57.

18. *An Essay on the Commercial Habits of the Jews*, 34.

19. *An Essay on the Commercial Habits of the Jews*, 35.

20. *An Essay on the Commercial Habits of the Jews*, 38–41.

21. *An Essay on the Commercial Habits of the Jews*, 39–41.

22. *An Essay on the Commercial Habits of the Jews*, 70–82.

23. *An Essay on the Commercial Habits of the Jews*, 68.

24. "Introduction," in *Five Restoration Adaptations of Shakespeare*, ed. Christopher Spencer (Urbana: University of Illinois Press, 1965), 29–32. Shapiro says there were forty performances in thirty-five years, *Shakespeare and the Jews*, 214.

25. "Jew of Venice," in *Five Restoration Adaptations of Shakespeare*, ed. Christopher Spencer , 363.

26. "Jew of Venice," 364.

27. "Jew of Venice," 365–71.

28. John Gross, *Shylock: Four Hundred Years in the Life of a Legend* (London: Chatto and Windus, 1992), 51.

29. Michael Ragussis, *Theatrical Nation: Jews and Other Outlandish Englishmen in Georgian Britain* (Philadelphia: University of Pennsylvania Press, 2010), 112.

30. Richard Cumberland, *The Jew; or, Benevolent Hebrew: A Comedy* (Boston: John West, 1795).

31. For commentary on Lessing's *Die Juden* and *Nathan der Weise*, see Michael Scrivener, *The Cosmopolitan Ideal in the Age of Revolution and Reaction, 1776–1832* (London: Pickering & Chatto, 2007), 150–54. A good modern translation of the play: Gotthold Ephraim Lessing, *Nathan the Wise*, trans., ed., intro. Ronald Schechter (Boston and New York: Bedford/St. Martin's, 2004).

32. Richard Cumberland, *The Jew: A Comedy* (London: C. Dilly, 1794), 6.

33. Cumberland, *The Jew: A Comedy*, 12.

34. Cumberland, *The Jew: A Comedy*, 75.

35. Richard Hole, "An Apology for the Character and Conduct of Shylock," in *Essays, By a Society of Gentlemen, At Exeter* (Exeter: Trewman and Son, 1796), 552.

36. Hole, "An Apology for the Character," 557.

37. Judith W. Page, *Imperfect Sympathies: Jews and Judaism in British Romantic Literature and Culture* (New York: Palgrave/Macmillan, 2004), 68–69.

38. Page, *Imperfect Sympathies*, 67–68.

39. George Farren, *An Essay on Shakespeare's Character of Shylock, Originating in An Examination of the Laws and Customs of Moses, and of the Primitive Christians, with Reference to Enumerations*

of Population, and the Rate of Interest of Money (London: Pelham Richardson, 1833), 20–21.

40. Alexander, *Memoirs of the Late Benjamin Goldsmid*, 22.

41. Alexander, *Memoirs of the Late Benjamin Goldsmid*, 28.

42. Alexander, *Memoirs of the Late Benjamin Goldsmid*, 27.

43. Alexander, *Memoirs of the Late Benjamin Goldsmid*, 98.

44. Mark L. Schoenfield, "Abraham Goldsmid: Money Magician in the Popular Press," in *British Romanticism and the Jews: History, Culture, Literature*, ed. Sheila A. Spector (New York: Palgrave Macmillan, 2002), 37–60.

45. This section appeared first in a slightly different form and is published here with permission. "The Philosopher and the Moneylender: The Relationship between William Godwin and John King," in *Godwinian Moments: From Enlightenment to Romanticism*, ed. Robert M. Maniquis and Victoria Myers (University of Toronto Press, 2010), 333–62.

46. The reliably informative sources on John King are Todd M. Endelman, Iain McCalman, and David B. Ruderman. Endelman's "The Chequered Career of 'Jew' King: A Study in Anglo-Jewish Social History," in *From East and West: Jews in a Changing Europe, 1750–1870*, ed. Frances Malino and David Sorkin (Oxford: Basil Blackwell, 1990), 151–81, situates King in the context of Anglo-Jewish history, while McCalman's discussion in *Radical Underworld: Prophets, Revolutionaries, and Pornographers in London, 1795–1840* (Oxford: Clarendon Press, 1993), 35–38, 66–67, positions King in relation to the "unrespectable" radicalism of the 1790s and early nineteenth century. Ruderman's *Jewish Enlightenment in An English Key: Anglo-Jewry's Construction of Modern Jewish Thought* (Princeton: Princeton University Press, 2000), 144–46, locates King in the specifically Anglo-Jewish context of deist and politically radical thought. On King's giving money to the treason trial defendants, see John King, *Mr. King's Apology; or a Reply to his Calumniators* (London: Thomas Wilkins, 1798), 36–37.

47. Godwin's diary, Oxford, Bodleian MS Abinger, e. 6. I am quoting and making reference to the diary with the permission of The Bodleian Library, University of Oxford, whose generosity in granting me permission I wish to acknowledge. I also want to thank Professor Victoria Myers, Pepperdine University, for her invaluable assistance in making the transcription of the relevant diary sections available to me.

48. For the relationship between Robinson and King, as well as Robinson and Godwin, see Paula Byrne, *Perdita: The Literary, Theatrical, Scandalous Life of Mary Robinson* (New York: Random House, 2004), 31–37 and 253 (King), 321–23 and 390 (Godwin).

49. William St. Clair, *The Godwins and the Shelleys: The Biography of a Family* (New York and London: W.W. Norton, 1989), 353.

50. C. Kegan Paul, *William Godwin: His Friends and Contemporaries*, 2 vols. (London: Henry S. King, 1876), 1:146–47, 155–57.

51. John Taylor, *Records of My Life* (New York: Harper, 1833), 423–25. Taylor was not the only memoirist who fondly recalled the King dinners that Godwin frequented. Captain Gronow (1794–1865) recalls King as a man of wit and elegant taste, whose dinners were attended by the rich, powerful, and artistic, including Richard Brinsley Sheridan (1751–1816). See *The Reminiscences and Recollections of Captain Gronow, Being Anecdotes of the Camp, Court, Clubs and Society, 1810–1860*, ed. John Raymond (London: Bodley Head, 1964), 110–13.

52. John King, *Letters from France* (London: M. Jones, 1802), 161–66. Godwin and Holcroft were inseparable and passionate friends until Mary Wollstonecraft entered Godwin's life in 1796, after which the friendship cooled. In 1802 they resumed their friendship, but in 1805 they became bitterly estranged over Godwin's *Fleetwood*; they reconciled shortly before Holcroft's death. See St Clair, *The Godwins and the Shelleys*, 207, 275–78.

53. King, *Letters from France*, 174–80.

54. [John King], *Letters from Perdita to a Certain Israelite, and His Answers to Them* (London: J. Fielding and J. Stockdale and J. Sewell, 1781). On the cultural norms relating to courtesans and actresses in the eighteenth century, see Cindy McCreery, *The Satirical Gaze: Prints of Women in Late Eighteenth-Century England* (Oxford: Clarendon Press, 2004), 80–114.

55. John King, *Thoughts on the Difficulties and Distresses in Which the Peace of 1783, Has Involved the People of England; on the Present Disposition of the English, Scots, and Irish, to Emigrate to America; and on the Hazard They Run (without Certain Precautions) of Rendering Their Condition More Deplorable. Addressed to the Right Hon. Charles James Fox* 5th ed. (London: T. Davies, J. Southern, W. Deane, 1783).

56. Endelman, "The Chequered Career," 171.

57. William Godwin, "The History of the Life of William Pitt, Earl of Chatham," in *Political Writings I*, ed. Martin Fitzpatrick, vol. 1 of *Political and Philosophical Writings of William Godwin*, 7 vols., gen. ed. Mark Philp (London: Pickering & Chatto, 1993), 32. This edition is hereafter cited as *PPW*, with volume and page numbers.

58. Godwin, "History of the Life of Pitt," *PPW* 1:52.

59. King, *Thoughts on the Difficulties*, 1–28.

60. King, *Thoughts on the Difficulties*, 10.

61. King, *Thoughts on the Difficulties*, 22–24.

62. William Godwin, "Critique of the Administration of Mr. Pitt," *Political Writings* I, ed. Martin Fitzpatrick, *PPW* 1:207–11; King, *Thoughts on the Difficulties*, 22–28.

63. Fox's power and influence in the political and literary circles in which Godwin traveled hardly needs to be documented.
64. Godwin's diary, Oxford, Bodleian MS Abinger e. 6.
65. Godwin's diary, e. 7.
66. Endelman, "The Chequered Career," 172–23.
67. For Sampson Perry, see Michael T. Davis, Iain McCalman, and Christina Parolin, eds., *Newgate in Revolution: An Anthology of Radical Prison Literature in the Age of Revolution* (London and New York: Continuum, 2005), 116–19.
68. Godwin too is seen as a Girondin by Mark Philp in *Godwin's Political Justice* (London: Duckworth, 1986), 100.
69. *The Autobiography of Francis Place (1771–1854)*, ed. Mary Thrale (Cambridge: Cambridge University Press, 1972), 174.
70. *The Autobiography of Francis Place*, 236–39.
71. McCalman, *Radical Underworld*, 66–67.
72. McCalman, *Radical Underworld*, 38.
73. McCalman, *Radical Underworld*, 35.
74. Godwin's diary, Oxford, Bodleian MS Abinger e. 7.
75. Godwin's diary, e. 7.
76. Godwin's diary, e. 6.
77. Godwin's diary, e. 7.
78. Godwin's diary, e. 7, e. 10.
79. Godwin's diary, e. 13, e. 14, and e. 22.
80. St. Clair, *The Godwins and the Shelleys*, 498 and 541 n. 4.
81. St. Clair, *The Godwins and the Shelleys*, 353; Scrivener, "'Zion Alone is Forbidden': Historicizing Antisemitism in Byron's The Age of Bronze," *Keats-Shelley Journal*, 43 (1994): 87 n. 31.
82. William Godwin, *St. Leon*, ed. and intro. William D. Brewer (Peterborough, ON: Broadview Press, 2006), 36. Hereafter cited parenthetically by page number.
83. N.a., *Authentic Memoirs, Memorandums, and Confessions. Taken from the Journal of His Predatorial Majesty, The King of the Swindlers* (London: W. Hatton, n.d. [1798]). King sued the publisher John Parsons and won a judgment of 50 pounds. See Israel Solomons, "Jew King," *Notes and Queries* 11 (June 5, 1915): 437–38. Most of the material in *Authentic Memoirs* seems genuine, especially the diary extracts, but the editor's summaries are moralistic and prejudiced.
84. The scholarly edition of Pinto is Fernão Mendes Pinto, *The Travels of Mendes Pinto*, ed., intro., and trans. Rebecca D. Catz (Chicago and London: University of Chicago Press, 1989).
85. Pinto, "Introduction," xxviii–xxix.
86. Pinto, "Introduction," xxii–xxiii.
87. Cecil Roth, *A History of the Jews in England*, 3rd ed. (Oxford: Oxford University Press, 1964), 68–90.

88. For Cagliostro, see Iain McCalman, *The Last Alchemist: Count Cagliostro, Master of Magic in the Age of Reason* (New York: HarperCollins, 2003).

89. Godwin, *St. Leon*, 213 n. 1.

90. For an account of Lessing's *Nathan der Weise*, see Scrivener, *The Cosmopolitan Ideal*, 150–54.

91. "Of Religion," May 7, 1818, in *Religious Writings*, ed. Mark Philp, *PPW* 7:63.

92. On Woolston, see James A. Herrick, *The Radical Rhetoric of the English Deists: The Discourse of Skepticism, 1680–1750* (Columbia: University of South Carolina Press, 1997), 77–101. See also William H. Trapnell, *Thomas Woolston: Madman and Deist?* (Bristol: Thoemmes Press, 1994).

93. The full prayer is in William Wollaston, *The Religion of Nature Delineated* (London: Samuel Palmer 1724), 120–21. King's citing of it is in David Levi, *Dissertations on the Prophecies of The Old Testament*, 2 vols., rev. and intro. John King (London: John King, 1817), 1:xii–xiii.

94. Endelman, "The Chequered Career," 167.

95. Endelman, "The Chequered Career," 176.

96. King, *Mr. King's Apology*, 38–42.

97. Joanna Southcott, *An Account of the Trials on Bills of Exchange, Wherein the Deceit of Mr. John King and His Confederates, Under the Pretence of Lending Money, Is Exposed, and Their Arts Brought to Light* (London: S. Rousseau, 1807).

98. For Levi, see Ruderman, *Jewish Enlightenment*, 57–88, and Michael Scrivener, "British-Jewish Writing of the Romantic Era and the Problem of Modernity: The Example of David Levi," in *British Romanticism and the Jews: History, Culture, Literature*, ed. Sheila Spector (New York: Palgrave Macmillan, 2002), 159–78.

99. William Godwin, "The Genius of Christianity Unveiled," in *Religious Writings*, ed. Mark Philp, *PPW* 7:81.

100. King, *Mr. King's Apology*, 21.

CHAPTER 5

1. Ann Lemoine, ed. *Laugh When You Can; or The Monstrous Droll Jester* (London: Ann Lemoine, n. d.), 10.

2. For the Donaldson decision and its consequences, see William St. Clair, *The Reading Nation in the Romantic Period* (Cambridge: Cambridge University Press, 2004). For the Lackington literary circle, see Michael Scrivener, British-Jewish Writing of the Romantic Era and the Problem of Modernity: The Example of David Levi, in *British Romanticism and the Jews: History, Culture, Literature*, ed. Sheila A. Spector (New York: Palgrave/Macmillan, 2002), 164.

3. David Sorkin, *The Transformation of German Jewry 1780–1840* (Detroit: Wayne State University Press, 1999), 20.

4. Todd M. Endelman, *The Jews of Georgian England 1714–1830: Tradition and Change in a Liberal Society* (Ann Arbor: University of Michigan Press, 1999), 142.

5. Endelman, *The Jews of Georgian England*, 119–65.

6. Sorkin, *The Transformation of German Jewry*, 72.

7. David B. Ruderman, *Jewish Enlightenment in An English Key: Anglo-Jewry's Construction of Modern Jewish Thought* (Princeton and Oxford: Princeton University Press, 2000).

8. Lisa Lampert, *Gender and Jewish Difference from Paul to Shakespeare* (Philadelphia: University of Pennsylvania Press, 2004), 14–15.

9. Janet Adelman, *Blood Relations: Christian and Jew in The Merchant of Venice* (Chicago and London: University of Chicago Press, 2008), 88.

10. Lampert, *Gender and Jewish Difference from Paul to Shakespeare*, 160–63; Adelman, *Blood Relations*, 95–96.

11. Lampert, *Gender and Jewish Difference*, 165; Adelman, *Blood Relations*, 74.

12. Ezra Mendelsohn, *Painting a People: Maurycy Gottlieb and Jewish Art* (Hanover and London: Brandeis University Press, 2002), 125.

13. Michael Ragussis, *Figures of Conversion: The Jewish Question and English National Identity* (Durham and London: Duke University Press, 1995).

14. Nadia Valman, *The Jewess in Nineteenth-Century British Literary Culture* (Cambridge: Cambridge University Press, 2007).

15. Cynthia Scheinberg, *Women's Poetry and Religion in Victorian England: Jewish Identity and Christian Culture* (Cambridge: Cambridge University Press, 2002).

16. Judith W. Page, *Imperfect Sympathies: Jews and Judaism in British Romantic Literature and Culture* (New York: Palgrave/Macmillan, 2004), 105–32, 204–05.

17. Gotthold Ephraim Lessing, *Nathan the Wise*, trans., ed., intro. Ronald Schechter (Boston and New York: Bedford/St. Martin's, 2004), 112.

18. Maria Edgeworth, *Harrington*, ed. Susan Manly (Peterborough: Broadview Press, 2004), 136–37.

19. Edgeworth, *Harrington*, 137.

20. Edgeworth, *Harrington*, 138.

21. Frank Felsenstein, *Anti-Semitic Stereotypes. A Paradigm of Otherness in English Popular Culture, 1660–1830* (Baltimore and London: Johns Hopkins University Press, 1995), 303, n. 84.

22. Valman, *The Jewess in Nineteenth-Century British Literary Culture*, 2.

23. For an English translation, Eugène Scribe, *La Juive: The Jewess. In Four Acts. The Music by Halevy* (New York: Palmer & Co., 1860). The untranslated opera was actually in five acts.

24. Valman, *The Jewess in Nineteenth-Century British Literary Culture*, 2–3.
25. Julia Reinhard Lupton, *Citizen-Saints: Shakespeare and Political Theology* (Chicago and London: University of Chicago Press, 2005),76, 99, 80; Susan A. Handelman, *The Slayers of Moses: The Emergence of Rabbinic Interpretation in Modern Literary Theory* (Albany: SUNY Press, 1982).
26. Walter Scott, *Ivanhoe*, ed. Graham Tulloch (London: Penguin, 2000), 82–83. Valman calls Rebecca's Ashby performance provocative and unrestrained, *The Jewess in Nineteenth-Century British Literary Culture*, 29.
27. Mildred Starr Witkin, The Jewess in English Literature: A Mediating Presence, Ph.D. Diss. (New York: City University of New York, 1988), 123.
28. Witkin, The Jewess in English Literature, 129.
29. Scott, *Ivanhoe*, 295.
30. Scott, *Ivanhoe*, 293.
31. Scott, *Ivanhoe*, 445.
32. Valman, *The Jewess in Nineteenth-Century British Literary Culture*, 42.
33. Ragussis, *Figures of Conversion*, 95.
34. *The History of Mary Prince, A West Indian Slave. Related by Herself* (London: F. Westley and A.H. Davis, 1831).
35. Amelia Bristow, *Emma De Lissau; A Narrative of Striking Vicissitudes, and Peculiar Trials.* 2nd ed., 2 vols. (London: T. Gardiner and Son, 1829), 1: viii.
36. Ragussis, *Figures of Conversion*, 137.
37. Witkin, The Jewess in English Literature, ch. 3, focuses on the influence of Marlowe's Abigail.
38. Edward Lytton Bulwer, *Leila: or, The Siege of Granada* (Philadelphia: Carley, Lea, and Blanchard, 1838), 252.
39. Valman, *The Jewess in Nineteenth-Century British Literary Culture*, 63–65.
40. Madame Brendlau, *Tales of a Jewess: Illustrating The Domestic Manners and Customs of the Jews. Interspersed with Original Anecdotes of Napoleon. First Series* (London: Simpkin, Marshall and Co., 1838), v–x.
41. Brendlau, *Tales of a Jewess*, 6.
42. Brendlau, *Tales of a Jewess*, vi.
43. Ragussis, *Figures of Conversion*, 15–56.
44. Brendlau, *Tales of a Jewess*, 80–82.
45. Brendlau, *Tales of a Jewess*, 69–70.
46. Brendlau, *Tales of a Jewess*, 3.
47. Brendlau, *Tales of a Jewess*, 89–90.
48. Brendlau, *Tales of a Jewess*, 35.

49. Valman, *The Jewess in Nineteenth-Century British Literary Culture*, 15–16.
50. [Mary] Leman Grimstone, *Character; or, Jew and Gentile: A Tale*, 2 vols. (London: Charles Fox, 1833), 1: iii–iv.
51. Maria Polack, *Fiction Without Romance; or, The Locket-Watch*, 2 vols. (London: Effingham Wilson, 1830).
52. Julius Ursinus Niemcewicz, *Levi and Sarah; or The Jewish Lovers. A Polish Tale* (London: John Murray, 1830), xix.
53. Henry Hart Milman, *The History of the Jews*, 3 vols. (New York: J and J. Harper, 1830), 3: 278.
54. Thomas Wade, *The Poems and Plays of Thomas Wade*, ed., John L. McLean (Troy, NY: Whitston Publishing Company, 1997), 483–84.
55. Ernst J. Schlochauer, "Thomas Wade: Forgotten Champion of English Jewry," *Jewish Social Studies* 13.3 (1951): 231.
56. Wade, *The Poems and Plays of Thomas Wade*, 479.
57. Wade, *The Poems and Plays of Thomas Wade*, 480.
58. Wade, *The Poems and Plays of Thomas Wade*, 502.
59. *Authentic Memoirs, Memorandums, and Confessions. Taken from the Journal of His Predatorial Majesty, The King of the Swindlers* (London: W. Hatton, n.d. [1798]), 27–28.
60. Jerome McGann, *The Poetics of Sensibility: A Revolution in Literary Style* (Oxford: Clarendon Press, 1996), 1–9.
61. Because the biographical information on the King family has sometimes been unreliable I want to clarify a few details. The birth dates for Sophia and Charlotte are not documented with certainty. Confusion was sown after Charlotte died in 1825 when her age was given as 53, which would make her birth date around 1772, well before John King and his wife Sara Lara married in 1776. Making his wife older was perhaps Nicholas Byrne's attempt to obscure the fact he was two decades older than his wife. In Sophia's *Cordelia* (1799) the heroine, modeled after the author, is said to be two years younger than her sister (ch. 15). (That Charlotte is the eldest is also suggested by the order of names in the dedication to their father in *The Trifles of Helicon* [1798]). Joined with the information in the Preface to Sophia's *Fatal Secret* (1801) that she is nineteen years old, the available evidence suggests a birth date for Charlotte 1779/80 and for Sophia 1781/82. Their birth dates could be much closer than Sophia suggests because in Charlotte's *Hours of Solitude* she identifies her age as twenty-three, which would make her birth in 1782. Younger brother Charles was born in 1783; his birth and circumcision are recorded in the synagogue records, *The Birth Register (1767–1881) of the Spanish & Portuguese Jews' Congregation*, ed. Miriam Rodrigues-Pereira and Chloe Loewe (London: The Spanish and Portuguese Jews' Congregation, 1993), 62, 129. In 1801 Sophia married and had three children with Charles Fortnum (1770–1860),

related to but not the son of the famous Charles (1738–1815) of Fortnum and Mason. It is not certain when Sophia dies, but her last publication is in 1805 and husband Charles remarries in 1817, before which he has an irregular relationship with the widow of a General Roberts, according to Elizabeth Warburton, "C.D.E. Fortnum, DCL (Oxon), JP, FSA, of Hill House, Great Stanmore," *Journal of History of Collections*, 11.2 (1999): 130–31; there is a photo of Charles on p. 135.

62. Lord Byron, *Lord Byron. The Complete Poetical Works*, 7 vols, ed. Jerome McGann (Oxford: Clarendon Press, 1980), 1: 413.

63. Jerome McGann, " 'My Brain is Feminine': Byron and the Poetry of Deception [1990]," in *Byron and Romanticism*, ed. James Soderholm (Cambridge: Cambridge University Press, 2002), 56.

64. Lisa M. Wilson, "Female Pseudonymity in the Romantic 'Age of Personality': The Career of Charlotte King/Rose Matilda/Charlotte Dacre." *European Romantic Review* 9.3 (1998): 400.

65. George Daniel, *The Modern Dunciad: Virgil in London and Other Poems* (London: William Pickering, 1835), 6.

66. Albert H. Hyamson, *The Sephardim of England: A History of the Spanish and Portuguese Jewish Community 1492–1951* (London: Methuen, 1951), 210.

67. Adriana Craciun, "Introduction to *Waldorf*," in Sophia King, *Waldorf; or, The Dangers of Philosophy* (1798), ed., Adriana Craciun, *Anti-Jacobin Novels*, 10 vols., ed. W.M. Verhoeven (London: Pickering & Chatto, 2005), 9: xix.

68. King, *Waldorf*, 9: 4.

69. Craciun, "Introduction to *Waldorf*," 9: xvi.

70. Iain McCalman, *The Last Alchemist. Count Cagliostro, Master of Magic in the Age of Reason* (New York: HarperCollins, 2003).

71. Don Herzog, *Poisoning the Minds of the Lower Orders* (Princeton: Princeton University Press, 1998).

72. King, *Waldorf*, 9: 65.

73. King, *Waldorf*, 9: 87.

74. Craciun, "Introduction to *Waldorf*," 9: x.

75. King, *Cordelia; or, A Romance of Real Life*. 2 vols. (London: William Lane, 1799), 1: 8.

76. King, *Cordelia*, 1: 8–12.

77. King, *Cordelia*, 2: 190.

78. Sophia King, *The Fatal Secret, or, Unknown Warrior; A Romance of the Twelfth Century, With Legendary Poems* (London: J.G. Barnard and J. Fiske, 1801), i–vii.

79. Jane Austen, *Northanger Abbey*, ed. Susan Fraiman (New York: W.W. Norton, 2004), 22–23.

80. Diane Long Hoeveler, "Charlotte Dacre's *Zofloya*: A Case Study in Miscegenation as Sexual and Racial Nausea," *European Romantic Review* 8.2 (1997), 185–99, and "Charlotte Dacre's *Zofloya*:

The Gothic Demonization of the Jew," in *The Jews and British Romanticism: Politics, Religion, Culture*, ed. Sheila A. Spector (New York: Palgrave/Macmillan, 2005), 165–78; Craciun, "Unnatural, Unsexed, Undead: Charlotte Dacre's Gothic Bodies," in *Fatal Women of Romanticism* (Cambridge: Cambridge University Press, 2003), 110–53. For gothic's affinity with xenophobia and anti-Semitism, see Carol Margaret Davison, *Antisemitism and British Gothic Literature* (New York: Palgrave/Macmillan, 2004).

81. James A. Dunn, "Charlotte Dacre and the Feminization of Violence," *Nineteenth-Century Literature* 53.3 (1998): 318.

82. Anne Mellor, *Romanticism and Gender* (New York and London: Routledge, 1993), and *Mothers of the Nation: Women's Political Writing in England, 1780–1830* (Bloomington: University of Indiana Press, 2000).

83. Kim Ian Michasiw, Introduction, Charlotte Dacre, *Zofloya, or The Moor* (Oxford and New York: Oxford University Press, 1997), vii–xxx.

84. Wordsworth and Coleridge plundered Charlotte Smith (1749–1806), and Keats Mary Tighe (1772–1810), as described by feminist literary historians since the 1980s such as Marlon B. Ross's *The Contours of Masculine Desire: Romanticsm and the Rise of Women's Poetry* (New York: Oxford University Press, 1989), and Anne K. Mellor's *Romanticism and Gender* (London and New York: Routledge, 1992).

85. Charlotte King [Rosa Matilda], *Confessions of the Nun of St. Omer: A Tale*, 3 vols. (London: J.F. Hughes, 1806), 1: 62–63.

86. Charlotte Dacre [King], *The Libertine*, 4 vols., 2nd ed (London: T. Cadell & W. Davies, 1807) 2:178.

87. Rosa Matilda [Charlotte King], *The Passions*, 4 vols. (London: T. Cadell & W. Davies, 1811), 1: 209–10.

88. Matilda, *The Passions*, 2: 220–21.

89. Matilda, *The Passions*, 2: 252.

90. Matilda, *The Passions*, 1: 279.

91. Charlotte and Sophia King, *Trifles of Helicon* (London: James Ridgway, 1798), 42.

92. Judith Pascoe, *Romantic Theatricality: Gender, Poetry, and Spectatorship* (Ithaca and London: Cornell University Press, 1997), 28: 130–62.

93. Pascoe, *Romantic Theatricality*, 68–94.

94. Dacre [King], *Hours of Solitude*, 2 vols. (London: Hughes and Ridgeway, 1805), 1: 132–33.

95. Dacre, *Hours of Solitude*, 1: 134–36.

96. Dacre, *Hours of Solitude*, 1: 13.

97. Dacre, *Hours of Solitude*, 1: 19–20.

98. Dacre, *Hours of Solitude*, 1: 126–29.

Chapter 6

1. Nineteenth-century Reform Judaism rejected the Zionist return and favored making one's home the sacred place. After the Shoah Reform Judaism strongly has supported Zionism and the State of Israel. Michael Meyer, *Response to Modernity: A History of the Reform Movement in Judaism* (New York: Oxford University Press, 1988).

2. Walter Laqueur, *A History of Zionism* (New York: Schocken Books, [1972] 1989).

3. George K. Anderson, *The Legend of the Wandering Jew* (Providence, RI: Brown University Press, 1965), 13.

4. E.S. Shaffer, *Kubla Khan and The Fall of Jerusalem: The Mythological School in Biblical Criticism and Secular Literature 1770–1880* (Cambridge: Cambridge University Press, 1975), 37.

5. Eitan Bar-Yosef, *The Holy Land in English Culture 1799–1917: Palestine and the Question of Orientalism* (Oxford: Clarendon Press, 2005).

6. Morton D. Paley, *Apocalypse and Millennium in English Romantic Poetry* (Oxford: Clarendon Press, 1999), 8.

7. David B. Ruderman, *Connecting the Covenants: Judaism and the Search for Christian Identity in Eighteenth-Century England* (Philadelphia: University of Pennsylvania Press, 2007), 52, 167.

8. William Blake, *The Complete Poetry and Prose of William Blake,* rev. ed. David V. Erdman (New York: Doubleday, 1988), 617.

9. David B. Ruderman, *Jewish Enlightenment in An English Key: Anglo-Jewry's Construction of Modern Jewish Thought* (Princeton: Princeton University Press, 2000), 23–88.

10. S.T. Coleridge, *Lectures 1795 On Politics and Religion,* ed. Lewis Patton and Peter Mann. *The Collected Works of Samuel Taylor Coleridge,* 1 vol. (London: Routledge and Kegan Paul, and Princeton: Princeton University Press, 1971), 126.

11. Coleridge, *Lectures 1795,* 122–45.

12. Nicholas Roe, *Wordsworth and Coleridge: The Radical Years* (Oxford: Clarendon Press, 1988).

13. Parts of this section on Thomas Spence are from my *Seditious Allegories: John Thelwall and Jacobin Writing* (University Park: Pennsylvania State University Press, 2001), 102–10, 131–38. I have made numerous changes.

14. H.T. Dickinson, *The Political Works of Thomas Spence* (Newcastle-upon-Tyne: Avero, 1982), 94.

15. Dickinson, *The Political Works of Thomas Spence,* ii. Biographical information on Spence is culled from Dickinson (vii–xviii) but corrected by the early nineteenth-century sources.

16. Dickinson, *The Political Works of Thomas Spence,* viii.

17. Dickinson, *The Political Works of Thomas Spence,* 41–44.

18. The title is cited in Olive D. Rudkin, *Thomas Spence and His Connections* (New York: A.M. Kelley, [1927] 1966), 222. The title page, which I have not seen, is apparently in the Francis Place Collection in the British Library, Add. MSS., 27808.

19. Olivia Smith, *The Politics of Language 1791–1819* (Oxford: Clarendon Press, 1984), ch. 4.

20. William Blake, *The Complete Poetry and Prose of William Blake,* ed. David V. Erdman, newly revised ed. (New York: Doubleday, 1988), 95.

21. Marcus Wood, *Radical Satire and Print Culture 1790–1822* (Oxford: Clarendon Press, 1994), 85.

22. Second Report from the Commons' Committee of Secrecy on the State of Ireland, and the Proceedings of Certain Disaffected Persons in Both Parts of the United Kingdom, *Parliamentary History of England*, 1800–1801 (London: Hansard, 1819), 35: 1307.

23. P.M. Ashraf *The Life and Times of Thomas Spence* (Newcastle-upon-Tyne: Frank Graham, 1983), 190.

24. Ashraf, *The Life and Times of Thomas Spence*, 104 n. 45.

25. Eneas. Mackenzie, *A Descriptive and Historical Account of the Town and County of Newcastle upon Tyne, Including the Borough of Gateshead* (Newcastle upon Tyne: Mackenzie & Dent, 1827), 399.

26. Don Locke, *A Fantasy of Reason: The Life and Thought of William Godwin* (London, Boston, & Henley: Routledge & Kegan Paul, 1980), 16–17.

27. Dickinson, *The Political Works of Thomas Spence*, 59.

28. Michael Scrivener, *Poetry and Reform: Periodical Verse from the Democratic Press, 1792–1824* (Detroit: Wayne State University Press, 1982), 63–65.

29. Malcolm Chase, *The People's Farm: English Radical Agrarianism 1775–1840* (Oxford: Clarendon Press, 1988), 54–55.

30. For popular millenarianism at this time, see J.F.C. Harrison, *The Second Coming: Popular Millenarianism, 1780–1850* (New Brunswick: Rutgers UP, 1979); Jon Mee, *Dangerous Enthusiasm: William Blake and the Culture of Radicalism in the 1790s* (Oxford: Clarendon Press, 1992).

31. Marsha Keith Schuchard, "Lord George Gordon and Cabalistic Freemasonry: Beating Jacobite Swords into Jacobin Ploughshares," in *Secret Conversions to Judaism in Early Modern Europe*, ed. Richard H. Popkin and Martin Mulsow (Leiden and Boston, Brill. 2004), 230.

32. Christopher Hibbert, *King Mob: The Story of Lord George Gordon and the Riots of 1780* (London, New York, Toronto: Longmans, Green, 1958), 166. Cecil Roth's unpersuasive account of Gordon's conversion dismisses it as a product of enthusiasm rather than deep conviction. *Essays and Portraits in Anglo-Jewish History* (Philadelphia: Jewish Publication Society of America, 1962), 183–210.

33. Iain McCalman, "New Jerusalems: Prophecy, Dissent and Radical Culture in England 1786–1830," in *Enlightenment and Religion: Rational Dissent in Eighteenth-Century Britain*, ed. Knud Haakonssen (Cambridge: Cambridge University Press, 1996), 314.

34. McCalman, "Mad Lord George and Madame La Motte: Riot and Sexuality in the Genesis of Burke's Reflections on the Revolution in France," *Journal of British Studies* 35 (1996): 357–59.

35. "The Trials of George Gordon. 6 June 1787," in *A Complete Collection of State Trials and Proceedings for High Treason*, ed. Thomas Jones Howell, vol. 22 (London: T. C. Hansard, 1817), 189–90.

36. "The Trials of George Gordon," 195.

37. "The Trials of George Gordon," 193.

38. Erdman, *Complete Poetry and Selected Prose of William Blake*, 213.

39. "The Trials of George Gordon," 189, 191.

40. "The Trials of George Gordon," 192–94.

41. "The Trials of George Gordon," 194.

42. McCalman, "Controlling the Riots: Dickens, *Barnaby Rudge* and Romantic Revolution," *History* 84 (1999): 466.

43. Louis Ginzburg, *Legends of the Jews*, trans. Henrietta Szold and Paul Rudin, 7 vols. (Philadelphia: Jewish Publication Society of America, 1956), 6: 377 n. 117; Hayim Nahman Bialik and Yehoshua Hana Ravnitzky, eds., *The Book of Legends: Sefer Ha-Aggadah. Legends from the Talmud and Midrash*, trans. William G. Braude (New York: Schocken Books, 1992), 627.

44. Michael Galchinsky, *The Origin of the Modern Woman Jewish Writer: Romance and Reform in Victorian England* (Detroit: Wayne State University Press, 1996), 74–81.

45. Galchinsky, *The Origin of the Modern Woman Jewish Writer*, 73–74.

46. [Review of *Miscellaneous Poems*], *Monthly Review*, 70 (February 1813): 214. A similarly condescending treatment is in the *Critical Review*, 2 n. s. (August 1812): 216. For another essay on Lyon's poetry, see my *Cosmopolitan Ideal in the Age of Revolution and Reaction, 1776–1832* (London: Pickering & Chatto, 2007), 174–94.

47. Israel Solomons, "Lord George Gordon's Conversion to Judaism," *Transactions of the Jewish Historical Society of England* 7 (1915): 256.

48. Celia and Marion Moss, *Early Efforts: A Volume of Poems* (Portsmouth: Whittaker & Co., and John Miller, 1839).

49. [Review of Christian Gottfried Körner, *The Life of Carl Theodor Körner*], *The London Literary Gazette and Journal of the Belles Lettres* 548 (July 21, 1827): 470.

50. Emma Lyon, *Miscellaneous Poems* (Oxford: J. Bartlett, 1812), vii–viii.

51. Lyon, *Miscellaneous Poems*, 1–2. The book is available online through the University of California at Davis British Women Romantic Poets site.

52. Lyon, *Miscellaneous Poems*, 3–7.

53. *London Times,* September 16. 1812. Emma Lyon and Mrs. French testified in court on behalf of Daniel French. For biographical information on Lyon, see Naomi Cream, "Isaac Leo Lyon: The Free Jewish Migrant to Australia?" *Journal of Australian Jewish Historical Society* 21.1 (1993): 3–16, Revd Solomon Lyon of Cambridge, 1755–1820, *Jewish Historical Studies* 36 (1999–2000): 31–69.
54. Lyon, *Miscellaneous Poems,* 119–22.
55. Mitchell Dahood, S.J., ed., *The Anchor Bible. Psalms I. 1–50* (Garden City: Doubleday, 1966), 121.
56. Lyon, *Miscellaneous Poems,* 146–52.
57. Immanuel Kant, "Perpetual Peace: A Philosophical Sketch (1795)," in *Kant: Political Writings,* ed. H. Reiss, trans. H.B. Nisbet, 3rd ed. (Cambridge: Cambridge University Press, 1991), 93–130.
58. Scrivener, *The Cosmopolitan Ideal,* 239, n. 108.
59. Galchinsky, *The Origin of the Modern Woman Jewish Writer,* 107.
60. Nadia Valman, *The Jewess in Nineteenth-Century British Literary Culture* (Cambridge: Cambridge University Press, 2007), 120.
61. Valman, *The Jewess in Nineteenth-Century British Literary Culture,* 118–19.
62. Galchinsky, *The Origin of the Modern Woman Jewish Writer,* 111.
63. Benjamin Disraeli *Alroy: A Romance* (Leipzig: Bernhard Tauchnitz, 1846), 122.
64. *Athenaeum,* 280 (March 9, 1833), 150–51; quoted in electronic edition of *Alroy* edited by Sheila A. Spector. http://www.rc.umd.edu/editions/alroy/contexts/reviews/athenaeum.html
65. Celia and Marion Moss, *The Romance of Jewish History,* 3 vols. (London: Saunder and Otley, 1840), 2: 13–75.
66. Celia and Marion Moss, *The Romance of Jewish History,* 2: 65.
67. William St. Clair, *The Reading Nation in the Romantic Period* (Cambridge: Cambridge University Press, 2004), 323–38.
68. Grace Aguilar, *Essays and Miscellanies,* ed. Sarah Aguilar (Philadelphia: A. Hart, Carey & Hart, 1853), 302–09.
69. For Aguilar's literary career, see Michael Galchinsky, "Introduction," in *Grace Aguilar: Selected Writings* (Peterborough: Broadview Press, 2003), 11–47.
70. Aguilar, *Essays and Miscellanies,* 304–05.
71. Aguilar, *Essays and Miscellanies,* 273.
72. Galchinsky, *Grace Aguilar,* 167.
73. Martha Nussbaum, *Poetic Justice: The Literary Imagination and Public Life* (Boston: Beacon Press, 1997).
74. Galchinsky, *Grace Aguilar,* 151.
75. Anne Nichols, 'Woman's Sphere in the Law of God': Biblical Women and Domesticity in the Writings of Felicia Hemans, Grace Aguilar, Harriet Beecher Stowe, and Elizabeth Cady Stanton, Ph.D Diss. (Detroit: Wayne State University, 2010), 74.

76. Galchinsky, *The Origin of the Modern Woman Jewish Writer*, 166.
77. Galchinsky, *The Origin of the Modern Woman Jewish Writer*, 167.
78. Galchinsky, *Grace Aguilar*, 85.
79. Aguilar, *Essays and Miscellanies*, 306.
80. Aguilar, *Essays and Miscellanies*, 306–09.
81. Aguilar, *Essays and Miscellanies*, 302–03.
82. Galchinsky, "Introduction," 18.
83. Galchinsky, *The Origin of the Modern Woman Jewish Writer*, 167.
84. Michael Ragussis, *Figures of Conversion: The Jewish Question & English National Identity* (Durham, NC: Duke University Press, 1995), 143, 147.
85. Elizabeth Fay, "Grace Aguilar: Rewriting Scott Rewriting History, in *British Romanticism and the Jews: History, Culture, Literature*," ed. Sheila A Spector (New York: Palgrave Macmillan, 2002), 217.
86. Fay, "Grace Aguilar: Rewriting Scott Rewriting History," 227.
87. Aguilar, *The Vale of Cedars; or, The Martyr* (New York and Philadelphia: Appleton, 1850), 66.
88. Aguilar, *The Vale of Cedars*, 66–67.
89. Aguilar, *The Vale of Cedars*, 20.
90. Ragussis, *Figures of Conversion*, 145.
91. Aguilar, *The Vale of Cedars*, 42.
92. Aguilar, *The Vale of Cedars*, 21.
93. Aguilar, *The Vale of Cedars*, 253.
94. Aguilar, *Women of Israel*, 2 vols. (New York: Appleton, 1851), 1: 107–33.
95. Fay, "Grace Aguilar: Rewriting Scott Rewriting History," 221–23.
96. Cf. Fay's discussion of martyrdom, which differs somewhat from my own, 228–29.
97. Ragussis, *Figures of Conversion*, 146.
98. Valman, *The Jewess in Nineteenth-Century British Literary Culture*, 105–07.
99. Glachinsky, *The Origin of the Modern Woman Jewish Writer*, 165.
100. Traci Michele Klass, 'Writing' Home: Grace Aguilar and the Jews, Ph.D. diss. (Miami: University of Florida Diss. 2005), 136.
101. Aguilar, *The Vale of Cedars*, 222.
102. Aguilar, *Essays and Miscellanies*, 245–49; cf. Henry Hart Milman, *The History of the Jews* 3 vols. (New York: J. and J. Harper, 1830), 3: 273–74.
103. Fay, "Grace Aguilar: Rewriting Scott Rewriting History," 226; Galchinsky, *The Origin of the Modern Woman Jewish Writer*, 166; Ragussis, *Figures of Conversion*, 150.
104. Ragussis, *Figures of Conversion*, 145.
105. Aguilar, *The Vale of Cedars*, 83.
106. Fay, "Grace Aguilar: Rewriting Scott Rewriting History," 224–28.

Conclusion

1. Frank Felsenstein, *Anti-Semitic Stereotypes: A Paradigm of Otherness in English Popular Culture, 1660–1830* (Baltimore and London: Johns Hopkins University Press, 1995), 86–87.

2. The edition of the poem produced by Bedford St. Martin's compellingly illustrates the hermeneutic gymnastics the poem can inspire. S.T. Coleridge, *Rime of the Ancient Mariner*, ed. Paul H. Fry (New York: Bedford St. Martin's, 1999).

3. Judith W. Page, *Imperfect Sympathies: Jews and Judaism in British Romantic Literature and Culture* (New York: Palgrave/Macmillan, 2004), 159–66; William Galperin, "Romanticism and/or Antisemitism," in *Between Race and Culture: Representations of "the Jew" in English and American Literature*, ed. Bryan Cheyette (Stanford: Stanford University Press, 1996), 19–20.

4. Page, *Imperfect Sympathies*, 1–2, 33, 166–67.

5. William Cobbett, "Good Friday; or, The Murder of Jesus Christ by the Jews," in *Thirteen Sermons* (New York: John Doyle, 1834), 227–28.

6. Sheila A. Spector, *"Glorious Incomprehensible:" The Development of Blake's Kabbalistic Language* (Lewisburg, PA: Bucknell University Press, 2001) and *"Wonders Divine": The Development of Blake's Kabbalistic Myth* (Lewisburg, PA: Bucknell University Press, 2001).

7. William Blake, *The Complete Poetry and Prose of William Blake*, rev. ed. David V. Erdman (New York: Doubleday, 1988), 13, plate 18.

8. Karen Shabetai, "The Question of Blake's Hostility Toward the Jews," *ELH* 63.1 (1996): 139–52.

9. Bryan Shelley, *Shelley and Scripture: The Interpreting Angel* (Oxford: Clarendon Press, 1994), vii.

10. P.B. Shelley, *The Complete Works of Shelley*, ed. Roger Ingpen and Walter E. Peck (New York: Gordian Press, 1965), 7: 47.

11. Nora Crook, "Shelley's Jewish 'Orations,' " *Keats-Shelley Journal* 59 (2010): 43–64.

12. P.B. Shelley, *Shelley's Poetry and Prose*, 2nd ed., ed. Donald H. Reiman and Neil Fraistat (New York: W.W. Norton, 2002), 448.

13. Sheila A. Spector, *Byron and the Jews: A Study in Translation* (Detroit: Wayne State University Press, 2010).

14. Scrivener, " 'Zion Alone is Forbidden': Historicizing Antisemitism in Byron's The Age of Bronze," *Keats-Shelley Journal* 43 (1994): 75–97.

15. Lord Byron, *The Complete Poetical Works*, 7 vols., ed. Jerome J. McGann (Oxford: Oxford University Press, 1980–93), 7: 22.

16. Felsenstein, *Anti-Semitic Stereotypes*, 12; Walter Lippmann, *Public Opinion* (New York: Harcourt, Brace & Co., 1922), 81: 79–158.

17. Leonard Dinnerstein, *Antisemitism in America* (New York: Oxford University Press, 1994), 78–104.

18. Todd M. Endelman, *The Jews of Georgian England 1714–1830: Tradition and Change in a Liberal Society* (Ann Arbor: University of Michigan Press, 1999), 94–96.
19. See Dominick LaCapra's discussion of working-through (durcharbeiten) as it relates to traumatic memories of the Shoah, *History, Theory, Trauma: Representing the Holocaust* (Ithaca and London: Cornell University Press, 1994), ch 1.

BIBLIOGRAPHY

PRIMARY TEXTS

Abramovitsh, S.Y. (Mendele Moykher Sforim), *Tales of Mendele the Book Peddler. "Fishke the Lame" and "Benjamin the Third."* Edited by Dan Miron and Ken Frieden. Translated by Ted Gorelick and Hillel Halkin. New York: Schocken Books, 1996.

Aguilar, Grace. *Essays and Miscellanies.* Edited by Sarah Aguilar. Philadelphia: A. Hart, Carey & Hart, 1853.

———. *Selected Writings.* Edited by Michael Galchinsky. Peterborough, ON: Broadview Press, 2003.

———. *The Vale of Cedars; or, The Martyr.* New York and Philadelphia: Appleton, 1850.

———. *Women of Israel,* 2 vols. New York: Appleton, 1851.

Alexander, Levy. *Memoirs of the Life and Commercial Connections, Public and Private, of the Late Benaminj Goldsmid, Esq, of Roehampton; Containing a Cursory View of the Jewish Society and Manners. Interspersed with Interesting Anecdotes of Several Remarkable Characters.* London: Levy Alexander, 1808.

Austen, Jane. *Northanger Abbey.* Edited by Susan Fraiman. New York: W.W. Norton, 2004.

Authentic Memoirs, Memorandums, and Confessions. Taken from the Journal of His Predatorial Majesty, The King of the Swindlers. London: W. Hatton, n.d. [1798].

Barrett, C.F. *Allanrod* (180?), *The Shipwreck* (1803), *Douglas Castle* (1803), *The Black Castle* (1800), and *Tracey Castle* (1800).

Bialik, Hayim Nahman and Yehoshua Hana Ravnitzky, eds. *The Book of Legends: Sefer Ha-Aggadah. Legends from the Talmud and Midrash.* Translated by William G. Braude. New York: Schocken Books, 1992.

Blake, William. *The Complete Poetry and Prose of William Blake.* Revised edition by David V. Erdman. New York: Doubleday, 1988.

Brendlau, Madame. *Tales of a Jewess: Illustrating the Domestic Manners and Customs of the Jews. Interspersed with Original Anecdotes of Napoleon.* First Series. London: Simpkin, Marshall and Co., 1838.

Bristow, Amelia. *Emma De Lissau; A Narrative of Striking Vicissitudes, and Peculiar Trials.* 2nd ed., 2 vols. London: T. Gardiner and Son, 1829.

———. *Sophia de Lissau; A Portraiture of the Jews, Of the Nineteenth Century; Being An Outline of Their Religious and Domestic Habits: With Explanatory Notes.* London: T. Gardiner and Son, 1829.

Bulwer, Edward Lytton. *Leila; or, The Siege of Granada*. Philadelphia: Carley, Lea, and Blanchard, 1838.

Byron, Lord. *Lord Byron. The Complete Poetical Works*, 7 vols. Edited by Jerome McGann Oxford: Clarendon Press, 1980–93.

Cahan, Abraham. *Yekl and The Imported Bridegroom and Other Stories of Yiddish New York* [1896]. Edited by Bernard G. Richards. New York: Dover, 1970.

Cobbett, William. "Good Friday; or, The Murder of Jesus Christ by the Jews." In *Thirteen Sermons*. 226–42. New York: John Doyle, 1834.

Coleridge, S.T. *Lectures 1795 On Politics and Religion*. Edited by Lewis Patton and Peter Mann. *The Collected Works of Samuel Taylor Coleridge*, 1 vol. London: Routledge and Kegan Paul, and Princeton: Princeton University Press, 1971.

———. *Rime of the Ancient Mariner*. Edited by Paul H. Fry. New York: Bedford St. Martin's, 1999.

Collier, Thomas. *A Brief Answer to Some of the Objections and Demurs Made Against the Coming in and Inhabiting of the Jews in this Common-wealth*. London: Thomas Brewster, 1656.

Cumberland, Richard. *The Jew; or, Benevolent Hebrew: A Comedy*. London: C. Dilly, 1794.

———. *The Jew; or, Benevolent Hebrew: A Comedy*. Boston: John West, 1795.

Dahood, Mitchell. S.J., ed., *The Anchor Bible: Psalms I. 1–50*. Garden City: Doubleday, 1966.

Daniel, George. *The Modern Dunciad: Virgil in London and Other Poems*. London: William Pickering, 1835.

Dibdin, Charles. *The Pedlar: A Miscellany, in Prose and Verse, by C.I. Pitt*. London: Harrison & Co., 1796.

Dickens, Charles. *Oliver Twist*. Edited by Philip Horne. London: Penguin, 2003.

———. *The Works of Charles Dickens*, 34 vols. Edited by Andrew Lang. New York: Charles Scribner's Sons, 1900.

Dickinson, H.T. *The Political Works of Thomas Spence*. Newcastle-upon-Tyne: Avero, 1982.

Disraeli, Benjamin. *Alroy: A Romance*. Leipzig: Bernhard Tauchnitz, 1846.

———. *Alroy*. Edited by Sheila A. Spector. Electronic Editions, Romantic Circles. http://www.rc.umd.edu/editions/alroy/toc.html

Dury, John. *A Case of Conscience, Whether It Be Lawful to Admit Jews into a Christiancommonwealth? Resolved by Mr. John Dury: Written to Samuel Hartlib, Esq*. London: Richard Wodenothe, 1656, rpt. *The Harlelian Miscellany; or, A Collection of Scarce, Curious, and Entertaining Pamphlets and Tracts, As Well in Manuscript As in Print, Found in the Late Earl of Oxford's Library*. Edited by William Oldys, 6: 438–44. London: Robert Dutton, 1810.

Edgeworth, Maria. *Harrington*. Edited by Susan Manly. Peterborough: Broadview Press, 2004.

———. *Maria Edgeworth in France and Switzerland: Selections from the Edgeworth Family Letters.* Edited by Christian Colvin. Oxford: Clarendon Press, 1979.

Eliot, George. *Daniel Deronda.* Edited by Terence Cave. London: Penguin, 1996.

An Essay on the Commercial Habits of the Jews. London: Samuel Tipper and J. Hatchard, 1809.

Farren, George. *An Essay on Shakespeare's Character of Shylock, Originating in An Examination of the Laws and Customs of Moses, and of the Primitive Christians, with Reference to Enumerations of Population, and the Rate of Interest of Money.* London: Pelham Richardson, 1833.

Finch, Henry. *The Worlds Great Restavration.* London: William Gouge, 1621.

Ginzburg, Louis. *Legends of the Jews.* 7 vols. Translated by Henrietta Szold and Paul Rudin. Philadelphia: Jewish Publication Society of America, 1956.

Godwin, William. Godwin's diary, Oxford, Bodleian MS Abinger, e. 6–22.

———. *Political and Philosophical Writings of William Godwin.* 7 vols. Edited by Mark Philp. London: Pickering & Chatto, 1993.

———. *St Leon.* Edited and introduction by William D. Brewer. Peterborough, ON: Broadview Press, 2006.

Granville, George. "Jew of Venice," (1701). In *Five Restoration Adaptations of Shakespeare.* Edited by Christopher Spencer, 345–402. Urbana: University of Illinois Press, 1965.

Grimstone, [Mary] Leman. *Character; or, Jew and Gentile: A Tale.* 2 vols. London: Charles Fox, 1833.

Gronow, Rees Howell. *The Reminiscences and Recollections of Captain Gronow, Being Anecdotes of the Camp, Court, Clubs and Society, 1810–1860.* Edited by John Raymond London: Bodley Head, 1964.

Harrington, James. *"The Commonwealth of Oceana" and "A System of Politics."* Edited by J.G.A. Pocock. Cambridge: Cambridge University Press, 1992.

Hazlitt, William. *The Works of William Hazlitt.* 20 vols. Edited by P.P. Howe. London and Toronto: J. M. Dent, 1930.

The History of Mary Prince, A West Indian Slave. Related by Herself (London: F. Westley and A.H. Davis, 1831).

Hole, Richard. "An Apology for the Character and Conduct of Shylock." In *Essays, By a Society of Gentlemen, At Exeter.* 552–73. Exeter: Trewman and Son, 1796.

Jessey, Henry. *A Narrative of the Late Proceedings at Whitehall, Concerning the Jews.* London: L. Chapman, 1656, rpt. *Harleian Miscellany; or, A Collection of Scarce, Curious, and Entertaining Pamphlets and Tracts, As Well In Manuscript As In Print, Found in the Late Earl of Oxford's Library.* Edited by William Oldys, 6: 445–54. London: Robert Dutton, 1810.

Kant, Immanuel. "Perpetual Peace: A Philosophical Sketch" (1795). *Kant: Political Writings.* Translated by H. B. Nisbet. 3rd ed. Edited by H. Reiss, 93–130. Cambridge: Cambridge University Press, 1991.

King, Charlotte [Rosa Matilda]. *Confessions of the Nun of St. Omer. A Tale*, 3 vols. London: J. F. Hughes, 1806.

———. [Charlotte Dacre]. *Hours of Solitude*, 2 vols. London: Hughes and Ridgeway, 1805.

———. [Charlotte Dacre, Rosa Matilda]. *The Libertine*, 4 vols., 2nd ed. London: T. Cadell & W. Davies, 1807.

———. [Rosa Matilda]. *The Passions*, 4 vols. London: T. Cadell & W. Davies, 1811.

———, and Sophia King. *Trifles of Helicon*. London: James Ridgway, 1798.

King, John. ed., David Levi, *Dissertations on the Prophecies of The Old Testament*. 2 vols. Edited and introduction by John King. London: John King, 1817.

———. *Letters from France*. London: M. Jones, 1802.

———. *Letters from Perdita to a certain Israelite, and His Answers to them*. London: J. Fielding and J. Stockdale and J. Sewell, 1781.

———. *Mr. King's Apology; or A Reply to his Calumniators*. London: Thomas Wilkins, 1798.

———. *Thoughts on the Difficulties and Distresses in Which the Peace of 1783, Has Involved the People of England; on the Present Disposition of the English, Scots, and Irish, to Emigrate to America; and on the Hazard They Run (without Certain Precautions) of Rendering Their Condition More Deplorable. Addressed to the Right Hon. Charles James Fox*. 5th ed. London: T. Davies, J. Southern, W. Deane, 1783.

King, Sophia. *Cordelia; or, A Romance of Real Life*. 2 vols. London: William Lane, 1799.

———. *The Fatal Secret, or, Unknown Warrior; A Romance of the Twelfth Century, With Legendary Poems*. London: J.G. Barnard and J. Fiske, 1801.

———. *Waldorf; or, The Dangers of Philosophy* (1798). Edited by Adriana Craciun. Anti-Jacobin Novels, vol. 9. Edited by W. M. Verhoeven. London: Pickering & Chatto, 2005.

Körner, Christian Gottfried. *The Life of Carl Theodor Körner*. Translated by G. F. Richardson. London and Dublin: T. Hurst, Westley and Tyrrell, 1827.

L., D. *Israels Condition and Cause Pleaded; or Some Arguments for the Jews Admission into England*. London: William Larner and Jonathan Ball, 1656.

Lemoine, Ann, ed., *Laugh When You Can; or The Monstrous Droll Jester*. London: Ann Lemoine, n.d.

Leskóv, Nikolai. "Fish Soup Without Fish." In *Satirical Stories of Nikolai Leskóv*. Edited and translated by William B. Edgerton. New York: Pegasus, 1969.

Lessing, Gotthold Ephraim. *Nathan the Wise*. Translated, edited, and introduction by Ronald Schechter. Boston and New York: Bedford/St. Martin's, 2004.

Levi, David. *Dissertations on the Prophecies of The Old Testament.* 2 vols. Edited and introduction by John King. London: John King, 1817.

London Times, September 16, 1812.

Lyon, Emma. *Miscellaneous Poems.* Oxford: J. Bartlett, 1812.

MacDonald, Edgar E. ed., *The Education of the Heart: The Correspondence of Rachel Mordecai Lazarus and Maria Edgeworth.* Chapel Hill: University of North Carolina Press, 1977.

Mackenzie, Eneas. *A Descriptive and Historical Account of the Town and County of Newcastle upon Tyne, Including the Borough of Gateshead.* Newcastle upon Tyne: Mackenzie & Dent, 1827.

Macklin, Charles. *Four Comedies by Charles Macklin.* Edited by J.O. Bartley. London and Hamden, CT: Sidgwick & Jackson, Archon, 1968.

Mendelsohn, Ezra. *Painting a People: Maurycy Gottlieb and Jewish Art* Hanover and London: Brandeis University Press, 2002.

Milman, Henry Hart. *The History of the Jews.* 3 vols. New York: J. and J. Harper, 1830.

Montefiore, C.G. and H. Loewe, eds., *A Rabbinic Anthology.* New York: Schocken Books, 1974.

Moss, Celia and Marion. *Early Efforts: A Volume of Poems.* Portsmouth: Whittaker & Co., and John Miller, 1839.

———. *The Romance of Jewish History,* 3 vols. London: Saunder and Otley, 1840.

Niemcewicz, Julius Ursinus. *Levi and Sarah; or The Jewish Lovers. A Polish Tale.* London: John Murray, 1830.

Old Bailey Proceedings Online, www.oldbaileyonline.org

Pinto, Fernão Mendes. *The Travels of Mendes Pinto.* Translated, edited, and introduction by Rebecca D. Catz. Chicago and London: University of Chicago Press, 1989.

Place, Francis. *The Autobiography of Francis Place (1771–1854).* Edited by Mary Thrale. Cambridge: Cambridge University Press, 1972.

Polack, Maria. *Fiction Without Romance; or, The Locket-Watch,* 2 vols. London: Effingham Wilson, 1830.

Prynne, William. *A Short Demurrer to the Jewes Long discontinued Remitter into England.* London: Edward Thomas, 1655.

["Review of Benjamin Disraeli, *Alroy*"]. *Athenaeum* 280 (March 9, 1833): 150–51.

["Review of Christian Gottfried Körner, *The Life of Carl Theodor Körner*"], The London Literary Gazette and Journal of the Belles Lettres 548 (July 21, 1827): 470.

["Review of Emma Lyon, *Miscellaneous Poems*"]. *Critical Review* 2 n.s. (August 1812): 216.

["Review of *Miscellaneous Poems*"]. *Monthly Review* 70 (February 1813): 213–14.

"Second Report from the Commons' Committee of Secrecy on the State of Ireland, and the Proceedings of Certain Disaffected Persons in Both

Parts of the United Kingdom." 35: 1302–23; *Parliamentary History of England*, 1800–1801. London: Hansard, 1819.

Scott, Walter. *Ivanhoe*. Edited by Graham Tulloch. London: Penguin, 2000.

Scribe, Eugène. *La Juive: The Jewess. In Four Acts. The Music by Halevy*. New York: Palmer & Co., 1860.

Shakespeare, William. *The Merchant of Venice*. Edited by M. Lindsay Kaplan. Boston: Bedford/St. Martin's, 2002.

Shelley, P.B. *The Complete Works of Shelley*. 10 vols. Edited by Roger Ingpen and Walter E. Peck. New York: Gordian Press, 1965.

———. *Shelley's Poetry and Prose*. 2nd ed. Edited by Donald H. Reiman and Neil Fraistat.New York: W.W. Norton, 2002.

Southcott, Joanna. *An Account of the Trials on Bills of Exchange, Wherein the Deceit of Mr. John King and His Confederates, Under the Pretence of Lending Money, Is Exposed, and Their Arts Brought to Light*. London: S. Rousseau, 1807.

Spence's Songs. London: Seale and Bates, n.d.

Taylor, John. *Records of My Life*. New York: Harper, 1833.

"The Trials of George Gordon. 6 June 1787." In *A Complete Collection of State Trials and Proceedings for High Treason*. Edited by Thomas Jones Howell, 22: 175–236. London: T.C. Hansard, 1817.

The Torah: A Modern Commentary. Edited by W. Gunther Plaut. New York: Union of American Hebrew Congregations, 1981.

Universal Songster, 3 vols. London: John Fairburn, Simpkin and Marshall, Sherwood,Gilbert, and Piper, 1825.

Wade, Thomas. *The Poems and Plays of Thomas Wade*. Edited by John L. McLean. Troy, NY: Whitston Publishing Company, 1997.

Wolf, Lucien, ed. *Menasseh Ben Israel's Mission to Oliver Cromwell: Being a Reprint of the Pamphlets Published by Menasseh Ben Israel to Promote the Re-admission of the Jews to England 1649–1656*. London: Jewish Historical Society of England and Macmillan, 1901.

Woodfall, William. Parliamentary Register; or An Impartial Report of the Debates, vol. 2 London: T. Chapman, T. Woodfall, T. Bellamy, H.D. Symonds, 1798.

Wollaston, William. *The Religion of Nature Delineated*. London: Samuel Palmer 1724.

Wordsworth, William. *The "Ruined Cottage" and "The Pedlar."* Edited by James Butler. Ithaca: Cornell University Press, 1979.

———. *Translations of Chaucer and Virgil*. Edited by Bruce E. Graver. Ithaca and London: Cornell University Press, 1998.

SECONDARY TEXTS

Adelman, Janet. *Blood Relations: Christian and Jew in "The Merchant of Venice."* Chicago and London: University of Chicago Press, 2008.

Adorno, Theodor W. and Max Horkheimer. *Dialectic of Enlightenment* (1944). Translated by John Cumming. New York: Continuum, 1972.

Anderson, George K. *The Legend of the Wandering Jew.* Providence, RI: Brown University Press, 1965.

Ashraf, P.M. *The Life and Times of Thomas Spence.* Newcastle-upon-Tyne: Frank Graham, 1983.

Bailey, Quentin. "'Dangerous and Suspicious Trades': Wordsworth's Pedlar and the Board of Police revenue." *Romanticism* 13.3 (2007): 244–56.

Bar-Yosef, Eitan. *The Holy Land in English Culture 1799–1917: Palestine and the Question of Orientalism.* Oxford: Clarendon Press, 2005.

Batten, J. Minton. *John Dury: Advocate of Christian Reunion.* Chicago: University of Chicago Press, 1920.

Benis, Toby R. *Romantic Diasporas: French Emigrés, British Convicts, and Jews.* New York: Palgrave/Macmillan, 2009.

Benjamin, Walter. *Illuminations.* Edited by Hannah Arendt. Translated by Harry Zohn. New York: Schocken, 1969.

Bennett, Anthony. "Sources of Popular Song in Early Nineteenth-Century Britain: Problems and Methods in Research." *Popular Music* 2 (1982): 69–89.

Bhabha, Homi K. "Joking Aside: The Idea of a Self-Critical Community." In *Modernity, Culture and "the Jew."* Edited by Byran Cheyette and Laura Marcus, xv–xx. Stanford: Stanford University Press, 1998.

———. *The Location of Culture*, new ed. London and New York: Routledge, 2004.

Biberman, Matthew. *Masculinity, Anti-Semitism and Early Modern Literature: From the Satanic to the Effeminate Jew.* Aldershot and Burlington: Ashgate, 2004.

Boyarin, Jonathan and Daniel. *Powers of Diaspora: Two Essays on the Relevance of Jewish Culture.* Minneapolis: University of Minnesota Press, 2002.

Butler, James. "Introduction." *"The Ruined Cottage" and "The Pedlar" by William Wordsworth.* Edited by James Butler, 3–35. Ithaca: Cornell University Press, 1979.

Butler, Marilyn. *Maria Edgeworth: A Literary Biography.* Oxford: Clarendon Press, 1972.

Byg, Barton. "*Holocaust* and West German 'Restoration.'" *Telos* 42 (1979–80): 143–49.

Byrne, Paula. *Perdita: The Literary, Theatrical, Scandalous Life of Mary Robinson.* New York: Random House, 2004.

Calisch, Edward N. *The Jew in English Literature, As Author and As Subject.* Richmond, VA: Bell Book and Stationery, 1909.

Cardozo, Jacob Lopes. *The Contemporary Jew in the Elizabethan Drama.* 1925. Reprint. New York: Burt Franklin, 1968.

Chase, Malcolm. *"The People's Farm": English Radical Agrarianism 1775–1840.* Oxford: Clarendon Press, 1988.

Chazan, Robert. *Medieval Stereotypes and Modern Antisemitism.* Berkeley: University of California Press, 1997.

Cheyette, Bryan. *Constructions of "the Jew" in English Literature and Society: Racial Representations, 1875–1945.* Cambridge: Cambridge University Press, 1993.

———. and Laura Marcus, eds. *Modernity, Culture and "the Jew."* Stanford: Stanford University Press, 1998.

———. "On Being a Jewish Critic." *Jewish Social Studies* 11.1 (2004): 32–51.

Coleman, Edward D. *The Jew in English Drama. An Annotated Bibliography.* Preface by Joshua Bloch (1943). With Edgar Rosenberg. *The Jew in Western Drama: An Essay and a Check List.* New York: The New York Public Library and Ktav Publishing House, 1968.

Craciun, Adriana. "Introduction to *Waldorf.*" In Sophia King, *Waldorf; or, The Dangers of Philosophy* (1798). Edited by Adriana Craciun, 9: vii–xxvii. *Anti-Jacobin Novels.* 10 vols. Edited by W.M. Verhoeven. London: Pickering & Chatto, 2005.

———. "Unnatural, Unsexed, Undead: Charlotte Dacre's Gothic Bodies." In *Fatal Women of Romanticism.* Cambridge: Cambridge University Press, 2003.

Cream, Naomi. "Isaac Leo Lyon: The Free Jewish Migrant to Australia?" *Journal of Australian Jewish Historical Society* 21.1 (1993): 3–16.

———. "Revd Solomon Lyon of Cambridge, 1755–1820." *Jewish Historical Studies* 36 (1999–2000): 31–69.

Crook, Nora. "Shelley's Jewish 'Orations.'" *Keats-Shelley Journal* 59 (2010): 43–64.

Davis, Michael T., Iain McCalman, and Christina Parolin, eds., *Newgate in Revolution: An Anthology of Radical Prison Literature in the Age of Revolution.* London and New York: Continuum, 2005.

Davison, Carol Margaret. *Antisemitism and British Gothic Literature.* New York: Palgrave/Macmillan, 2004.

Devereaux, Simon. "The City and the Sessions Paper: 'Public Justice' in London, 1770–1800." *Journal of British Studies* 35 (1996): 466–503.

Dinnerstein, Leonard. *Antisemitism in America.* New York: Oxford University Press, 1994.

Dunn, James A. "Charlotte Dacre and the Feminization of Violence." *Nineteenth-Century Literature,* 53.3 (1998): 307–27.

Endelman, Todd M. *The Jews of Britain, 1656 to 2000.* Berkeley, Los Angeles, and London: University of California Press, 2002.

———. "The Chequered Career of 'Jew' King: A Study in Anglo-Jewish Social History." In *From East and West: Jews in a Changing Europe, 1750–1870.* Edited by Frances Malino and David Sorkin, 151–81. Oxford: Basil Blackwell, 1990.

———. *The Jews of Georgian England 1714–1830: Tradition and Change in a Liberal Society.* Ann Arbor: University of Michigan Press, 1999.

Fay, Elizabeth. "Grace Aguilar: Rewriting Scott Rewriting History." In *British Romanticism and the Jews: History, Culture, Literature*. Edited by Sheila A. Spector, 215–34. New York: Palgrave/Macmillan, 2002.

Feldman, David. *Englishmen and Jews: Social Relations and Political Culture, 1840–1914*. New Haven: Yale University Press, 1994.

Felsenstein, Frank. *Anti-Semitic Stereotypes: A Paradigm of Otherness in English Popular Culture, 1660–1830*. Baltimore and London: Johns Hopkins University Press, 1995.

Fiedler, Leslie A. "What Can We Do About Fagin? The Jew-Villain in Western Tradition." *Commentary* 7 (May 1949): 412–13.

Fisch, Harold. *The Dual Image: The Figure of the Jew in English and American Literature*. New York: Ktav Publishing House, 1971.

Foucault, Michel. "What Is An Author?" In *Critical Theory Since 1965*. Edited by Hazard Adams and Leroy Searle, 138–48. Tallahassee: University Presses of Florida, 1986.

Freedman, Jonathan. *The Temple of Culture: Assimilation and Anti-Semitism in Literary Anglo–America*. New York: Oxford University Press, 2000.

Galchinsky, Michael. "Africans, Indians, Arabs, and Scots: Jewish and Other Questions in the Age of Empire." *Jewish Culture and History* 6.1 (2003): 46–60.

———. "Introduction." In *Grace Aguilar: Selected Writings*. Edited by Michael Galchinsky, 11–47. Peterborough, ON: Broadview Press, 2003.

———. *The Origin of the Modern Woman Jewish Writer: Romance and Reform in Victorian England*. Detroit: Wayne State University Press, 1996.

Galperin, William. "Romanticism and/or Antisemitism." In *Between Race and Culture: Representations of "the Jew" in English and American Literature*. Edited by Bryan Cheyette, 16–26. Stanford: Stanford University Press, 1996.

Gilman, Sander L. *Jewish Frontiers: Essays on Bodies, Histories, and Identities*. New York: Palgrave/Macmillan, 2003.

———. *Jewish Self-Hatred: Antisemitism and The Hidden Language of the Jews*. Baltimore: Johns Hopkins University Press, 1986.

———. *The Jew's Body*. New York and London: Routledge, 1991.

Glaser, Eliane. *Judaism Without Jews: Philosemitism and Christian Polemic in Early Modern England*. New York: Palgrave Macmillan, 2007.

Goldhagen, Daniel Jonah. *Hitler's Willing Executioners: Ordinary Germans and the Holocaust*. New York: Vintage Books, 1997.

Graver, Bruce. "Introduction." In *Translations of Chaucer and Virgil by William Wordsworth*. Edited by Bruce E. Graver, 3–29. Ithaca and London: Cornell University Press, 1998.

Gross, John. *Shylock: Four Hundred Years in the Life of a Legend*. London: Chatto and Windus, 1992.

Grossman, Jonathan H. "The Absent Jew in Dickens: Narrators in *Oliver Twist, Our Mutual Friend, and A Christmas Carol*." *Dickens Studies Annual: Essays on Victorian Fiction* 24 (1996): 37–57.

Handelman, Susan A. The Slayers of Moses: *The Emergence of Rabbinic Interpretation in Modern Literary Theory.* Albany: SUNY Press, 1982.

Harrison, J.F.C. *The Second Coming: Popular Millenarianism, 1780–1850.* New Brunswick: Rutgers University Press, 1979.

Henriques, H.S.Q. *The Return of the Jews to England: Being a Chapter in the History of English Law.* London: Macmillan, 1905.

Herrick, James A. *The Radical Rhetoric of the English Deists: The Discourse of Skepticism, 1680–1750.* Columbia: University of South Carolina Press, 1997.

Herzog, Don. *Poisoning the Minds of the Lower Orders.* Princeton: Princeton University Press, 1998.

Hibbert, Christopher. *King Mob: The Story of Lord George Gordon and the Riots of 1780.* London, New York, and Toronto: Longmans, Green, 1958.

Higgins, Lori. "Wayne State University Drops Helen Thomas Diversity Award over Journalist's Controversial Remarks." *Detroit Free Press* (December 4, 2010), online.

Hoeveler, Diane Long. "Charlotte Dacre's *Zofloya*: A Case Study in Miscegenation As Sexual and Racial Nausea." *European Romantic Review* 8.2 (1997): 185–99.

———. "Charlotte Dacre's *Zofloya*: The Gothic Demonization of the Jew." In *The Jews and British Romanticism: Politics, Religion, Culture.* Edited by Sheila A. Spector, 165–78. New York: Palgrave/Macmillan, 2005.

Hyamson, Albert H. *The Sephardim of England: A History of the Spanish and Portuguese Jewish Community 1492–1951.* London: Methuen, 1951.

Julius, Anthony. *Trials of the Diaspora: A History of Anti-Semitism in England.* Oxford and New York: Oxford University Press, 2010.

Kaplan, Yosef, Henry Méchoulan, and Richard H. Popkin, eds. *Menasseh Ben Israel and His World.* Leiden, New York, København, and Köln: E. J. Brill, 1989.

Karp, Jonathan. *The Politics of Jewish Commerce: Economic Thought and Emancipation in Europe, 1638–1848.* Cambridge: Cambridge University Press, 2008.

Katz, David S. *The Jews in the History of England 1485–1850.* Oxford: Clarendon Press, 1994.

———. "Menasseh ben Israel's Christian Connection: Henry Jessey and the Jews." In *Menasseh Ben Israel and His World.* Edited by Yosef Kaplan, Henry Méchoulan, and Richard H. Popkin, 117–38. Leiden, New York, København, and Köln: E. J. Brill, 1989.

———. *Philo-Semitism and the Readmission of the Jews to England 1603–1655.* Oxford: Clarendon Press, 1982.

Kaufman, Heidi. *English Origins, Jewish Discourse, and the Nineteenth-Century British Novel: Reflections on a Nested Nation.* University Park: Pennsylvania State University Press, 2009.

Klass, Traci Michele. "'Writing' Home: Grace Aguilar and the Jews." Ph.D Diss., Miami: University of Florida, 2005.

LaCapra, Dominick. *History, Theory, Trauma: Representing the Holocaust.* Ithaca and London: Cornell University Press, 1994.

Lampert, Lisa. *Gender and Jewish Difference from Paul to Shakespeare.* Philadelphia: University of Pennsylvania Press, 2004.

Landa, M[eyer] J. *The Jew in Drama.* New York: William Morrow, 1927.

Lanzmann, Claude. "From the Holocaust to *The Holocaust*." *Telos* 42 (Winter 1979–80),137–43.

Laplanche, J. and J.-B. Pontalis. *The Language of Psycho-Analysis.* Translated by Donald Nicholson-Smith. New York: W.W. Norton and Co., 1973.

Laqueur, Walter. *A History of Zionism.* New York: Schocken Books, [1972] 1989.

Lippmann, Walter. *Public Opinion.* New York: Harcourt, Brace & Co., 1922.

Locke, Don. *A Fantasy of Reason: The Life and Thought of William Godwin.* London. Boston, & Henley: Routledge & Kegan Paul, 1980.

Lupton, Julia Reinhard. *Citizen-Saints: Shakespeare and Political Theology.* Chicago and London: University of Chicago Press, 2005.

Manly, Susan. "Introduction." In *Maria Edgeworth, Harrington.* Edited by Susan Manly, 7–57. Peterborough: Broadview Press, 2004.

Massey, Irving. *Philo-Semitism in Nineteenth-Century German Literature.* Tübingen: Max Niemeyer Verlag, 2000.

McCalman, Iain. *The Last Alchemist: Count Cagliostro, Master of Magic in the Age of Reason.* New York: HarperCollins, 2003.

———. "Controlling the Riots: Dickens, *Barnaby Rudge* and Romantic Revolution." *History* 84 (1999): 458–76.

———. "Mad Lord George and Madame La Motte: Riot and Sexuality in the Genesis of Burke's *Reflections on the Revolution in France*." *Journal of British Studies* 35 (1996): 343–67.

———. "New Jerusalems: Prophecy, Dissent and Radical Culture in England 1786–1830." In *Enlightenment and Religion: Rational Dissent in Eighteenth-Century Britain.* Edited by Knud Haakonssen, 312–35. Cambridge University Press, 1996.

———. *Radical Underworld: Prophets, Revolutionaries, and Pornographers in London, 1795–1840.* Oxford: Clarendon Press, 1993.

McCreery, Cindy. *The Satirical Gaze: Prints of Women in Late Eighteenth-Century England.* Oxford: Clarendon Press, 2004.

McGann, Jerome. " 'My Brain Is Feminine': Byron and the Poetry of Deception [1990]." In *Byron and Romanticism.* Edited by James Soderholm, 53–76. Cambridge: Cambridge University Press, 2002.

———. *The Poetics of Sensibility: A Revolution in Literary Style.* Oxford: Clarendon Press, 1996.

McLane, Maureen. *Balladeering, Minstrelsy, and the Making of British Romantic Poetry.* Cambridge: Cambridge University Press, 2008.

Méchoulain, Henry, and Gérard Nahon, "Introduction." In *Menasseh Ben Israel, The Hope of Israel: The English Translation by Moses Wall, 1652.* New York: Oxford University Press, 1987, 1–95.

Mee, Jon. *Dangerous Enthusiasm: William Blake and the Culture of Radicalism in the 1790s.* Oxford: Clarendon Press, 1992.

Mellor, Anne. *Gender and Romanticism.* New York and London: Routledge, 1993.

———. *Mothers of the Nation: Women's Political Writing in England, 1780–1830.* Bloomington: University of Indiana Press, 2000.

Meyer, Michael. *Response to Modernity: A History of the Reform Movement in Judaism.* New York: Oxford University Press, 1988.

Michasiw, Kim Ian. "Introduction." Charlotte Dacre, *Zofloya, or The Moor.* Oxford and New York: Oxford University Press, 1997, vii–xxx.

Michelson, H[ijman]. *The Jew in Early English Literature.* Amsterdam: H.J. Paris, 1926.

Modder, Montagu Frank. *The Jew in the Literature of England to the End of the Nineteenth Century.* Philadelphia: Jewish Publication Society of America, 1939.

Naggar, Betty. *Jewish Pedlars and Hawkers, 1740–1940.* Camberley and Surrey: Porphyrogenitus, 1992.

Nichols, Anne. " 'Woman's Sphere in the Law of God': Biblical Women and Domesticity in the Writings of Felicia Hemans, Grace Aguilar, Harriet Beecher Stowe, and Elizabeth Cady Stanton," Ph.D Diss., Michigan: Wayne State University, 2010.

Nussbaum, Martha. *Poetic Justice: The Literary Imagination and Public Life.* Boston: Beacon Press, 1997.

Page, Judith W. *Imperfect Sympathies: Jews and Judaism in British Romantic Literature and Culture.* New York: Palgrave/Macmillan, 2004.

Paley, Morton D. *Apocalypse and Millennium in English Romantic Poetry.* Oxford: Clarendon Press, 1999.

Pascoe, Judith. *Romantic Theatricality: Gender, Poetry, and Spectatorship.* Ithaca and London: Cornell University Press, 1997.

Paul, C. Kegan. *William Godwin: His Friends and Contemporaries,* 2 vols. London: Henry S. King, 1876.

Penslar, Derek J. *Shylock's Children: Economics and Jewish Identity in Modern Europe.* Berkeley, Los Angeles, and London: University of California Press, 2001.

Philp, Mark. *Godwin's Political Justice.* London: Duckworth, 1986.

Philipson, David. *The Jew in English Fiction.* 4th ed. New York: Bloch Publishing, 1918.

———. *My Life As An American Jew: An Autobiography.* Cincinnati: John G. Kidd & Son, 1941.

Pocock, J.G.A. *The Machiavellian Moment: Florentine Political Thought and the Atlantic Republican Tradition.* Princeton: Princeton University Press, 1975.

———. *Virtue, Commerce and History: Essays on Political Thought and History Chiefly in the Eighteenth Century.* Cambridge: Cambridge University Press, 1985.

Popkin, Richard H. "Hartlib, Dury and the Jews." In *Samuel Hartlib and Universal Reformation: Studies in Intellectual Communication.* Edited by Mark Greengrass, Michael Leslie, and Timothy Raylor, 118–36. Cambridge: Cambridge University Press, 1994.

———. and Gordon M. Weiner, eds. *Jewish Christians and Christian Jews: From the Renaissance to the Enlightenment.* London, Dordrecht, and Boston: Kluwer Academic Publishers, 1992.

———. "The Rise and Fall of the Jewish Indian Theory." In *Menasseh Ben Israel and His World.* Edited by Yosef Kaplan, Henry Méchoulan, and Richard H. Popkin, 63–82. Leiden, New York, København, Köln: E.J. Brill, 1989.

Ragussis, Michael. *Figures of Conversion: "The Jewish Question" and English National Identity.* Durham and London: Duke University Press, 1995.

———. "Passing for a Jew, On Stage and Off: Stage Jews and Cross-Dressing Gentiles in Georgian England." In *The Jews and British Romanticism: Politics, Religion, Culture.* Edited by Sheila A. Spector, 41–60. New York: Palgrave/Macmillan, 2005.

———. "The 'Secret' of English Anti-Semitism: Anglo-Jewish Studies and Victorian Studies." *Victorian Studies* 40.2 (1997): 295–307.

———. *Theatrical Nation: Jews and Other Outlandish Englishmen in Georgian Britain.* Philadelphia: University of Pennsylvania Press, 2010.

Rodrigues-Pereira, Miriam, and Chloe Loewe, eds. *The Birth Register (1767–1881) of the Spanish & Portuguese Jews' Congregation.* London: The Spanish and Portuguese Jews' Congregation, 1993.

Roe, Nicholas. *Wordsworth and Coleridge: The Radical Years.* Oxford: Clarendon Press, 1988.

Rosenberg, Edgar. *From Shylock to Svengali: Jewish Stereotypes in English Fiction.* Stanford: Stanford University Press, 1960.

Ross, Marlon B. *The Contours of Masculine Desire: Romanticism and the Rise of Women's Poetry.* New York: Oxford University Press, 1989.

Roth, Cecil. *Essays and Portraits in Anglo-Jewish History.* Philadelphia: Jewish Publication Society of America, 1962.

———. *A History of the Jews in England*, 3rd ed. Oxford: Oxford University Press, 1964.

———. *A Life of Menasseh Ben Israel: Rabbi, Printer, and Diplomat.* Philadelphia: Jewish Publication Society of America, 1934.

Rubinstein, W.D. *A History of the Jews in the English-Speaking World: Great Britain.* Basingstoke, London and New York: Macmillan and St. Martin's, 1996.

Ruderman, Daniel B. *Connecting the Covenants: Judaism and the Search for Christian Identity in Eighteenth-Century England.* Philadelphia: University of Pennsylvania Press, 2007.

Ruderman, Daniel B. *Jewish Enlightenment in An English Key: Anglo-Jewry's Construction of Modern Jewish Thought.* Princeton: Princeton University Press, 2000.

Rudkin, Olive D. *Thomas Spence and His Connections*. New York: A.M. Kelley, [1927] 1966.

Saltman, Avrom. *The Jewish Question in 1655: Studies in Prynne's "Demurrer."* Ramat-Gan and Jerusalem: Bar-Ilan University Press, 1995.

Scheinberg, Cynthia. "Introduction: Re-mapping Anglo-Jewish Literary History." *Victorian Literature and Culture* 27.1 (1999): 115–24.

———. *Women's Poetry and Religion in Victorian England: Jewish Identity and Christian Culture*. Cambridge: Cambridge University Press, 2002.

Schlochauer, Ernst J. "Thomas Wade: Forgotten Champion of English Jewry." *Jewish Social Studies* 13.3 (1951): 227–34.

Schoenfield, Mark L. "Abraham Goldsmid: Money Magician in the Popular Press." In *British Romanticism and the Jews: History, Culture, Literature*. Edited by Sheila A. Spector, 37–60. Basingstoke and New York: Palgrave/Macmillan, 2002.

Scholem, Gershom G. *Major Trends in Jewish Mysticism*, 3rd ed. New York: Schocken Books, 1961.

Schorsch, Ismar. "From Messianism to Realpolitik: Menasseh Ben Israel and the Readmission of the Jews to England." *Proceedings of the American Academy for Jewish Research* 45 (1978): 187–208.

Schuchard, Marsha Keith. "Lord George Gordon and Cabalistic Freemasonry: Beating Jacobite Swords into Jacobin Ploughshares." In *Secret Conversions to Judaism in Early Modern Europe*. Edited by Richard H. Popkin and Martin Mulsow, 183–232. Leiden and Boston, Brill. 2004.

Scrivener, Michael. "British-Jewish Writing of the Romantic Era and the Problem of Modernity: The Example of David Levi." In *British Romanticism and the Jews: History, Culture, Literature*. Edited by Sheila A. Spector, 159–78. New York: Palgrave/Macmillan, 2002.

———. *The Cosmopolitan Ideal in the Age of Revolution and Reaction, 1776–1832*. London: Pickering & Chatto, 2007.

———. "The Philosopher and the Moneylender: The Relationship between William Godwin and John King." In *Godwinian Moments: From Enlightenment to Romanticism*. Edited by Robert M. Maniquis and Victoria Myers, 333–62. Toronto: University of Toronto Press, 2011.

———. *Poetry and Reform: Periodical Verse from the Democratic Press, 1792–1824*. Detroit: Wayne State University Press, 1982.

———. "Rethinking Margin and Center in Anglo-Jewish Literature." In *Romanticism/Judaica: A Convergence of Cultures*. Edited by Sheila A. Spector. Farnham and Burlington: Ashgate, 2011, 157–68.

———. *Seditious Allegories: John Thelwall and Jacobin Writing*. University Park: Pennsylvania State University Press, 2001.

———. "'Zion Alone is Forbidden': Historicizing Antisemitism in Byron's *The Age of Bronze*." *Keats-Shelley Journal* 43 (1994): 75–97.

Shabetai, Karen. "The Question of Blake's Hostility Toward the Jews." *ELH* 63.1 (1996): 139–52.

Shaffer, E.S. *"Kubla Khan" and The Fall of Jerusalem: The Mythological School in Biblical Criticism and Secular Literature 1770–1880.* Cambridge: Cambridge University Press, 1975.

Shapiro, James. *Shakespeare and the Jews.* New York: Columbia University Press, 1996.

Shelley, Bryan. *Shelley and Scripture: The Interpreting Angel.* Oxford: Clarendon Press, 1994.

Smith, Olivia. *The Politics of Language 1791–1819.* Oxford: Clarendon Press, 1984.

Solomons, Israel. "Jew King." *Notes and Queries* 11 (June 5, 1915): 437–38.

———. "Lord George Gordon's Conversion to Judaism." *Transactions of the Jewish* Historical Society of England 7 (1915): 222–71.

Sorkin, David. *The Transformation of German Jewry 1780–1840.* Detroit: Wayne State University Press, 1999.

Spector, Sheila A. "Alroy As Disraeli's 'Ideal Ambition.'" In *British Romanticism and the Jews: History, Culture, Literature.* Edited by Sheila A. Spector, 235–48. New York: Palgrave/Macmillan, 2002.

———, ed. *British Romanticism and the Jews: History, Culture, Literature.* New York: Palgrave/Macmillan, 2002.

———. *Byron and the Jews: A Study in Translation.* Detroit: Wayne State University Press, 2010.

———. *"Glorious Incomprehensible": The Development of Blake's Kabbalistic Language.* Lewisburg, PA: Bucknell University Press, 2001.

———, ed. *The Jews and British Romanticism: Politics, Religion, Culture.* New York: Palgrave/Macmillan, 2005.

———, "The Other's Other: The Function of the Jew in Maria Edgeworth's Fiction." *European Romantic Review* 10.3 (1999): 326–33.

———. *"Wonders Divine": The Development of Blake's Kabbalistic Myth.* Lewisburg, PA: Bucknell University Press, 2001.

Spencer, Christopher. "Introduction." In *Five Restoration Adaptations of Shakespeare.* Edited by Christopher Spencer, 29–32. Urbana: University of Illinois Press, 1965.

St. Clair, William. *The Godwins and the Shelleys: The Biography of a Family.* New York and London: W.W. Norton, 1989.

———. *The Reading Nation in the Romantic Period.* Cambridge: Cambridge University Press, 2004.

Tobias, J.J. *Prince of the Fences: The Life and Crimes of Ikey Solomons.* Foreword Ewen Montagu. London: Vallentine, Mitchell, 1974.

Trapnell, William H. *Thomas Woolston: Madman and Deist?* Bristol: Thoemmes Press, 1994.

Valman, Nadia. *The Jewess in Nineteenth-Century British Literary Culture.* Cambridge: Cambridge University Press, 2007.

———. "Semitism and Criticism: Victorian Anglo-Jewish Literary History." *Victorian Literature and Culture* 27.1 (1999): 235–48.

Van der Veen, H[arm]. Reijndert]. S[ientjo]. *Jewish Characters in Eighteenth-Century English Fiction and Drama (1935). With Edgar Rosenberg. Tabloid Jews and Fungoid Scribblers.* New York: Ktav Publishing, 1972.

Vreté, Mayir. "The Restoration of the Jews in English Protestant Thought 1790–1840." *Middle Eastern Studies* 8 (1972): 3–50.

Warburton, Elizabeth. "C.D.E. Fortnum, DCL (Oxon), JP, FSA, of Hill House, Great Stanmore." *Journal of History of Collections* 11.2 (1999): 129–47.

Wilensky, Mordecai L. "Thomas Barlow's and John Dury's Attitude Towards the Readmission of the Jews to England." *Jewish Quarterly Review*, n.s., 50.3 (1960): 256–68.

Williams, Bill. "The Anti-Semitism of Tolerance: Middle-Class Manchester and the Jews 1870–1900." In *City, Class and Culture: Studies of Social Policy and Cultural Production in Victorian Manchester.* Edited by Alan J. Kidd and K.W. Roberts, 74–102. Manchester: Manchester University Press, 1985.

Wilson, Lisa M. "Female Pseudonymity in the Romantic 'Age of Personality': The Career of Charlotte King/Rose Matilda/Charlotte Dacre." *European RomanticReview* 9.3 (1998): 393–420.

Wisse, Ruth R. *The Modern Jewish Canon: A Journey Through Language and Culture.* Chicago: University of Chicago Press, 2000.

Witkin, Mildred Starr. "The Jewess in English Literature: A Mediating Presence." Ph.D. Diss., New York: City University of New York, 1988.

Wood, Marcus. *Radical Satire and Print Culture 1790–1822.* Oxford: Clarendon Press, 1994.

INDEX

Note: 'N' following a page number indicates an endnote.

Fox, Charles James, 98, 100
Frankenstein (Shelley), 144
French, Daniel, 177–79

Galchinsky, Michael
  on Aguilar's "The Escape," 190
  on Aguilar's *The Perez Family*, 188
  on Aguilar's *The Vale of Cedars*,
    194, 195
  on Anglo-Jewish women
    writers, 117
  on failure of *Jewish Sabbath
    Journal*, 175
  and Jewish conversion, 13
  on Moss sisters, 183
  on philosemitism, 2
gambling, 104–5
Garrow, William, 52–55, 61
The Genius of Christianity
  (Godwin), 109
Gilman, Sander, on Jewish self-
  hatred, 3, 12, 20
Glaser, Eliane, 29, 38
Glover, John, 56
Godwin, William
  background of, 95
  The Genius of Christianity, 109
  parallels with King's life, 95–97
  personal relationship with King,
    97–104
  Political Justice, 109
  publications compared to King's,
    98–102
  Of Religion, 109
  religious views of, 109–11
  St. Leon, 104–9
  Sophia King's influence on, 141
Goldhagen, Daniel Jonah, 1
Goldsmid, Abraham, 94
Goldsmid, Benjamin, 92–95
*Good Friday; or, the Murder of Jesus
  Christ by the Jews* (Cobbett),
  200–201
Gordon, George
  and Cagliostro, 106
  conversion to Judaism, 171

Jewish scripture's influence on,
    162–63, 173–74
  as pacifist, 206
  *Prisoners Petition to the Right
    Hon. Lord George Gordon*,
    171–74
gothicism, 145–46, 148
Gottlieb, Maurycy, 116, 208–9
Granville, George, 88–89
Green, Gerald, 19
Grimmelshausen, Hans Jakob, 108
Grimstone, Mary Leman, 132–33
Gross, John, 89
Grossman, Jonathan H., 5

Halévy, Fromental, 121
Handelman, Susan, 123
"The Happy Jew" (song), 68–70
Harrington, James, 27–29,
    42–43, 85
Harrington (Edgeworth), 23,
    71–77, 119–21
Harwood, Thomas, 55
Haywood, Eliza, 147
Hebrew Melodies (Byron), 204
Hebrew republicanism, 6, 162,
    166–70
Hellas (Shelley), 203–4
Herzog, Don, 143
Hibbert, Christopher, 171
The History of Mary Prince
  (Strickland), 126
The History of the Jews
  (Milman), 135
History of the Jews in England
  (Aguilar), 185–86, 189
Hitler's Willing Executioners
  (Goldhagen), 1
Holcroft, Thomas, 97–98
Hole, Richard, 91
The Holocaust (TV miniseries), 19
*The Holy Land in English Culture
  1799–1917* (Bar-Yosef), 14
The Hope of Israel (Menasseh), 30
Howard, Juliana, 60–62
Huldah, 174